To Gisela:
May your spirit of love
and efforts toward social
equality prosper.
Love,
X Dombuso

Youth and Identity Politics in South Africa, 1990–1994

Sibusisiwe Nombuso Dlamini

UNIVERSITY OF TORONTO PRESS
Toronto Buffalo London

© University of Toronto Press Incorporated 2005
Toronto Buffalo London
Printed in Canada

ISBN 0-8020-3911-1

Printed on acid-free paper

Library and Archives Canada Cataloguing in Publication

Dlamini, S. Nombuso, 1962–
    Youth and identity politics in South Africa, 1990–1994 / Sibusisiwe
Nombuso Dlamini.

    Includes bibliographical references and index.
    ISBN 0-8020-3911-1

    1. Youth, Black – South Africa – KwaZulu-Natal – Political activity.
    2. Zulu (African people) – Ethnic identity.   3. KwaZulu-Natal (South
Africa) – Politics and government.   4. Zulu (African people) – Politics and
government – 20th century.   5. South Africa – Politics and government –
1978–1989.   6. South Africa – Politics and government – 1989–1994.   I. Title.

    HQ799.S62K92 2005   305.242'089'96398609684   C2004-905060-5

This book has been published with the help of a grant from the Canadian
Federation for the Humanities and Social Sciences, through the Aid to
Scholarly Publications Programme, using funds provided by the Social
Sciences and Humanities Research Council of Canada.

University of Toronto Press acknowledges the financial assistance to its
publishing program of the Canada Council for the Arts and the Ontario
Arts Council.

University of Toronto Press acknowledges the financial support for its
publishing activities of the Government of Canada through the Book
Publishing Industry Development Program (BPIDP).

To my mother, Doreen Thandazile
In memory of my brother, Nkonzenhle Sibusiso
and my father, Michael David Dlamini

Contents

Acknowledgments

The dedication to produce this book came in the form of the death and memory of my brother, whose questions and challenges about formal politics and its effects in everyday life, and his trust in my scholarship, were instrumental to the collection of the data. Writing as I was in pain and memory, angels of various forms appeared to guide and encourage me to pursue and complete this work.

First and most gratefully I must thank my husband Errol Swan, whose angelic wings I use to fly when my feet can no longer carry me. His love, support, and enduring patience sustain me through this writing journey in which I tread. My daughter Nothando Swan brightens the day when it turns dark and desolate. Her heart I use when mine fails and her spirit I borrow when mine perishes. Her love, joy, and laughter I cherished throughout the writing of this book. Ursula Kelly, my academic angel whose exemplary light I continue to gaze at in all projects I undertake, made it possible for me to complete this work. Her compassion and faith in my ability to write this and many other books she has in store for me kept me focused and dedicated.

Members of my family in South Africa deserve my special thanks. I thank my sisters Sihle and Skhumbuzo for their love, encouragement, and humour. Their children, my nephews, continue to be great sources of information on identity politics; through them I have been able to understand and follow youth practices in the post-apartheid era. For this I am thankful. My mother has been a guiding angel in all that I have done and in what I have become. Her love, care, and integrity are with me always. *Kine nonke bakwa Dlamini nabakwa Swan, ngiyabonga.*

Finally, I extend my appreciation to the many young people with whom I worked and are the subject of this book. To them I am for ever indebted.

YOUTH AND IDENTITY POLITICS IN
SOUTH AFRICA, 1990–1994

chapter 1

Introduction

This book encapsulates the different historic socio-cultural practices that have shaped the social identities of youth in South Africa. First coined by Bishop Desmond Tutu, the notion of South Africa as a rainbow nation is now widely used. This rainbow image suggests variety and non-homogeneity of the people who constitute this nation. It is also an image associated with the premise of safety that followed the biblical flood and thus is a symbol of reconciliation following a difficult period. Yet as a physical phenomenon the rainbow is both ephemeral and highly stratified. That is, each colour in the spectrum always stands in the same relation to others. In this sense the rainbow's promise of hope is complex, suggesting fixed, stratified positions even within a period of change. The image of a rainbow nation, then, can be read to include recognition of South Africa's diverse population, the interconnectedness of the people within this nation, and acknowledgment of continuing power relations within the South African state. This image can also be seen to be cognizant of the idea that identity is fluid, constantly in the process of construction as subjects move from one context to another. This introduction is an examination of the processes of identity construction that laid the foundation for the possibility of considering South Africa as a rainbow nation, paying particular attention to the role that language, social practices, and ethnicity played in the construction of identities in apartheid South Africa.

The first process of identity formation in apartheid South Africa came in the form of government-sanctioned legislation designed to determine who people were and what geopolitical spaces they could occupy. This process, sometimes referred to as 'ethnicity from above' (Pieterse 1992) or 'imposed ethnicity' (Zegeye 2001), has been well documented in educational scholarship. Under apartheid, ethnicity, colour, and language were key determinants of a person's identity. This form of identification was put into place under the Population Registration Act of 1950, which divided South Africans into four racial groups: white, black, Indian, and coloured. These categories were distinguished from each other through descent – that is, through classification of the natural father and through social acceptance as members of a particular subgroup. Such a racial categorization was upheld as the fundamental basis for 'separate development,' as each group was to occupy different areas and to participate differently in the country's economy and in the production and consumption of material and symbolic resources.

To further promote apartheid, the racial groups were compartmentalized into ten black nations and three non-black nations. Since whites constituted a minority of South Africa's population, the most effective way to rule was to prevent the 75 per cent black population from cohering into a unified group. A key means of achieving this was through an active state-controlled and state-sponsored African tribalism. This led to the creation of tribal bantustans, later known as homelands, each tied to a separate black 'nation' with its own language and bureaucratic structure. Though the implementation of these bantustans was widely resisted, it managed to create divisions within anti-apartheid organizations, since, as will later be seen, these organizations differed in their interpretation of the meaning of these homelands and in their participation in them. Furthermore, these basically rural bantustans were characterized by high unemployment rates and poverty, and served as labour reserves for the urban sectors. A black person who wanted to move from his/her homeland could only do so by entering into a work contract with a member of the white urbanized population, and was prohibited from bringing his/her family into the urban sectors. This practice resulted in the creation of a large urban-rural migrant labour population. In a nutshell, the bantustans were mostly populated by unemployed, disenfranchised people who, economically, had little to lose by involving themselves in the struggle against apartheid.

The second process of identity formation was a result of the struggle against apartheid, which took different forms of resistance from low-intensity war to mass mobilization. This struggle brought together apartheid opponents in a common assertion of a non-racial South Africa. In this way, black South Africans were unified in a struggle against a system of oppression and colonialism, which, to some degree, helped form a certain sense of 'African-ness' found in the unity of oppression.

Zegeye asserts that political organizations which participated in the anti-apartheid struggle contributed in the creation of this African identity by 'jointly and actively undermining apartheid notions of whiteness as representing political superiority and non-whiteness as representing political inferiority' (2001, p. 5).

As political organizations embarked on the struggle against apartheid, a third process of identity formation emerged. In the early stages of apartheid and the struggle against it, it was easy to define the struggle as one of black against white and to ignore what being black actually meant. However, as the struggle intensified, and as it became important to define the character of a post-apartheid state, opposition groups were divided in their ways of defining a post-apartheid South Africa and in identifying the position each political organization was to occupy within that future South Africa. Therefore, as the struggle intensified and as it became clear that the days of apartheid were almost over, the struggle became multi-focused. From one perspective, the focus was on the eradication of apartheid and on a move towards democratic elections. From another perspective, however, the struggle focused on the conflict between Xhosa and Zulu people, or between the African National Congress (ANC) and the Zulu-based Inkatha. At this juncture, the dominant perception believed the focus was on the conflict between ANC and Inkatha, the two leading black political parties in the country. During this period, political organizations were important agents of identity formation and influenced the decisions people made about who they were and with whom they were to relate. The manner in which political organizations shaped identities led to the concept of a 'politicized ethnicity' (Louw 1991).

This book is about the manner in which individuals negotiated all three processes of identity formation, thus giving birth to yet another process born out of the struggle against apartheid and consequently out of the struggle for envisioned power in post-apartheid South Africa. The emphasis here is on the importance of these historical, conflict-laden processes and I will argue that these processes laid the foundation for the construction of identities in post-independent South Africa. The focus is on youth processes of identity construction and negotiation in the region of KwaZulu/Natal where the majority of those who identified as Zulu lived. The book presents youth life stories of survival and identity negotiation in a region where to be youthful and politically active was associated with membership in the ANC and to be elderly and politically active was associated with membership in Inkatha. While the book presents a case study of KwaZulu/Natal youth identity formation and negotiation, media reports during this period indicated that issues of youth in this region mirrored a trend of events happening throughout the country. However, the discussion is designed to stand as an illustration, as opposed to a model of youth practices in changing political societies. The discussion here is limited to a comparison of identity formation within a few townships in South Africa. While broader generalizations require broader bases of comparison, it is hoped that the framework provided in this study might be useful for future undertakings on youth culture and identity construction in South Africa and elsewhere.

The Study of Youth, Identity, and Politics

I undertook this study in order to address the different socio-cultural practices that shaped youth social identitities in South Africa and to investigate the in-school and out-of-school activities of black African high-school students living in two townships of KwaZulu/Natal. The central issues are the construction, meaning, and negotiation of Zulu identity, and the manner in which this identity intersected with formal politics, encompassing the actions of political parties and other interest groups in competition for access to power in a post-apartheid state; and how it intersected with interpersonal politics, that is, the negotiation of relations of power and solidarity between individuals.

Media reports indicate that youths were considered a central problem in liberation politics, and it was anticipated that this problem would continue in a post-apartheid era. The media depicted youths as the perpetrators of the political violence that characterized the region in the mid-1980s and early 1990s. Even though these portrayals were, to some extent, true representations of the violence that characterized this era, some important aspects of youth activities were not presented. These unreported events included the struggles of youths trying to survive the social and economic hardships that marked this era, and the suffering that accompanied such struggles. Therefore, it has been necessary to uncover these practices and to understand the strategies and techniques that enabled youths to survive such hardships. A secondary objective, which was informed by my experiences working with youth in the region, was to demonstrate that their actions were in response to and an attempt to adapt to socio-political conditions that emanated from both state practices and, to some extent, practices in formal politics.

To understand the manner in which youths constructed and negotiated Zulu identity during this period of political transformation, it is important to outline the forces that shaped this identity. Twentieth-century Zulu identity was constructed from a number of important symbolic resources, including language, history, and culture. In my study I examine the use of these resources and the manner in which the South African state, black political organizations, and individuals used them to legitimize their practices and to locate these practices within a defined, though contradictory, Zulu identity.

The history of political consolidation under Shaka, the great Zulu leader who orchestrated armed resistance to British colonialism in the late 1800s, and the existence of the Zulu kingdom with its successful and continued resistance to colonial domination was one important and very complex set of resources.[1] As a result of this history, the name and the house of Shaka and the term Zulu kingdom were historical concepts that individual Africans, as well as African politicians, continued to draw on as a way of constructing their identities and of defining and legitimizing their socio-political and economic struggles. However, within these historic resources emerged both complexities and ambiguities that individuals had to negotiate.

The first complexity emerged as the South African state used this history to justify the racially motivated homeland structure of KwaZulu. The homeland system was an invention of the South African Nationalist Party, which formed the government in 1948. This policy divided people along racial/ethnic lines and differentially allocated to these groups economic resources that later contributed to the power struggle among these groups. Official segregation through the apartheid system included a certain degree of homeland independence within the broader apartheid state. KwaZulu was one such structure within the apartheid state, created as a home for those people defined by the Nationalist Party as linguistically and racially/ethnically Zulu and therefore as making up a Zulu 'nation.'

The second complexity involved the use of history by African nationalist leaders, whose efforts from the mid-1960s onwards focused on gaining state recognition for the Zulu monarchy and for territorial, political, and cultural rights for the Zulu people. These nationalist leaders included Chief Mangosuthu Buthelezi, whose leadership of the then Zulu Cultural Movement, Inkatha, was recognized by both the South African state and liberation organizations such as the African National Congress (ANC).[2] It was to such nationalist leaders that the idea of the KwaZulu homeland appeared attractive and worth embracing. Thus, to pursue and legitimize the existence of KwaZulu and their participation in it, it became important for these leaders to present the Zulu people as a homogeneous and well-defined linguistic and cultural group. To some extent, these politicians viewed KwaZulu as a strategy for the establishment of democratic political institutions, which addressed the socio-political and economic needs of the population in the region that could not be done within the larger South African structures. However, Kwa-Zulu was to respond only to the political and economic needs of the population, not to cultural reconstruction, because to these politicians, a specific Zulu identity, centring on the Zulu monarchy and its history, was already in place. The presentation of Zulu history by these African politicians was in itself full of contradictions. The first contradiction had to do with the presentation of the Zulu people as a unified group, which then ignored or suppressed the presentation of the history of other sub-groups in KwaZulu/Natal (and elsewhere) that were dominated and then destroyed by the Zulu warriors during the Shaka wars of conquest. A second contradiction related to the issue of leadership. Were the Zulu king and the Zulu royal house the legitimate representatives of the Zulu people or were politicians and their organizations, some of whom were closely related to Zulu royalty, the legitimate leaders?

A third complexity that arose with the use of this history was its association with a specific political party, the Inkatha Freedom Party (Inkatha), whose activities occurred alongside and often in conflict with those of the African National Congress. The ANC was formed in 1912 initially as a political organization looking after the interests of all black South Africans, while Inkatha originated in the 1920s as a cultural movement taking care of Zulu cultural interests that seemed to be undermined by industrialization and other socio-economic changes. Although there was no direct nexus between these two organizations, both used the symbols of the Zulu monarchy and its history in legitimizing their aims. They drew on the same membership and had the same effect of factionalizing KwaZulu/Natal within Zulu nationalist and class-based movements. Later, beginning in the 1950s, the same symbols and histories used to construct the KwaZulu nation gave form to the ANC and Inkatha, and were utilized by these organizations in the struggle against apartheid.

The national government's creation of the KwaZulu homeland added another layer of complexity to the use of this history by political organizations. First, it resulted in the claim by the KwaZulu homeland authority that they were the legitimate 'owners' of this history. This in turn meant that only those political parties, such as Inkatha, that supported and were simultaneously supported by KwaZulu had the legitimate right to use this history. Still another layer of complexity was added by individuals who saw themselves as owners of this history but who did not belong to KwaZulu-supported political organizations, or to any political organization for that matter. Did this mean that these individuals were no longer of Zulu heritage? Since this history was also used to distinguish the Zulu from non-Zulu, to which historical group did such individuals belong?

In addition to history, other symbolic resources, such as language, were highly idealized and controversial in KwaZulu/Natal. Linguistic and cultural practices played a crucial role in the social and political organization of the region, as well as in strategies for the restructuring of a post-apartheid South Africa. This symbolic role of language, and of cultural material in general, was particularly true in Durban, KwaZulu/Natal's largest city, where the ANC and Inkatha were competing for political control over the townships that surround it.

One such resource was the colour and style of clothing, with both sides adopting green and gold. Yellow and black berets were associated with the ANC; the khaki colour was associated with Inkatha. Survivors – that is, those not killed in the violence that came with the struggle for control – wore none of these. As well, the tradition that older men and women carried walking sticks had ended, since these sticks were associated with Inkatha and rendered their users liable to attack from ANC supporters. Survivors carried nothing. Language accents were also important. Someone who spoke Zulu with a 'slang' dialect called *tsotsi-taal* or Johannesburg Zulu was suspected of being an ANC supporter. Someone who spoke with a 'deep' or 'rural' Zulu accent was thought to support Inkatha. Survivors spoke little in public. In a nutshell, any display that was considered provocative was avoided by the prudent.

Symbolic resources, the establishment and practices of the KwaZulu authority, and political organizations, created a number of ambiguities and paradoxes that individuals had to comprehend in order to negotiate township life. Thus, since not all black people agreed on the notion of a KwaZulu homeland as a legitimate administrative structure and a legitimate political locale from which their struggles could be fought, groups emerged that aimed at fighting both the Pretoria and KwaZulu levels of governments. The result was a conflict within and between liberation groups, which later erupted into violence, the so-called black-on-black violence.

But who exactly were involved in this conflict, and what were the criteria used to identify them? In a simplistic analysis, the conflict was between the supporters of the ANC and Inkatha, the two leading political parties in the region, and involved youths, who were believed to make up the majority of ANC followers in KwaZulu/Natal, and adults, who were believed to constitute the majority of Inkatha membership. First, the ANC and Inkatha differed in the strategies they employed in fighting against white domination. This difference became increasingly articulated in the last stages of apartheid and, therefore, in defining the character of a post-apartheid (KwaZulu) state. To the ANC, a post-apartheid state meant a South Africa that realized equality for all groups, a 'nonracial' democratic state. Inkatha, however, envisioned a post-apartheid state organized according to ethnic constituencies and accommodating group rights and group vetoes which would ensure that the Zulus maintained control over the resources that they were allocated under the apartheid state. As Lowe notes: 'Big capitalists and the state even now reward Inkatha aspirant accumulators for their pro-capitalist stance with access to capital and joint investment schemes; ethno-regionalism would also allow Inkatha's chiefs to retain their neo-traditional authoritarian powers and means of accumulation' (1991, p. 198).

To the ANC, however, such a state would be a duplication of apartheid methods of governing, which divided people into racial/ethnic groups. To mobilize in the region, therefore, the ANC had to convince the Zulus that their rights both as Zulus and as South Africans would not be eroded if it came to power. Inkatha, however, went on a mission to paint the ANC as anti-Zulu, an agent of the Xhosa bent on the genocide of the Zulu.[3] These differences were played out in the politics of identity in KwaZulu/Natal and influenced the way individuals positioned themselves politically/linguistically and ethnically, and by so doing contributed to the formation of the political economic character of a post-apartheid state. It was in such a political conflict that the activities of youths rendered themselves profitable to both sides and resulted in the killing of hundreds of innocent bystanders.

The involvement of youth in liberation politics, especially from the well-documented 1976 student uprising[4] and onwards, provided the state with an ever-increasing problem of managing and protecting apartheid and its structures. And despite state efforts to suppress opposition, youth involvement in political activity increased. By 1990 the activity of youths in the liberation struggle was now a concern for both the South African state and opposition groups.

Initially, youth activity in the liberation struggle involved peaceful ways of protesting, such as demonstrations and marches. As the struggle continued, youth militancy became, from the point of view of the state, ungovernable, and to political organizations, a point of great concern. The state viewed youth as a problem to be controlled, managed, or suppressed. Political parties were also continuously in search of positive solutions to alleviate what became known as the 'youth problem.'

In KwaZulu/Natal, the proliferation of youth activity could be traced to the political unrest that swept over the townships and rural areas in the 1980s. The township uprisings of the mid-1980s were based on the attempts of the United Democratic Front (UDF) – then considered as the inner wing of the then exiled ANC – to render the townships ungovernable. This campaign evolved into violent efforts to destroy the structures of the state and its clients, including the police, suspected informers, township counsellors seen as puppets of the apartheid government, and homeland officials. The result was a conflict between ANC and Inkatha supporters.

Yet political killings accounted for only a small fraction of the violence that swept over South Africa in the mid-1980s and early 1990s. Estimates indicated that purely criminal murders outnumbered politically motivated murders by five to one. The media reported that unemployment surpassed 40 per cent among black South Africans and in some areas reached 90 per cent among the so-called lost generation. These were the black youth who had been militant in the township uprisings of the 1980s and were now ill-equipped to compete in an economy that had been shrinking because of economic sanctions and other factors. The failing economy drove hundreds of people from the rural areas into the crowded townships, which escalated the problem of housing shortages, lack of schools and transportation, and the breakdown of family structures and other sources of authority. As a result, organized crime flourished, with the youth running gambling rackets, drugs, and, above all, guns.

The interrelationship between the political struggle and crime was complicated as political parties competed for access to political power in the region of KwaZulu/Natal. It became difficult to distinguish those for whom behaviour that would usually be considered criminal was justified by the struggle from those for whom the struggle was a pretext. For instance, warlords who were part of Inkatha and had either emerged as gangsters or served a vigilantes against crime (or both) were inevitably drawn into the political struggle. The ANC produced many township toughs, with tax bases of their own. Criminals who, in the name of the struggle, looted, extorted, and murdered for personal gains exploited the struggle against apartheid. Lines of authority were blurred, and legal accountability for abuses did not exist.

It was at the height of this political and criminal militancy and turmoil that I undertook this study. Basically, I sought to uncover how youth, at this historical juncture, navigated township lives. For many of these young people, any positive sense of their future, or even the notion that they had a future, was disabled or deflected by the violence in their lives. Despite the harsh realities they experienced, the media portrayed them as an ever-growing problem for the future South Africa and reinforced the inevitability of their continued poverty in a transformed society. Portrayals of their vanishing communities, depressed economies, and disappearing families did little to foster more positive models of a successful future.

Research Questions and Objectives

How, then, did youth living in the townships of KwaZulu/Natal construct and pursue alternatives that enriched their lives – alternatives that provided them with images of a productive and meaningful future? How did young people navigate the anarchistic tendencies of township life and construct positive identities and perceptions of themselves as members of society? Was the violence in the townships a means to an end or an end in itself?

These questions revealed a key element of youth survival in the townships: the emerging social groups made up of youths struggling to make life a meaningful experience for themselves. The historical, political, and economic conditions of this era underscored the different values attributed to the various groups. These same political and economic conditions influenced the positions of specific groups of people in specific ways. This book focuses on the practices of individuals who belonged to self-defined groups and demonstrates how the socio-political and economic experiences of such individuals were both hallmarks to the formation of the groups themselves and to group identity and practices. These individuals operated in particular social spaces – that is, not the geographically defined spaces in which the groups were found but to the experiential spaces that made it possible to enact group practices. Social space, therefore, encompasses both practice and locale. For example, to the soccer group, the soccer field was a geographically defined space in which members of this group were commonly found. But soccer as a social space refers to those practices, beliefs, behaviours, and values that were allowed within the group. The group might have changed their geographic location and decided to play along the riverside, but their values and beliefs – the rules regulating what and how members of the group behaved – remained the same despite shifts in geographic location.

Once these social groups were located, it then became important to ask what it was that some groups offered that others did not. To answer this question, it became important to have information about the ecology of the social groups and about the ways that township politics, financial possibilities, and other related issues affected them. What was the form and content of these youth groups? What were the socio-political, cultural, and linguistic practices that defined each of them as groups? How did their practices construct their ethnolinguistic identities? And in which spaces did different aspects of their identities become important? Specifically, how did youths negotiate the labels imposed on them, first, by the state; second, by political organizations; and third, by their own practices? How did they deal with the dominant categories of Zulus versus Xhosa and of Inkatha versus ANC? How fluid was the boundary between these categories, and how did youth deal with this fluidity?

It also became important to know how these social groups were embedded in layers – from their local township to regional politics to the larger state – which shaped their institutional and individual identities, and how the diverse conceptions of youth expressed in various spaces within the township joined together (or did not join together) to produce possibilities for a better life in a post-apartheid era. There was also concern about socio-political structures and how these existing structures constrained or enhanced the ways in which social groups operated in dealing with township life and providing possibilities for the future.

In the first section of the book, chapters two to five provide background information necessary for contextualizing the ethnographic material that is presented in the second section. Chapter two describes methods used for data collection; chapter three details the historic development of the region of KwaZulu/Natal and the evolution of Inkatha and the ANC; chapter four undertakes a specific look at the townships in which the study was done; and chapter five sets out the tensions that existed in KwaZulu/Natal at the time of the study, tensions which necessitated crucial strategies for youth survival. The second section of the book discusses the youth groups in the townships, the spaces they occupied, the social and political practices they engaged in, and the strategies they embarked on to navigate township life. Three youth groups are presented in chapters six to nine: tsatsatsa, soccer, and church-based groups. The conclusion in chapter ten synchronizes the different practices of the youths and relates the underlying substance of these practices to issues of symbolic representation, formal politics, and the construction of identity. In particular, this chapter informs the struggles involved in the constant negotiation of symbolic meaning, representation, and practice in the construction of youth identity.

chapter 2

Methodology

Identifying the Site and Participants

My intended site for data collection had been the townships in Pieter-maritzburg, Natal's provincial capital. This choice had been made for two reasons. First, I had lived and worked in Pietermaritzburg for a number of years before migrating to Canada in 1988. Second, I had returned to Pietermaritzburg to collect data for my master's thesis for a period of three months in 1989. Based on my experience in this area, I felt that it would be a suitable one to address the central theme in this study: the construction and negotiation of identity at a time of political turmoil.

Upon arriving in Pietermaritzburg, I contacted friends with whom I had worked as a teacher and in the liberation struggle. Although I approached them at different times, they all agreed on one issue: Pieter-maritzburg was no longer a safe place to conduct research because violence in the area had increased since the last time I had collected data there. In 1989 the estimated number of deaths per day was twenty; by 1992 it had increased to about sixty. A number of friends suggested that I consider some of the townships in Durban, and recommended Umlazi as a comparatively stable place. I have close relatives and friends in Durban, and had in fact frequented the place as a safe haven on weekends and holidays during the time I worked in Pietermaritzburg. Further-more, these two cities are only seventy kilometres apart. I welcomed this suggestion and left for Umlazi.

Both my relatives and friends welcomed my arrival at Umlazi, although my relatives were not very enthusiastic about my research agenda, especially after they heard some of the issues that I planned to investigated, which they interpreted as a search for trouble. This was the beginning of my lessons about the political history of Umlazi at that time. With the help of friends who were involved in soccer, I established contact with a soccer group in the area and I developed close contacts with a few individuals who became key informants. In turn, these soccer informants introduced me to other youth groups, and to other individuals at Umlazi whom they knew even though they did not closely associate with them. As the introductions continued, I also established relations with individuals who were not residents of Umlazi. These were people who, for a variety of reasons, attended school at Umlazi, but were residents of another Durban township, KwaMashu. It became important to familiarize myself with KwaMashu also in order to pursue data collection in this township. In most cases, my first introduction was as a relative of a friend, or a friend of a friend; it was only at the school that I introduced myself primarily as a researcher. I never introduced myself as a member of the ANC; however, as I worked along, it became important to state my political orientation in order to gain the trust of the people I worked with. With the exception of one group of youths, I approached individuals without any knowledge of their political affiliations.

In both Umlazi and KwaMashu, I developed about ten close relationships that made up the first circle of key informants. The second circle was made up of twenty or more people with whom I had regular relations. Most, although not all, of these people in these two circles were between the ages of twenty and thirty-five. It is probably significant to my analysis that these were often people whom I felt to be like me in important ways – that is, were involved in similar social and political practices as myself. My key informants were drawn from a single political persuasion, the ANC. This was partly because that was the party that I belonged to, and also because it would have been impossible to work closely with individuals from a variety of political parties. KwaZulu/ Natal had been so highly politicized that political neutrality did not exist, and those who claimed to have no sympathies for any political party were told by their associates to which political party they belonged. The relationship between members of Inkatha and the ANC was so hostile that it would have been impossible for me to work with participants from both organizations. I chose to work with participants from the ANC, and for my safety and the safety of those I worked with, I distanced myself from working with people of opposing parties. The fact that the people I worked closely with were of a single political persuasion may have biased the views presented by this study. Nonetheless, none of my participants should be held responsible for these views.

Beyond these two groups of participants is another circle of about a dozen people from KwaMashu with whom I met more than once. This group was diverse in political and class background, as well as in age. I owe a great deal of what I know about KwaMashu to this group of people who helped me understand the politics of this township by providing me with detailed oral information which I could otherwise not have obtained. Most of the political and criminal activities of KwaMashu between the years 1985 and 1992 are yet to be documented.

The Relevance of My Identity to the Research

I grew up with what I would call a strong Zulu background since my parents upheld Zulu tradition and culture.[1] My mother is a product of the missionaries and grew up in a Christian family with aspirations of progress and social mobility, which could only be attained through missionary education. My mother's father was one of the few educated men of the early 1900s and for a variety of reasons was considered a 'true convert' (meaning he had fully abandoned the African religion from which he was converted) by both the missionaries and the community. Because of his German-missionary education, he was able to translate the German Lutheran hymnbook into Zulu, and his name appears at the end of many of the songs in this book.

My father, on the other hand, came from what I would term a traditional family – traditional in the sense that although his mother had heard of the Christian religion and in fact supported and practised it, she had not abandoned the Zulu traditional ways of worship, the ancestral beliefs. So while my mother came from a family of converts, the *amaKholwa*, my father was a product of both missionary education and African ways of existing. Furthermore, while Mother was born into missionary education, Father came into contact with education only through working as a garden boy for the missionaries in the area. My parents' different backgrounds have had a profound influence on the ways they brought up our family.

As children, we listened to a lot of biblical stories from my mother and a lot of traditional oral stories from my father. For a variety of reasons, we loathed those days in which my mother had to tell us stories before bedtime. The biblical stories of David and Goliath, interesting as they may be, were no match for the legendary African stories that my father told. Like most Zulu children, I grew up with Zulu stories of war and conquest, as well as of resistance and defeat. I knew the names of Shaka, Dingane, Cetshwayo and other Zulu kings, of Mkabayi, Nandi, and other Zulu heroes, not by reading any textbook but through the stories that my parents told us.[2]

For reasons associated with apartheid, and the countrywide depression of the 1960s, my family left South Africa for Swaziland in 1967 but returned in 1975 when Inkatha was resurrected. Like many, my parents considered Inkatha a genuine locale from which to fight apartheid, and viewed it as the inner wing of the ANC. My parents were at the forefront of Inkatha activities in the Nongoma region of KwaZulu. Yet Inkatha was torn with divisions from the very beginning, as individuals competed for power and positions within the organization. These positions translated into economic benefits as prominent Inkatha members took over private businesses with financial backing from Ithala, KwaZulu's financial institution.

From 1978 to 1981 my father was also the president of the Natal African Teachers' Union (NATU), an Inkatha affiliate. This position made it easy for him to organize both Inkatha and NATU activities in the Nongoma region. His activities, however, were not well received by the Inkatha regional coordinator, who viewed my father as a threat to his position and portrayed him at the Inkatha head office in Ulundi as a 'foreigner,' that is, someone who had worked for the ANC in Swaziland. However, since Ulundi wanted to maintain good relations with NATU, of which my father was still president, it became difficult for its officials to deal with this accusation. My father died in August 1981 in the midst of this conflict. My mother moved the family to Melmoth, Natal, my father's birthplace.

I started at the University of Swaziland the year my father died. Attending a university, particularly the University of Botswana and Swaziland, which, because of its British standards, was considered one of the best in the Southern African region, probably speaks to my privileged background. It was during my university years that my involvement in politics took a different turn. I evaluated the lessons and politics of Inkatha that I had learned through my parents. By this time, Inkatha's politics had shifted and the ties it had with the ANC had been broken. More important, however, it was during this time that Inkatha expressed its first violent response to criticism and opposition. For example, in 1980, a group of students from the University of Zululand protested the appearance at the graduation ceremony of Chief Buthelezi, then

Inkatha's president and KwaZulu's chief minister, and chancellor of the university. Buthelezi's response was to send in a group of *amabutho* (Zulu regiments), who, on the day of the ceremony, attacked and killed six of the protesting students. It was at the height of such incidents that the United Democratic Front (UDF) was formed as the inner wing of the ANC, and many like myself, who were already disillusioned with Inkatha' s path, joined it.

After finishing my degree, I worked for the Department of the Chief Minister as an education officer at Ulundi for two years. Initially, there seemed to have been no problem with my UDF activities at Ulundi. I formed relations with a group of women who had started working for the department around the same time as myself, and had also graduated from universities in 1985. For reasons that I no longer remember, we soon were referred to by our colleagues as the 'academic clique.' It is probably our close friendship that brought us trouble with KwaZulu authorities, for, as our circle matured, KwaZulu authorities began to look into our backgrounds in search of reasons for our associations. Moreover, many of our practices differed from those of most civil servants, some of whom were not members of Inkatha but casually participated in its activities. For example, one of the things that was expected of civil servants, especially of those who worked at the Department of the Chief Minister, was to volunteer 'collecting' or putting together for distribution, the chief minister's speech whenever there was a big Inkatha conference. None of the members of the academic clique participated in this, and at one time when I was asked to do so by the chief education officer, I responded by saying that I was going to do so only if I was going to be paid for working overtime. Similarly, when we were expected to prepare for upcoming Inkatha conferences, we systematically scheduled ourselves to be working outside Ulundi in other Kwa-Zulu projects which were part of the department.

Our refusal to be involved in Inkatha-related events led KwaZulu authorities to discover that all of us had, at one time or another, participated in anti-apartheid demonstrations organized by our respective universities, and a few had spent nights in prison for such activities. For example, immediately after the death of Swaziland's King Sobhuza II in 1982, South African authorities took advantage of this time, and entered then kidnapped those South Africans who had been given political refuge by the Swaziland government. As a student at the University of Swaziland, I was involved in organizing marches, partly to protest the actions of the South African regime, and also urged Swaziland authorities to act on behalf of those who had been taken to be tortured in South Africa. One of those taken was a former president of the university student association. Although it was never clear why the Swaziland government was against these protest marches, it became clear to us that with the death of King Sobhuza, political relations that Swaziland had previously had with South Africa had dramatically changed. Swaziland police were involved in arresting and/or deporting those university students who were wanted by the South African government. The KwaZulu officials soon discovered my part in the protests at Swaziland and the political relations with South African universities that we had established for solidarity purposes. Once our political activities and affiliations were out in the open, they could not be tolerated by these officials, who viewed us as anti-authority, with the potential to mobilize against KwaZulu or Inkatha. Indeed, some of my friends in the clique had direct UDF records, which further contributed to us being categorized as UDF spies in KwaZulu. The details of what followed are not important; nevertheless, that same year all the members of the academic clique left Ulundi, and two of us sought work in Pietermaritzburg.

I lived with my mother's sister's family[3] in Pietermaritzburg and became involved in UDF activities. As a high school teacher, I became involved with community-based programs that aimed at encouraging youth to go back to school and to make something of themselves. These programs addressed, in part, the material needs of students, such as providing shelter for those whose homes had been destroyed by 'the enemy.' Such shelters were controversial, however, since they were also aligned with either Inkatha or the UDF. At the heart of my activity (and of many of my colleagues') was the belief that the youth were not to blame for the political chaos that engulfed KwaZulu/Natal at this time, and that their actions were a response and an attempt to adapt to sociopolitical conditions created by the apartheid state. I left Pietermaritzburg for studies in Canada in 1988, at the height of the UDF/Inkatha conflict, and at the height of my political activism.

I was seventeen years old the year my father died, yet a lot of what I write about Inkatha and its structures comes from the knowledge I gained during my father's prominence in the organization and with NATU before 1981; indeed, I was part of and participated in most of those activities. I also gained a lot of knowledge about Inkatha during the two years that I worked for the department of the Chief Minister at Ulundi, for this was Chief Buthelezi's headquarters, and the place where a lot of crucial decisions about Inkatha's activities were made. More importantly, I learnt a lot about the chief minister's office through my friends in the academic clique who worked as communication officers. None of these friends, however, are responsible for any of the views expressed about Inkatha in this study.

At the time that I worked at Ulundi, I lived with my brother Nkonzo, who is ten years younger than me, and was attending his first year of secondary education.[4] We shared a lot of ideas that ranged from formal politics to education to family matters. One day in 1986 he returned home from school and asked what I thought of the Shaka Day celebrations that were to take place at Stanger that September. My response was to the effect that Shaka is a celebrated figure because he consolidated the Zulu nation, and therefore a key historic symbol worth celebrating. He responded by stating that his teacher had told them that Shaka, like Napoleon, was nothing but a blood-hungry killer who butchered innocent people in the name of power. From this, my brother continued, he didn't think that the Zulu people need to put so much emphasis on the Shakan wars of conquest, or on celebrating Shaka Day for that matter. My immediate response was to come to the defence of Zulu history. I told my brother that even in Russia, Shaka's portrait appears on the walls of the parliamentary buildings as one of the bravest warriors of all time, and that if the Russians could acknowledge him as a hero, then the least we could do as Zulu people was to celebrate Shaka Day. My brother was not convinced and simply looked at me and said, '*Bengithi uyi UDF*' (I thought you were UDF).

That conversation started me thinking about the contradictions that were inherent in Zulu history itself. But more importantly, I thought about the changes that had occurred over the ten years that I was growing up. I had been brought up with respected and legitimized symbols in Zulu history that I would not dare challenge. Yet within my family was someone who questioned the legitimacy of that history and its symbols. Ironically, the criticisms and revaluations of Zulu historic symbols occurred within the proximity of KwaZulu headquarters, and was facilitated by Zulu teachers, in KwaZulu-controlled schools like the one my brother attended. Yet KwaZulu authority and Inkatha believed the enemy to be in places like Pietermaritzburg where anti-KwaZulu activities were at their peak. The overriding lesson for me that day however, was that my brother had clearly stated that UDF people such as myself could not support the traditional view of Zulu history; one was either UDF or Zulu, but not both. There existed a superficial border between Zulus who were viewed as Inkatha, and the UDF, which was believed to be constituted of any ethnic/linguistic groups other than Zulu.

My identity as I approached the townships of Durban for my research, therefore, was as a Zulu person trying to reconcile being UDF/ANC[5] and remaining Zulu. I had concerns about my political relations with those people close to me, especially my mother, who, despite great dissatisfaction and regrets about Inkatha, continued to support and be at the forefront of its activities. Indeed, I owe a lot of the information about Zulu history and of Inkatha in general, to her and her continued guidance. As I faced trouble at Ulundi, it was my mother's descent,[6] and her strong participation in Inkatha that protected me by making my case ambivalent. Even though I moved to Pietermaritzburg, I was still able to get employment in a KwaZulu-controlled area. Many of my friends in the academic clique whose parents were first-generation mmigrants in KwaZulu/Natal were not so lucky and had to seek employment outside of KwaZulu-controlled areas.[7]

My socio-political identity also led me to seek answers about the youths who were not as lucky as myself and did not have the support of family structures. I wanted to know how they survived the identity conflicts that affected even privileged people such as me. I had had a glimpse of this during my years of work in Pietermaritzburg, but was still in search of a fuller understanding of events. More importantly, however, I approached these townships looking for solutions to the youth problems, and seeking ways in which my understanding of youth activities could prevent future generations from experiencing similar hardships. This study then is my own testimony, as well as that of the youths involved; it is a testimony of the social, economic, and identity conflicts that young people had to deal with in order to achieve their goals in a period of political chaos.

Tenure of Fieldwork

I arrived at Umlazi in January 1992 and stayed until well after the end of the first school term in June the same year. I spent my first month and a half at observing different groups of youths who were participating in a variety of sports in one of Umlazi's soccer fields. I established contact with a player nicknamed Sugar and with some of his associates, who in turn introduced me to other youths, the tsatsatsa, who, however, did not participate in this soccer space. Towards the end of the second month I asked these youths if I could observe them in their school activities. They agreed. This then led me to two schools, Umganga High School at

Umlazi, and Greensburg High School, located in one of Durban's white suburbs.

I gained permission from the principals of both these schools to attend classes in order to observe the informants. This part of the research lasted from mid-February until the end of the school term in June. At Umganga I concentrated on two classrooms. One was made up of twenty-two students, six of whom were already key informants, and the other had forty students, two of whom became key informants. At Greensburg I also observed two classrooms of about thirty students each, and in each classroom was one key informant. I must add, though, that the teachers at Greensburg were concerned that I was interested in observing these students because, to them, they did not present a 'true' picture of what the school was about. So I was encouraged to observe other classrooms to give myself a sense of the school. This I agreed to do. I spent two full days each week at Umganga, and one day of the week at Greensburg. I often spent an extra day in Umganga just hanging out; that is, although I did not have any scheduled classroom observations, I observed the staff room, the library, music practices, and used to social-ize with a variety of people in the school.

I began my observations at Umganga, sitting at the back of the room and quietly observed the daily performance of the various classes. I moved between the two classrooms as opportunity permitted and usu-ally stayed with a class for a few periods each day. I focused on observing those classes that seemed most topically related to issues of language and nationalism/ethnicity, such as Zulu, English, and history. I did not attend science and mathematics classes, but on a few occasions I attended music classes since it was there that interesting interactions often occurred between students – interactions that focused on the meaning and legitimacy of the songs they practised. Towards the end of the school term, however, in one of the classes (the tsatsatsa class) I was invited by the key informants to share some of the discussions we had had around issues of language and ethnicity with the rest of the class. This I agreed to do, and we scheduled these discussions for the last school period. These discussions lasted for about two months.

Many of the high school teachers at Umganga were about my age or older, and this made it easy to socialize with them. Similarly, I found it easy to form friendships with the groups of students in the classes I attended. My original contact with the key informants had been inde-pendent of the school, so I was not viewed as a teacher or other author-ity figure. Also, I only worked with the most students who were in their last two years of high school. Many of these were mature students who had, for a variety of reasons at one stage in their lives, dropped out of school. They had returned to Umganga for an education they believed was to give them social mobility. As a result of their experiences, most of the students I worked with were between the ages of twenty-one and twenty-six. The age difference, then, between me and these students was not that great.

All this said, however, it is important to understand that the relations I had with these students were ones of respect. Although I viewed myself as one of them, I was constantly aware of the differences in interaction between them as a group, and between them and me as a researcher. For instance, although I was never referred to as 'teacher Dlamini' or 'teacher Nombuso' as they would have done with their teachers, they always referred to me as sisi Nombuso, a typical Zulu way of addressing those one respects.

The situation at Greensburg was slightly different. I had close relations with only those teachers whose classes I observed, although I did have a good rapport with the students I observed in this school. As the staff at Greensburg was all white, I felt a bit out of place. Moreover, both the key informants in this school were only fourteen, and although I became close to them as time went on, this relationship never resembled that which I had with the students at Umganga.

Participation

In this study I have followed a participation-observation approach, spending a great deal of time in the classrooms as well as in the homes of key informants. Classroom observations were not that complex, and followed the usual procedure in which the researcher sits at the back of the classroom recording verbal utterances, and waiting for something significant to happen. Initially, my presence in the classroom was a novelty and somewhat of a distraction, but over a course of a week or so, the students were more comfortable with my presence and resumed their normal behaviour. In many of these observations, I relied heavily on my ability to scratch down as many details and direct quotes as I was able to, as the classrooms were not conducive for tape recording.

A lot of my observations also took place outside of Umlazi, in situations where the key informants were found. For example, the tsatsatsa had jobs in the city centre and therefore established relationships with co-workers who did not live in the townships. Accordingly, tsatsatsa spent most of their out-of-school time outside the township and it became important to see them in these other spaces in order to understand their strategies of survival during this period.

Observations that occurred outside the classrooms were a complex undertaking, and my level of participation varied between groups. For instance, I could not participate as a player in the soccer groups, and my interactions were different, largely due to my status as an adult. The soccer teams involved individuals between the ages of twelve and sixteen, which meant that the age difference was a significant factor. Within this group though, I developed close relations with the two men who founded and were the organizers of these soccer teams.

The relationship I developed with tsatsatsa and their associates, and other individuals who were about the same age, was a different one, however. Initially, it was difficult to establish meaningful relations with this group, and with other individuals who were not in this group. First, I would make arrangements to observe them at an arranged place such as the playground, only to find that there was nobody there. In my next encounter I would ask about the previous appointment, only to be told that they had changed their minds and decided to go to watch a movie, but did not bother to inform me.

The first month of observations was full of frustrations, basically emanating from similar incidents, and perhaps from my own anxiety to get things going. My approach towards the groups was that of a researcher, eager to get as much information from the participants as I could, through setting up interviews that aimed at learning more about who these people were. Although I did speak and recorded the conversations with each of these individuals, none of the information they gave me was relevant beyond knowing their names and addresses. Once I put away my tape recorder and stopped asking questions, but instead observed and made comments when need be, things began to change. Towards the third month of data collection, I no longer had to ask these individuals about locales where I could find them, but instead they would phone and inform me about their weekend agendas.

I observed and participated in most of the activities of tsatsatsa and associates. Some of their activities involved organizing ANC rallies, demonstrations, and meetings. Although I initially attended these rallies on my own or with other friends, by the third month of data collection I was planning and doing most of these activities with them. They invited me to many of their social activities, such as movies, and I got to attend a number of their family events, including weddings and funerals. In the middle of all this participation was the issue of trust. The political atmosphere was so tense that people just did not talk to strangers. One of the reasons then that made it difficult to establish relations at the beginning was that people did not know who I was. It became important for me to open up to these young people and participate in their discussions so they could know my views about issues, and most importantly, my political associations. Once that was established, the atmosphere became conducive to research and our relationship could then be developed.

It is difficult to say how much even the people within the inner circle trusted me, because I was constantly accused of being secretive, and of not being honest enough with them. For example, an incident in one of the classrooms at Umganga centred on Inkatha's actions and respect for elders. At the end of one class, the teacher mentioned that she was not going to give the class homework because she knew that a lot of the students were going to the late Chris Hani's vigil service that was to be held at the city centre on a Friday.[8] 'Sesobonana khona-ke,' she said (We will see each other there). Since Friday was a school day – and perhaps since it was known that the KwaZulu Department of Education and Culture (KDEC) was against teachers' participating in ANC-oriented events – one student responded by saying 'uGatsha ngeke akuvume lokho' (Gatsha [Chief Buthelezi] won't agree to that). The teacher was enraged: 'umbizelani undunankulu ngegama? NgesiZulu uyabizwa na umuntu omdala ngegama?' (Why are you calling the chief minister by name? In Zulu do you call adults by name?) The student was then ordered to go to the principal's office to be disciplined. This teacher's actions caused debate and controversy in the school, especially among the students. In the tsatsatsa class, to which six of the key informants belonged, students questioned whether this teacher was a 'true' ANC. Some teachers argued that Inkatha treated students and even teachers with disrespect; therefore, it did not deserve respect. Others supported the teacher by arguing that no one should abandon his or her culture even when they are shown disrespect by people considered as authority in that culture. In my opinion, what this teacher seems to have been saying was that there are values and beliefs that Zulu people had to comply with irrespective of their political orientation.[9]

This incident was still the subject of later discussions inside the school. Tsatsatsa informants wanted to know whether I thought the teacher was correct to punish the student, or to make an issue out of the student's comment. My response was that I didn't know what to make of this incident because both parties seemed to have good reasons for doing what they did. 'You see, this is what we always say, you are never honest,' somebody concluded. People could not sit on the fence in Kwa-Zulu/Natal, they had to take sides, and a refusal to do so was interpreted as being dishonest or secretive. Thus, even though I had close relations with tsatsatsa, I continuously had to monitor my actions in order to meet with their demands as to how group interactions occurred.

Despite continued efforts on my part to understand the course of events in the townships, throughout the period of data collection incidents in these townships indicated to me that they were sometimes beyond my comprehension. A particular incident occurred on the last week of data collection that remains vivid in my mind. On my last visit to my cousin, who also lives at Umlazi, we discussed which political party might win the anticipated elections. I had previously visited my cousin's place frequently and had listened while my cousin and his friends mocked and made fun of Chief Buthelezi's manner of speaking. Although I had laughed at these sallies, I never disclosed my views about Inkatha or Chief Buthelezi. This was partly because the opportunity never presented itself, and partly because I thought it was understood that all those involved in these conversations were not Inkatha, otherwise why would they mock it? On this particular day, I joined the conversation and mentioned that, despite the ANC's weaknesses, I was confident that 'we' would win the elections, that the problem might be with the second elections since the ANC would have been given plenty of time to fulfil its promises, and that I was disillusioned about its potential to deliver these promises. By the time I finished saying my piece, everyone in the room was silent. My cousin turned around and asked me a rhetorical question, *'Mzala usho obani uma uthi 'sizowina'?'* (Cousin, who do you mean when you say 'we will win'?). I said, *'Thina, uyazi nje nawe ukuthi ngisho obani'* (Us, you know who I mean). *'Angazi, usho iANC?'* (No, I do not know. Do you mean the ANC?), he asked but did not wait for me to respond. *'Amambhuka awangeni lapha emzini wami'* (Traitors do not come to my house), he concluded. The conversation ended.

I had totally misread the actions of my cousin and his friends, thinking that their actions of mocking Inkatha's chief were motivated by the same ideas as my own. They also had trusted me well enough to carry on such conversations about Inkatha and indeed thought I was 'one of them.' My sister Sihle, who was with me during this visit, later mentioned that she thought I was naive to have made this assumption, *'Usho ukuthi awukazi namanje ukuthi abantu bakwaZulu bamthanda kanjani u Gatsha?'* (Do you mean to say you still don't know how much Zulu people like/support Gatsha?), she had asked. This incident illustrates the complexity of relationships that existed in the townships. This incident also speaks to the ambiguity of the meaning of Zulu itself. My sister's statement also implied that those people who did not support Chief Buthelezi, myself included, were not Zulus. This study is indeed full of ambiguities and constitute a significant part of this study.

My most regrettable shortcoming in this study is with respect to the group of Inkatha youths that existed in the townships. It would have been interesting to find out about the ideologies that governed their actions, and the manner in which these ideologies assisted them in navigating township lives. I believe that youths in general, whether of Inkatha or ANC formation, suffered a lot because of the political conflict that characterized the townships at this time.

Interviewing

The usefulness of formal interviews with both the youth and old people I spoke with was often restricted to the tangible details of their life histories, and their addresses. As a result, most of the interviews were informal, undertaken in such a way that people felt I was talking with them as opposed to asking them information about events. Moreover, during this historic period, asking questions was neither a profitable nor a safe thing to do. People were suspicious of those who asked questions, especially because often questions were asked by specific people for a specific political party. In most cases therefore, I was part of discussions, rather than a researcher armed with a specific set of questions.

Youths are the focus of this study. Yet it became important to interview and talk with older people – that is, people who were in their late forties and fifties who had a wealth of knowledge. These people were helpful in providing me with an analysis of events surrounding the political turmoil that enveloped the townships at this time. Many events that had occurred in the townships, especially KwaMashu, between 1985 and 1992 were not available in books for me to read. The discussions and interviews I had with the people of KwaMashu helped reconstruct these events. Part of the discussions about the political history of KwaMashu during this era is presented in the following two chapters.

Specific Forms of Data and Data Analysis

The data in this study were obtained through formal and recorded interviews and discussions, and also from brief comments people made about current events in the region. Specifically, I was interested in the way people spoke about the political conflict that engulfed KwaZulu/ Natal during this period and how they situated themselves in this conflict. I was particularly interested in statements that displayed the identity of either the speaker or others she/he knew. For example, often people referred to themselves as Zulu, and used this term to explain their actions. In some instances I asked for specific clarification of what they meant; in others, it was difficult to do so because people knew that I identified as Zulu and therefore expected me to at least be aware of these meanings.

In addition to specific statements of identity, I also observed everyday practices of the key informants, and of other people close to them. I looked specifically at behaviour, particularly practices of language use and how these positioned people within the categories Zulu, Inkatha, or ANC, whose meanings are explained in chapter six. I also looked at social/cultural practices, and the manner these positioned people within the three categories of Zulu, Inkatha, and ANC. In most of these observations, I asked those people who were involved in these practices to clarify why they were involved in them and how such practices positioned them in the ongoing struggle.

I also observed public political activities, specifically those of the ANC, which helped to inform me of the contradictions between what people said they did and their actual practices. I read newspapers, listened to the radio, spoke to friends and family who helped me understand some of these events. During observations, I depended entirely on my ability to take field notes, which I rewrote at the end of each day for consumption by a broader audience. Most of the notes were written in the Zulu language because most of the participants used Zulu.

Added to the above were two sets of interviews; the first set was conducted at the beginning of data collection, and was with individuals whom I had selected as key informants but had not yet started observing in their schools. These interviews were designed mainly to uncover information about these youths: who they were, what they did, and the spaces in which they participated. The second sets of interviews were conducted with the same key informants, and were completed in July 1992, the last month of data collection. These interviews aimed at analysing events that had occurred during the entire period of research. Some of these events were group-based, and some had occurred between the individual interviewee and myself. In short then, the last set of interviews helped not only with conceptualizing events, but also with analysing the data that I already had collected. Both sets of interviews were tape recorded, transcribed, and translated into English. The first set of interviews usually lasted between fifteen and twenty minutes; the second averaged an hour to an hour and a half.

There were a number of group discussions that I scheduled with the key informants, especially tsatsatsa. The first set of discussions addressed events that we experienced as we went along, mostly related to the activities of the ANC in which we all participated. Some were social events that nonetheless made us re-examine the way we thought about ourselves as ANC-Zulu people. The second set of discussions was classroom-based and occurred between tsatsatsa, their classmates, and myself. Classroom-based discussions usually lasted forty-five minutes and were often tape recorded, transcribed, and translated into English. Again, all these discussions were related to party politics and also to the way in which all those involved in the discussions located themselves in relation to the political struggle and the then up-coming elections. The third set of discussions though less formal, was with a number of KwaMashu residents who were related or associated with the key informant who lived in this township.

Unless otherwise stated, all of the interviews and discussions were in the Zulu language, and on a very few occasions, we used Sotho and Afrikaans. The translations from Zulu, or Sotho or Afrikaans to English are all mine. My knowledge of spoken rather than written Afrikaans necessitated that I later seek help from friends for translating my phonetically written Afrikaans to English. None of these friends, however, are to be held responsible for inaccuracies in this translation.

chapter 3

KwaZulu/Natal: A Historical Overview

In the nineteenth century, colonial forces in this region faced the Zulu kingdom, which was to hold out against colonial and capitalist demands for labour longer than any other in Southern Africa. Because of the nature of the resistance that the Zulu mounted against colonial forces, the imposition of colonial rule in KwaZulu/Natal took a different form from already existing colonial practices. The destruction of the Zulu kingdom by British forces in 1879, and the imposition of indirect rule from that year onwards, did not necessarily mean an end to the struggle against colonialism. Instead, indirect rule created space for the utilization of traditional Zulu structures as resources for continuing the anti-colonial struggle. The history of colonial South Africa is full of rebellions and uprisings, all of which were influenced by events taking place in KwaZulu/Natal, then referred to as the Natal province or Natal-Zululand. Again, it was in KwaZulu/Natal that the first black resistance groups emerged, including the African National Congress and Inkatha. When in 1948 the National Party came to power and imposed its philosophy of apartheid, it was these groups that pioneered the struggle against this new form of white domination. And as the struggle against apartheid intensified, making it important for groups to define the character of a post-apartheid state, it was in KwaZulu/Natal that the political difference between black resistance groups was articulated – an articulation that often resulted in the so-called black-on-black violence. This chapter therefore, traces the political developments of the region of KwaZulu/Natal since the early 1800s, bringing out those themes that have had a significant impact on current events and on the lives of the individuals in this study. (See also the appendix for a chronology of the major developments discussed in this chapter.)

The Zulu Kingdom, 1820–1879

The Zulu Dynasty

Located between the Drakensburg Mountains to the west, and the Indian Ocean to the east, Natal is one of the most geographically favoured areas in southern Africa. At the turn of the nineteenth century, it was the homeland of Bantu-speaking Nguni chiefdoms. Of these, the Zulu emerged as the most powerful and famous, incorporating most of the other peoples between the Portuguese territories to the north and the Umzimkhulu River to the south in a series of wars known as the *mfecane* (or the 'crushing') (see appended maps).

The story of Shaka, son of Senzangakhona and consolidator of the Zulu kingdom, has been told many times, and even though the literature has still to rid itself of ethnocentricity, exaggerations, and inaccuracies, the outlines of the narrative are well known. The first quarter of the nineteenth century was a period of great violence and disruption in southeast Africa as rival chiefdoms fought for territory and the extension of political control. Through his exceptional military talents, Shaka was able to assert the supremacy of the comparatively insignificant Zulu chiefdom over its major rivals and made himself the ruler of a vastly extended area later known as Natal-Zululand. The rise of the Zulu kingdom under Shaka can be attributed to the assimilation of weak tribes into the emerging Zulu nation. Guy (1980, p. 111) argues that social groups inhabiting Zululand during this period were faced with two ecological crises: a change in the nature of the pasture for cattle rearing which increased population pressure on available land, and severe drought, which forced people to congregate for security. This in turn led to the evolution of a social hierarchy, some of which, as we will see later, has been modified and incorporated into existing Inkatha structures. By the mid-1820s, the Zulu kingdom was considered the most formidable power in southern Africa.

Shaka was assassinated by his brother Dingane, who succeeded him in 1828. It was during Dingane's rule that the first white missionaries arrived and the first trading settlement was established. In the 1820s the area had witnessed the arrival of predominantly British settlers, who were later followed by the Boer Voortrekkers in 1837. From this period onwards the Boers and the British would compete for control over this region. The Voortrekkers were mainly interested in the occupation of pastoral land for farming, while the British were on a colonial mission, aiming at total control of the region. When the first whites entered the area, they faced the formidable Zulu military state, clustered mainly along the northeastern part of the region later known as Zululand, making it difficult for any invaders to enter uncontested. At first Dingane had tried to accommodate the newcomers, especially the trekkers, granting them parts of the southern area between the Tugela and Umzimkhulu rivers. When Dingane tried to exert his authority over the trekkers, he soon realized his mistake of assuming that they would regard themselves as his subjects. At this stage Dingane tried to annihilate the trekkers but was eventually unsuccessful, for by now the trekkers were familiar with the politics of the region and of the conflict between Dingane and his rival brother Mpande. Therefore, in the area later known as Zululand, the Voortrekkers were able to establish themselves by utilizing the tension between Dingane and Mpande and, allying with Mpande, the Boers were able to drive Dingane out, and to make themselves suzerains over the new Zulu king.

While the occupation of Zululand by the Voortrekkers was achieved with difficulty, their expansion into the southern parts of the region later known as Natal was made easier by the earlier Zulu wars of expansion. The first whites entered an area that was war-torn and desolated. Its inhabitants were scattered and had taken refuge in the mountains and caves. Shaka had previously deliberately declared Natal a 'no man's land,' a buffer against possible enemies. Thousands of refugees clustered between the Umzimkhulu and Umzimvubu rivers to the south, and Natal lay as an 'empty paradise' waiting for white colonists (Marks 1970). When the Natal inhabitants finally emerged from their hiding places, thousands found themselves on the vast farms that the Voortrekkers had allocated to themselves.

Thus, when the British annexed Natal in 1843 they had to establish a number of land commissions to sort out the controversial land issue between the Zulus and the Voortrekkers. Between the years 1843 and 1864 land was set aside for purely African occupation. Africans were grouped together under their hereditary chiefs and were governed according to customary law. This was the work of Theophilus Shepstone who had come to Natal from the Cape in 1846. Faced with the problem of administering the Africans of Natal, who had their social organization shattered by the Shaka wars and were often without their traditional chiefs, Shepstone set out to design his own version of segregation and indirect rule.[1] The number of fresh refugees from the mountains and caves of Natal-Zululand returning to lands already taken by white settlers made Shepstone's job difficult. However, through what Marks (1970, p. 69) refers to as 'a feat of considerable administrative and psychological skill,' Shepstone managed to settle the disorganized Zulu people on what was later called Reserve Land, and to restore some semblance of tribal authority over them. With this accomplishment, British rule was taking shape in Natal. Here then was the first experience of white domination over the African population in Natal.

In Zululand, Mpande had assumed victory over Dingane by forming an alliance with the Voortrekkers (Boers) who later made themselves rulers over him. It is not clear, however, whether Mpande saw himself as a Boer dependant. What is clear is that with the advent of the British in Natal in 1843, Mpande quickly switched alliances and regained complete independence. Mpande came to the throne in 1840 and was to rule the Zulu kingdom for over thirty years, sharing a boundary with the colony of Natal. He was to deal with civil war, traders, missionaries, and neighbouring governments that tried to undermine his authority and to bring about changes in Zululand. Unlike so many African societies, the Zulu kingdom retained its essential autonomy and self-sufficiency. When Cetshwayo, Mpande's son, succeeded him, he became the ruler of a powerful, independent African kingdom that was feared by neighbouring settler communities.

Cetshwayo was to rule for only eight years. Important economic changes such as the discovery of gold and other minerals were quickly forcing southern Africa into industrialization and into a different capital/market system; and the Zulu kingdom, because of its economic and military independence, came to be viewed as an obstacle hindering progress and peaceful development in the region. Thus in 1879 the kingdom was invaded by the British army, the Zulu king was exiled, and the Zulu military system was terminated. This was the beginning of years of white domination in the whole region of Natal-Zululand.

Socio-Political Structure of the Zulu Kingdom

There is a vast amount of literature that tries to analyse the factors and strategies that enabled the Zulu kingdom to rise to its supremacy. Most of this literature indicates that the reasons for that success can be laid at the door of the kingdom's social organization, structured along kinship lines; its political strength, centred around the king and the military; and its economic power, based on the Zulu patrilineal mode of production (see, for example, Marks and Atmore 1980; Marks and Rathbone 1982; Marks 1970; and Guy 1979, 1980).

At the first level of organization were the Zulu families, which were centred in the homestead. This consisted of the homestead head known as *umnumzane*, his wives and children, and his livestock. A homestead was divided into houses, or *imizi*, which were in the charge of the wives of the homestead. A homestead was formed when the eldest son of a house left to establish a homestead of his own. This process of structuring was expressed according to a lineage, or clan, grounded on the belief that members had descended through the male line, from a common founding ancestor (Guy 1982). Marks (1980, p. 11) warns against an approach that views lineages as of purely biological or genetic relations, and asserts that they should be viewed as 'specific social groupings of biological relations which have socially determined functions.' Meillassouse (1980) also suggests that clans should be seen as expressing the relations of production and reproduction in the societies in which they are found, and as providing their legitimizing ideology.

The homestead was economically self-sufficient and consumed most of its produce. Women worked in agriculture and performed domestic labour and men concentrated on tending livestock, undertaking heavier building tasks, and tilling the land. Some individuals concentrated on activities for which they were talented or produced goods from locally available raw material. With the exception of iron, exchange of goods was informal, and this exchange did not affect the structure of the homestead. It has been estimated that out of 250,000 people, 90 per cent lived in homesteads and the remaining 10 per cent lived a nomadic life (Guy 1980, p. 176).

At the heart of the Zulu society was the drive to accumulate cattle. The possession of a large herd of cattle testified to the political power of men of rank in the kingdom, and the daughters of such men of status commanded more cattle on marriage than those of commoners. Consequently, the homestead clearly marked the importance of cattle in that its establishment was dependent on the transfer of cattle first, from father to son through inheritance, and second, from a prospective husband to the father of the bride through bride wealth or lobolo. Thus, it was the movement of cattle from father to son that enabled sons to establish their own homesteads, while the movement of cattle into the founding homestead as daughters moved out as prosperous wives helped maintain the homestead. Guy (1982, p. 169) describes this social practice of homestead formation as having been dependent on a 'vertical link between father and son, and a horizontal one between husband and wife's father.'

At the second level of organization, homesteads of the kingdom were grouped into large administrative and political units referred to as chiefdoms. A chiefdom was a political as well as a territorial unit. Some of these chiefdoms had existed as powerful independent polities before Shaka incorporated them into the Zulu kingdom. Guy (1980) suggests that these chiefdoms had reached their position of dominance during the reigns of the Zulu kings, which suggests that these chiefdoms were allowed some degree of autonomy within the kingdom. The chief was responsible for good order within the chiefdom, the distribution of land, and the application of the law. He held judicial, administrative, and legislative authority over his people. He controlled both external and internal relations. His fees came from fines from his court and he received tribute from members of the homestead; this tribute was in the form of labour and produce. The chiefs delegated authority to district heads or *izinduna*, but responsibility still lay on homestead heads.

The general rule of succession was that the oldest son of the 'great wife' of the chief succeeded his father. The great wife was married late in a chief's life after he had acquired wealth and prestige, and her husband's followers usually paid for her lobolo. Furthermore, chiefs' families were usually divided into what is known as Left-hand houses and Right-hand houses, for the purposes of distribution of property. The wife of the Right-hand was the first to marry and her sons were in a better position to accumulate wealth and followers than those of the Left-hand house. As the oldest son of the chief, the first-born of the Right-hand wife was often appointed the advisor to the political heir (who was of the Left-hand house and son of the great wife). Disputes arose when the powerful advisor refused to make way for the heir when he attained his majority. It should be noted though that rules of succession were by no means inviolable and, as Marks (1970) points out, the history of the Zulu royal family itself more often illustrates the principle in the breach than in its observance. Shaka, for example, was not of the Left-hand house nor did he grow up in royalty, for at a very early age he and his mother were chased out of his father Senzangakhona's homestead and his mother's family, the Langa, brought him up.

At the third level of organization was the king who ruled in association with, but above, the chiefs of the kingdom. His power was derived from the Zulu military organization in the form of a regiment system known as amabutho, in which all males of the kingdom had to serve the king when they were between the ages marking puberty and marriage, which was between the age of sixteen and forty. The key to the expansion and consolidation of the Zulu kingdom lay in both Shaka's brilliant military strategies and in his formulation of age-grade regiments for warfare. In these regiments, men of the same age were formed into fighting units regardless of clan or chiefdom. They were appointed by and responsible to the king. As fresh peoples were conquered and incorporated into the kingdom, so their young men were drawn into the regiment system and into a large standing army created with loyalty to its commanders and through them to the king. The king used many ceremonies and rituals to strengthen his powers and to unite behind him the diverse peoples who made up the kingdom. Like the chiefs, a council assisted the king, although many of the king's advisors were eminent commoners who had come to the fore through their exceptional military ability rather than through their royal birth. In a few cases, chieftaincies were created for those who had loyally served the king. Thus, Ndlela, Shaka's famous warrior and later Dingane's deputy, was appointed chief over the Ntuli people and was given a large tract of land as a reward for his services. Similarly, at a later stage the large tract of land occupied by the Buthelezi people and their prominence in Zulu affairs was a result of their chief Mnyamane who was Cetshwayo's prime minister.[2] In addition to acting as a force for external warfare, defence, and internal coercion, the army also provided labour to the king; soldiers herded his cattle and worked in his fields. The substance and reproduction of these state servants was provided by the homesteads in which they were born. In this way, therefore, the Zulu state depended ultimately on the massive extraction of surplus labour from the homesteads of the kingdom. Furthermore, the fact that males were released from state service when they were given permission to marry meant that the king not only maintained and controlled labour, but also maintained control over the age of marriage and over population growth.

In spite of all this, the king was not beyond reach. Alternative power could be established from alternative claims to authority of other sons of the royal family who could then create divisions within the military by mobilizing those regiments of which they were in charge. If the king became too authoritative, the people rebelled against his power and assassinated him, a lesson that was drawn from Shaka's assassination and the murder of Dingane in exile. Even if the king was not assassinated, there existed a chance that he would lose his followers to a rival brother, as in the case of Mpande and Dingane. This political system lasted in Zululand until the Anglo-Zulu War of 1879.

Figure 1   Traditional Zulu Structure under the Zulu Kings

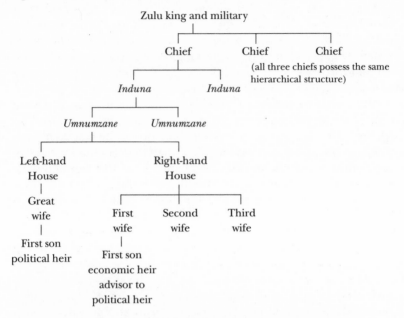

The Destruction of the Zulu Kingdom and Transformation in Restructuring of Zulu Society, 1879–1912

In the late 1870s the British had attempted to establish a political union, a confederation of southern Africa's different communities. This confederation would have, in part, facilitated capitalist production in the subcontinent (Guy 1982, p. 173). Given its strong economic independence and its political and military strength, the Zulu kingdom was viewed as a major obstacle to this plan and as a result the British invaded it in January of 1879. However, the British army could not deal with the Zulu military and suffered severe losses on the battlefield as Isandhlwana and Rorke's Drift. Thus at the end of the war, the Zulu were able to retain their land and their formal political independence. Again this was an unprecedented victory, an event that put into question the superiority of the British Empire. This record had to be corrected, so the British staged and won another battle at Ulundi in September 1879. It has been argued that, in fact, it was not because of British military might that the British were finally able to occupy Zululand, but that the peace that followed Ulundi was only attained by promising the Zulu people that they would retain possession of their land if they laid down their arms.[3] This however, was done at the price of the centralized state and the military system: the Zulu dynasty was terminated, Cetshwayo, sent into exile, and the country divided into thirteen chiefdoms.

The result of the 1879 'British settlement' of Zululand was a civil war. The British had proceeded to appoint new chiefs for the newly created chiefdoms and civil war broke out as supporters of the old Zulu order came into conflict with the newly appointed chiefs. The war eventually came to a halt in 1887. Britain divided Zululand, gave the Transvaal some territory in the northwest, and assumed sovereignty over the rest. This latter region became known as British Zululand until 1897 when it was incorporated into the Natal colony.

The incorporation of British Zululand into the Natal colony did not necessitate significant changes in administration, for from the very beginning Zulu land was dominated by its neighbour Natal. In the civil war, Natal officials had played a leading role in crushing supporters of the Zulu royal family and its administrative system, and the officials who implemented this had been drawn from the Natal's Department of the Secretary for Native Affairs which had been engineered by Theophilus Shepstone. By this time Shepstone had retired, but his administrative skills and his ideology of segregation were so valued in Natal, that up until his death in 1893, he acted as a resource person on matters dealing with governing Africans in the region. It was therefore the same Shepstone policies of Natal that were to influence the development of a policy for Zululand. The Natal officials had three main objectives for bringing control over the Zulu: to bring Zululand within the colony's economic circle; to ensure access to the African interior along a route to the east of the Transvaal; and to provide land for Natal's African population, for the trekkers had allocated for themselves most of the African land (Guy 1970).

Two competing explanations exist for the imposition of the Shepstone system in Zululand. The first supports the colonialist position arguing that the system made it possible to implement a policy that was in tune with the past. It was also argued that the recognition of the existing chiefly stratum and the traditional production system would free the Zulu people from the tyranny of the Zulu dynasty and that they would thus gladly accept the restoration of the 'natural' Nguni system of homestead production under chiefly rule.[4] Indeed, in Shepstone's view, there was no such thing as a Zulu nation, only autonomous tribes yearning for 'their ancient separate existence' and eager to throw off the 'terrible incubus of the Zulu Royal family' (cited in Marks 1970, p. 96). It was further argued that progress would be ensured by the overall authority of white magistrates and the right of appeal to their courts. Moreover, a tax that came to be known as the hut tax was introduced to substitute for the services provided by homesteads to the kingdom through the military system. It was also argued that the imposition of this tax would substitute the civilizing influence of wage labour for the barbaric demands of Zulu military service and would have the added advantage of covering the administrative costs of the colony.

The second explanation for the imposition of the Shepston system is offered by Guy (1982) who argues that the first concern of the administration was to devise a strategy to ensure that the colony could pay for its own administrative expenses. Therefore, through the hut tax, the Zulu covered the costs of their own coercion. Because Zululand was economically dependent on the Transvaal and other areas where minerals had been discovered, the hut tax had to be earned by wage labour outside of Zululand. Since Zulus had been forced out of their land, the colonial state anticipated that most were likely to emigrate permanently to places like the Transvaal. Such emigration could have jeopardized the state's economic plans and it therefore became important to tie migrants to continued homestead production by the hut tax.

With the introduction of hut tax, homestead males who had previously served in the Zulu army and had performed other services for the king were now forced to work for the colonial state. Each homestead was forced to pay a certain amount of money calculated according to the number of huts in the homestead (each hut was taken to represent one man). If migrants did not send back their share of earnings for the tax, their relatives in the homesteads were forced into free labour for the state, and sometimes had their property seized to make up for the payments. Thus attempts by the colonial state to ensure, for example, the continued existence of the homestead structure with its laws of marriage and production, the so-called recognition of native law under the Shepstone system was 'just a veneer covering total subordination.'

Guy also argues that, despite certain continuities of form with precolonial practices, the basic principles of the homestead structure were dramatically altered as soon as the colonial state was established. With the imposition and successful collection of hut tax in 1889, and more so after Dinizulu, son and successor to the last Zulu king, Cetshwayo, had been exiled, Zululand was fully locked into the colonial economy, and the number of migrants seeking work on the Rand in the Transvaal and elsewhere dramatically increased. Describing the transition that occurred in Zulu society as a result of colonial and capitalist forces, Guy states:

> The Zulu kingdom successfully resisted the intrusion of capitalist forces up to 1879. As a result it suffered first invasion and then a civil war during which the pre-capitalist system was effectively smashed. Reconstruction followed, but it was the reconstruction of a facade: a facade built from pieces carefully selected from the ruins it was meant to hide. Thus certain pre-capitalist features were retained if they enabled the colonial state to extract a surplus more effectively, and were rejected if they obstructed this. Capitalism dominated Zulu society from 1889, when the first hut-tax was successfully collected. From this time it was made to serve the interest of capitalist accumulation, whether mediated through the colonial state, or, as it happened later, mining capital through the South African state (1982, p. 190).

The years that followed marked continued transformation of Zulu society, and these changes were exacerbated by the upheaval of the civil war at the turn of the twentieth century, the depression that followed, natural disasters such as the drought of 1903, and diseases. By 1905, over 40 per cent of Zululand was opened to white settlement and access to land was soon to become a crucial factor as well.

Overall, therefore, it is evident that Shaka's political and economic structures were used by the British to establish a new colonial order: in place of the articulation of the 'lineage mode of production' and the 'tributary state' (Guy 1980), there was now an articulation between the lineage system and the colonial state which extracted surplus through rent, taxes, and, to some extent, labour. However, the colonizing state was never powerful enough to disrupt or totally restructure Zulu society, or to create a 'fully proletariat farm labour force' (Marks and Atmore 1980, p. 18). The homestead lineage mode of production could be seen to have provided the Zulu with a choice of how and for whom to produce surplus; ten years after the discovery of diamonds, the Zulu king could still boast that his people had not been to Kimberly to sell their labour. In short, the homestead lineage mode of production made it possible for the Zulu to withstand the political, military and, most importantly, the economic pressures of colonialism until late in the century.

British political penetration in Natal was made possible not, as we have noted, by direct coercion but by Shepstone's version of indirect rule. As long as the colonial state was small and weak it was forced to work within the already existing forms of Zulu administration. There was thus a considerable amount of continuity at both the political and ideological levels. Furthermore, it has been recently argued that it was these particular circumstances that led to the development of a policy and ideology of segregation, also known as apartheid, which provided late nineteenth-century policy-makers with useful, profound precedents (see, for example, Marks 1978). Some historians have even gone further to argue that apartheid is not just a product of Afrikaner nationalism, as it is most often believed, but rather that its antecedents are to be found in Natal (see, for example, Welsh 1971).

It has been argued that the essence of the 1879–87 civil war was between the representatives of the pre-capitalist and the capitalist social formations; between representatives of the old Zulu order working for the revival of the kingdom, and the colonialists who were trying to ensure political division as a prerequisite for subordination to capitalist production. Thus, while before 1879 the Zulu possessed land and controlled their produce, after 1884 they were losing both possession and control. The civil war has been often interpreted as solely a conflict within Zulu society whose many groups were deeply divided: once the authoritarian rule of the king was removed, these rivalries emerged in violence. This interpretation is partial as it fails to acknowledge other historical forces that can be deduced from the events in Zululand between 1879 and 1884: one force with its origin in the settler communities bordering Zululand, and the other from metropolitan Britain. Between and within these groups were factions moving towards capitalist domination of Zululand and factions attempting to revive and retain the pre-capitalist system. It was the tensions between these factions that drove the Zulu into civil war and the destruction of the old order.

The purpose of this section therefore, has not been to argue that pre-1879 Zulu society was essentially egalitarian with an organic social structure. It has been to demonstrate that pre-1879 Zulu social formation created in its people self-sufficiency and a sense of totality, which they knew was intrinsically valuable and was absent in the manner of existence that their enemies wished to force upon them. This was because those groups that had been absorbed into the Zulu kingdom had been given a certain degree of political independence to exist and be governed by their chiefs with very little interference from the king. It was only in times of war that the king, in conjunction with the chiefs, interfered directly with the affairs of the chiefdoms. And so, as the Zulu fought the British in 1879 and in the civil war in the years that followed, they were tragically conscious of what they were fighting for, and what they stood to lose. Thus, while the 1880s saw the physical destruction of the Zulu kingdom, the kingdom is still a symbolic, potent element in African life and continues to influence and direct politics in southern Africa. The memory of the kingdom, its history, its victories as well as its defeats, continues to influence events in a transformed situation. The survival of the kingdom up to the last quarter of the nineteenth century was viewed by the Africans in Natal as an articulation of resistance towards colonial rule. Searching for an acceptable program, alienated by their colonial backgrounds, and closely related to the Zulu, the Africans in Natal identified readily with the kingdom and its long history of independence. The house of Shaka has had an emotional appeal which remains an important factor in African thinking. Therefore, even though Zululand was incorporated into Natal in 1897, the Zulu continued to look towards the Zulu royal house for leadership. Risings and rebellions that were to follow became viewed as a centralizing device providing the African people with assistance and inspiration (Marks 1978). The first nationalist leaders identified with the Zulu royal house and supported it in their writing and speeches. Slogans such as Usuthu[5] that originated in the homestead of the Zulu King Cetshwayo over one hundred and fifty years ago were used in everyday gatherings against apartheid.

The Emergence of Black Resistance Groups, 1913–1960

White occupation of the land within Zululand did not begin until the early twentieth century, and this was 'later than almost every other case in southern Africa' (Beall et al 1986). The effect was to leave a legacy of unconsolidated land occupied by Africans, and the symbols of continuity, resistance, and apparent Zulu political and cultural coherence that could be used by subsequent regional leaders. While the Zulu kingdom was able to hold out against capitalist and colonial demands for labour and land for longer than most, when the collapse came, it had an overwhelming impact on the economic, social, and political life of the Africans. It benefited white farmers, industrialist and mining interests who now had access to cheap labour (Mare and Hamilton 1987). The actual turning point came with the Bhambatha rebellion in 1906, the last major resistance of an African chief against colonial encroachment. In light of the nineteenth-century history of the region, it is not surprising that it happened in Natal, now including Zululand (for a detailed discussion of the Bhambatha rebellion, see Marks 1970). The rebellion, which was basically about labour and the notorious hut tax, left over three thousand people dead, including Chief Bhambatha himself. His head was cut off and displayed to illustrate that the rebellion was over. In that same year, John Dube, who was later to become the first president of the African National Congress, started a newspaper in Natal, *Ilanga lase Natal* (literally, *Natal Sun*). This was the beginning of a new direction of political action.

The discriminatory practices established in Natal during the nineteenth century were formalized in the following years. Land allocations were given legislative form in the Land Acts of 1913 and 1936. These Land Acts allocated 35 per cent of Natal and 13 per cent of the total land area of South Africa to 80 per cent of the national population, the Africans (Mare and Hamilton 1987). Africans could now no longer purchase land, and moreover, isolated land already bought by Africans was made vulnerable to the charge that it was misplaced in white territory. Years later, this isolated land came to be called 'black spots' by the National Party government and Africans were forcibly removed from the white-owned areas which surrounded it. These Land Acts have been viewed by some as the beginning of the policy of separate homelands (see, for example, Marks 1986).

Therefore the first three decades of twentieth-century South Africa saw white appropriation of African land, the establishment of colonial rule and a new colonial order, and an intense industrialization of the country achieved with a cheap labour system and by racist ideologies. All these developments were met with intense African resistance which eventually gave rise to the first nationalist movements, the first being the African National Congress, founded in 1912 'to bring about and encourage mutual understanding in the country, to bring all people of the country together, and to defend the liberty, rights, and privileges of the people' (Walshe 1970, p. 89). Later, the ANC was to fight the 1936 Native Trust and Land Act, legislation that effectively forced blacks into migrant labour for white farmers and mine owners. Labour was also segregated according to race through such measures as the 1911 Mines and Works Act, with unskilled employment reserved for blacks. Although blacks did eventually gain the right to form trade unions, these were kept under strict government control.

African resistance in Natal was complex, giving rise not only to nationalist movements, but also to a Zulu ethnic consciousness. From about 1912 to 1930 three organizations dominated the politics of the Natal province: the ANC, the Industrial and Commercial Workers' Union (ICU), and Inkatha. Although there were no direct connections between these three organizations, their objectives were similar: the reconstruction of Zulu ethnic identity around symbols of the Zulu monarchy and its history in the service of resistance to white domination.

The relationship that the ANC sought between itself and the Zulu monarchy was based on the events that had led to its formation. The ANC had been formed in the wake of the 1913 Land Act, which segregated blacks in regions away from the rest of the population and strictly monitored their movements from these areas. The act primarily affected chiefs and their control over land, which they had had at the time of the Zulu kingdom. Alliance with the chiefs was important to the ANC; therefore chiefs and the Zulu king (then not recognised by the state) were drawn into ANC activity, which in turn brought strong rural membership. For example, Dube, who was then president of the ANC, had called on the Zulu paramount Chief Mshiyeni ka Dinizulu, to 'bring in his people' by blessing ANC recruitment (Mare and Hamilton 1987, p. 78).

The formation of the cultural organization Inkatha in the early 1920s added another feature to Natal's politics. (The exact year of origin is not clear. In her writings, Marks points to the years 1922–24, while others put it in 1928; see, for example, Mare and Hamilton 1987.) The formation of Inkatha can be attributed to two significant events of the 1920s. Following its victory in 1924, the National Party passed a 'Civilised Labour Policy' under which the Christian African community was stripped of its privileges, notably the right to purchase land. The Christian African community was a product of Sir George Grey's integrationist approach used by the British during the 1840 occupation of Natal (then excluding Zululand). This approach focused on changing and converting the Africans to 'civilization' and Christianity. As a result, missionary stations were established from which came a number of educated Africans who, because of their Christian faith, were given certain rights such as purchasing land. As small landowners were stripped of the right to purchase land, these Christian Africans saw the formation of Inkatha as a resource to enable them to cooperate with rural chiefs in the purchase and development of land. That is, Inkatha was seen as a means through which commercial agriculture could be started on land purchased ostensibly by a 'tribe,' since non-tribal land-buying syndicates had been practically outlawed following the 1913 Land Act. It was with this background that the Christian African community, the Natal intelligentsia, forged an alliance with Solomon ka Dinizulu, and formed the first Inkatha movement. The second event was the development of industries, which brought with it intense changes within Zulu communities. King Solomon himself viewed Inkatha as an important organization through which to preserve Zulu culture at a time when it seemed to be disintegrating in the face of industrialization and urbanization and also to fight for state recognition of the Zulu monarchy. So, while on the one hand Inkatha was meant to preserve Zulu culture, on the other hand it was meant to preserve the economic rights of the educated Christian Africans.

Thus, despite the undisputed popular support which the Zulu royal house enjoyed in the 1920s, the origin of Inkatha owed more to the deliberate reconstruction by the Zulu royal family and the Natal intelligentsia than to any spontaneous reaction of the Zulu people. Inkatha also drew much of its membership from the rural areas because it was in these areas that cultural practices were being affected and group norms redefined.

The Industrial and Commercial Workers' Union (ICU) was able to draw support in Natal because of the intense pressures the African rural population was then facing: changing conditions in agriculture, hunger because of the rising value of agricultural land, and the need for labour in white industries as the importation of indentured Indian labour had come to a halt. Therefore, at the beginning of the 1920s an increasing number of people were pushed into the towns in search of work, social relations in the countryside were transformed, and whole communities were disrupted. The cheap labour system and the racist ideologies which accompanied South Africa's industrialization exacerbated the tensions. The expansion of wattle plantations and sheep farming in the Natal countryside led to the eviction of tens of thousands of labour tenants and the increased exploitation of many more. It was the ICU under A.W.G. Champion (who was considered one of Natal's leading politicians) that organized these dislocated workers.

The union's mass militancy was expressed in the form of work stoppages, a demand for increased wages, and general insolence and insubordination. In response, angry white farmers burnt down the offices of the ICU and clamoured for state intervention against a movement which they viewed as a threat to rural stability. In Durban the ICU organized beer boycotts which resulted in the white mob attack on ICU headquarters in 1929, while a demonstration organised by the Communist party on Dingane's Day the following year was fired on by the police who shot the leader, Johannes Nkosi. Almost five years of unsuccessful militant action by Africans had resulted instead in passage of ever-increasing security measures such as the 1927 Native Administration Act and the 1930 Riotous Assemblies (Amendment) Act. The death of Nkosi, and the banishment of Champion, led to a lull in urban politics in the 1930s and 1940s.

There were a variety of reasons for this apparent quiescence. First were natural disasters: the world depression; drought between 1931 and 1936, and a malaria epidemic that raged in the early 1930s. Second, many of the unemployed who had fuelled the working-class militancy of the 1920s in Durban were removed from the city as the depression began to bite. However, a more important reason for the failure to revive this activism was the complex relationship between political groups in the region, and the divisions that existed within groups themselves.

From the very beginning, ideological differences created factions within the ANC. The radicals advocated a more militant approach, and adopted slogans that called for the killing of the white man and a return of the country to black South Africans. They considered any negotiations with the government to be futile. Eventually this difference in approach led to a split in the organization and to the formation of the Pan African Congress (PAC) in 1958.

A more conservative group within the ANC called for the return to a Zulu way of life. This group was led by the Reverend John Dube, who was considered Natal's leading political figure of the time. The existence of this faction eventually led to the existence of two branches of the ANC in Natal, one belonging to the national organization, and the other, a virtually autonomous Natal variant under Dube. Later, the formation of the ANC's military wing, Umkhonto weSizwe (Spear of the Nation) in 1960 by the national ANC executive, with Nelson Mandela appointed as its commander, exacerbated the tension between the ANC Natal leaders and the national executive. Lodge (1983, p. 227) writes that the problem seemed to have derived from the absence of any consultation by the ANC's national executive with lower echelons (notably those in Natal) when Umkhonto was established.

Therefore, at the time of the introduction of apartheid in 1948 black political activism had been reduced. By the 1940s, Inkatha had ceased to function as an effective organization, partly because King Solomon had died, and also because some Inkatha officials had defrauded the Zulu National Fund, the financial bastion of Inkatha. On the other hand, by 1960 the ANC had changed its strategy of non-violence after the Sharpville massacre that had been provoked by the hated pass laws. When non-violent methods of opposition to the apartheid regime were violently crushed, both the PAC and ANC formed military wings. This resistance movement was also soon crushed, with the imprisonment of Mandela and others in 1962.

Present-day KwaZulu/Natal is an amalgamation of the very different political ideologies that were constructed in this era. On the one hand, pre-colonial ideology focused around the Zulu king, as the symbol of unity of the nation; on the other hand were the aspirations of Christian converts imbued with nineteenth-century notions of progress, improvement, and assimilation to western norms and constitutional monarchy. While proclaiming the virtues of their past and the wholesomeness of tradition, the 'new African' was too much a product of the mission station and western culture to give unreserved approval to an unconditional return to tribal life. Moreover, precisely because the ideology constructed at this time was designed to forge an alliance between members of the Christian intelligentsia and landowners and the pre-colonial ruling class, it was never free of contradiction and tension.

Suppressed Resistance and the Implementation of Apartheid Structures, 1960–1975

The period between 1960 and 1975 saw an increase in state policy and legislation that suppressed African activism. This period also witnessed the implementation of apartheid structures. Legislation such as the Population Registration Act, the Reservation of Separate Amenities Act, the Bantu Education Act, and the Group Areas Act were quickly implemented, forming the infrastructure of apartheid. Among these laws the implementation of the Bantu Authorities Act is of importance to this study since it illuminates the creation of South Africa's Bantustans such as KwaZulu.

The Bantu Authorities Act was passed in 1951 and basically provided for the establishment of separate tribal, regional, and territorial authorities for blacks. Once these authorities were established, the Promotion of Bantu Self-Government Act was passed in 1959, which added administrative structures for what were now ethnically defined homelands. The 1959 act was introduced by the Minister of Bantu Administration, De

Wet Nel, who referred to it as 'cultural nationalism' and 'ethnic particularities' (attempting to move away, at least rhetorically, from racism). According to apartheid, different types of people were to be kept separate. Each group would have its own national territory and infrastructure (schools, media, and cultural bodies). Apartheid policy divided South Africa into ten black 'nations'[6] and three non-black 'nations.'[7] Afrikaners, especially from the 1970s onwards, justified apartheid by saying that they were merely giving to other 'nations' what they demanded for themselves, namely, cultural autonomy and *eiesoortigheid* (own-ness).

This policy was an attempt to defuse several pressures that were mounting against the central state. Growing worker militancy was reflected in the fourfold increase in the number of strikes involving African workers in the mid-1950s; the Trades Union Congress of South Africa which brought together most radical opposition to apartheid, was formed in 1955; and rapid urbanization of African people during the 1950s was making a racially exclusive system more untenable by the day. The winds of change of African nationalism that swept through the continent after the Second World War set an example as African states forced aside the direct control of colonial powers.

The apartheid policy was designed to meet all these threats to white supremacy and exclusive control over wealth and political power. Most importantly, it fulfilled the need to maintain separate areas for the social reproduction of the labouring class, where increasing poverty and a criminal imbalance in resource allocation could be justified in terms of 'dual economies' and 'Third World' components rather than sheer greed and the necessity of capitalist development (Mare and Hamilton 1987). From these separate areas, labour could also be allocated to the politically powerful but economically weak agricultural sector, where wages were too low to attract workers from the now dominant sector, mining.

This economic system rested heavily on what has euphemistically been called the 'principle of impermanence.' This meant that Africans outside a bantustan were in white-controlled areas either temporarily as migrants or commuters, or, if residents, would have no property or political rights, and would be subject to the same humiliations of pass checks as all other Africans. Wages could be kept low on the basis that this income was supplemented by family agriculture in the bantustans. Union organization was also made very difficult with a migrant workforce, and housing and other social facilities could be kept away from the obvious contrast with the standard of living of white South Africa, and from industrial areas, in case social unrest should spill out of the townships. In the 1960s profits of white-owned campanies were very high. Sharpville caused a brief scare and foreign capital flowed out of South Africa, but the trend was soon reversed as the state clamped down on opposition.

It was not only economic dominance that was to be safeguarded through apartheid. It was also to create or rekindle ethnic nationalisms. What became known as positive cultural nationalism was to take the place of the wider African nationalism, which was viewed as 'the monster, which may still perhaps destroy all the best things in Africa.' Cultural nationalism, on the other hand, meant that,

> the Bantu too will be linked together by traditional and emotional bonds, by their own language, their own culture their ethnic particularities: The Zulu is proud to be a Zulu and the Xhosa is proud to be a Xhosa and the Venda is proud to be a Venda, just as proud as they were a hundred years ago. The lesson we have learnt from history during the past three hundred years is that these ethnic groups, the whites as well as the Bantu, sought their greatest fulfilment, their greatest happiness and the best mutual relations on the basis of separate and individual development...the only bases on which peace, happiness and mutual confidence could be built up (de Wet Nel, cited in Moodie 1980, p. 266).

KwaZulu

The advent of apartheid in 1948 and its accompanying legislation brought significant changes to Natal's political administration. While much of the political rhetoric of Bantustan politics focuses on Natal resistance to the imposition of Bantu Authorities during the 1960s, the basis of that opposition is not clear. Nor is it clear whether chiefs and commoners opposed it for the same reasons. There are vague reports that some tribes wanted to wait and see how the implementation would work elsewhere, and that people resisted simply because they had not been consulted by the central government. There are also rumours that chiefs feared changes in the degree of local autonomy they had over such matters as the fines they imposed. It is possible that suspicion about loss of income and authority was behind their reluctance to accept the system. Nonetheless, the system was implemented. By 1966, 107 tribal authorities had been established throughout the Natal province for the over 282 government-recognized tribes (Mare and Hamilton 1987, p. 36). It was during this time also that Natal saw the rise of its leading political figure, Chief Mangosuthu Buthelezi.

Buthelezi had graduated from the University of Fort Hare, where he had been active as a member of the ANC Youth League. During his university years he had been warned by the state to stay clear of politics if he wanted to assume his hereditary position of being chief of the Buthelezi tribe. Temkin (1976, p. 39) argues that in order for Buthelezi to 'wipe out' his university activities he decided to join the Department of Native Affairs instead of serving his articles, as he had planned to do with Rowley Ainstern, 'a Durban lawyer who was a self-confessed communist.' Thus when the Bantu Authorities Act was passed, Buthelezi was employed with the Department of Native Affairs. He became acting chief of the Buthelezi tribe in 1953, and was officially installed in 1957.

Reasons for Buthelezi's move towards chieftainship are not clear, especially since an alternative was available for him through the ANC. Buthelezi himself presented the decision as a selfless choice to prevent a stooge from being appointed in his place. He also claimed he was destined to lead a Zulu nation that pre-existed apartheid and colonialism, covering a territory, a kingdom, and a state that dated back to the 1820s. Some analysts have argued that it was because this particular chieftainship could lead to the position of prime minister to the Zulu king, a post Buthelezi's father had held under King Solomon. It could thus expand Buthelezi's political horizons considerably, but only if the king should be restored to something of his previous central position (Mare and Hamilton 1987).

A wide 'Zuluness' with a distinct political definition had therefore to be created (or re-created). Chiefs, the Zulu royal house, and the symbol of the 'Zulu nation' were mobilized not only by successive colonial and apartheid administrators, but also by progressive and reactionary African interests. Thus in the 1950s Buthelezi became party to a broadly agreed-upon Zulu identity acknowledged by both members and outsiders. It is worth noting that this Zulu identity then existed in a much looser form; it mingled with an ANC-led national identity (with Chief Albert Luthuli symbolizing this as both a Zulu chief and the last president of the ANC before it was banned in 1960). Details of the events that took place between 1966 and 1970, which eventually led to the formation of the Zululand Territorial Authority, are beyond the scope of this study. Nevertheless, it is important to state that in 1970, Buthelezi came to head this Zululand Territorial Authority (ZTA), after being unanimously elected by regional authorities then in existence.

The period following the establishment of the ZTA was of enhanced political development in Natal. In 1972 the KwaZulu Legislative Assembly (KLA) was created to replace the ZTA. This was a major step forward in the state's constitutional planning for the bantustans, giving limited legislative as well as executive powers to regional administrators. The act under which the KLA was created, the Bantu Homelands Constitution Act (1971), makes provision for powers to be granted in two stages. During stage 1, which started in KwaZulu in 1972, an executive council was allowed which became a cabinet in the next stage. Excluded from stage 1 power were important areas such as the establishment of townships and business undertakings, the appointment and dismissal of chiefs, and educational syllabi uses. This status gave the Zulu protection, on an ethnic basis of resources, such as trading facilities which were to become a major issue during the mid 1970s. The KwaZulu Government Diary (1974, p. 10) carries a statement of policy in Buthelezi's foreword that speaks directly to the control of resources by the KLA: 'We firmly reject any policy or move which could have the tendency and/or ultimate result that the wealth, resources and commercial opportunities of Kwa-Zulu would no longer be reserved and developed exclusively for us.'

In 1972 a constitution was drafted for KwaZulu. In it the king was downgraded to a figurehead position at the insistence of Buthelezi and the other executive counsellors. This was against the wishes of such royalists as Prince Clement Zulu, who wanted an executive paramount chief (king) (Butler et al. 1977, p. 4; Schmahmann 1978, 93). The constitution also contained a pledge of respect for 'all laws applicable in the area of the KwaZulu Legislative Assembly' (Temkin 1976, p. 149).

In 1974 the KLA asked to move into stage 2 of self-government under the Bantu Homelands Constitution Act. The request was granted in 1977, and from this period onwards the KLA would have greater status and power than the Natal administrators to govern and direct those black people living in the Natal province.

Political developments in KwaZulu during this era need to be emphasized. The Bantu Authorities Act of 1951 committed the apartheid state to base its policy towards African people partly on a residue from the past. The 1959 Promotion of Bantu Self-Government Act confirmed that commitment and established the principle of ethnic fragmentation of the African people. It was under these two acts that Buthelezi became chief of the Buthelezi tribe, and later, the chief minister of KwaZulu. When the ZTA was established in 1970, its constitution provided for the chiefs or their representatives to dominate. This remained so even after the first elections to the KLA were held in 1978. Before this, the KLA was made up solely of regional authority representatives (chiefs or their alternatives). It was during these periods that new definitions of 'Zuluness' emerged which were drawn from the central state as well as from KwaZulu.

Revived African Activism, 1970–1980

The violence with which the resistance of the pre-1960s was crushed suppressed black resistance for a time. This resistance was revived first by the growth of the Black Consciousness Movement (BCM) and of Inkatha. In the early 1970s, the launching of Black Consciousness organizations, especially the South African Students Organisation (SASO), led by Steve Biko, who died in detention in 1977, awakened the peoples' longing for liberation. Black Consciousness demanded that the dominated group had to restore its past in order to regain its identity and establish pride in itself. The influence of SASO gave birth to various groups, such as Black Women's Federation, Black Parents' Association, Black Priests Solidarity Group, and others that propagated the philosophy of Black Consciousness. The message 'Blackman you are on your own,' articulated the anger and frustration of a generation of young blacks born since the Nationalist Party came to power.

The most significant challenge to apartheid by these organizations occurred on 16 June 1976 when over twenty thousand students marched to Orlando Stadium, Soweto, demonstrating against the imposition of Afrikaans as a medium of instruction. This demonstration turned into a massacre when police opened fire on the pupils. This uprising is estimated to have claimed over a thousand lives, spread nationwide, and very soon involved not just pupils, but their parents as well. The focus of students' demands turned from rejection of Afrikaans to a rejection of Bantu Education as a system. The government responded to this situation by banning over seventeen black organizations, most of which propagated the philosophy of Black Consciousness. However, blacks took the offensive, organized themselves and launched other political organisations.

Two points are worth noting. First, the philosophy of Black Consciousness did not have as much impact in KwaZulu/Natal as it did in the Transvaal, perhaps because KwaZulu/Natal already had a philosophy that fulfilled a similar function. *Ubuntu botho*, the philosophy promoted by Inkatha, strives for the promotion of African patterns of thought and the achievement of African humanism. Like Black Consciousness, ubuntu botho demanded that black people restore their past and use it to understand and fight the present. The difference was that the philosophy of ubuntu botho in KwaZulu/Natal was marked by another complex element: Zulu ethnicity.

Second, because of the school boycotts in the Transvaal at this time, especially after the 1976 uprisings, many parents started to look for alternative regions in which to send their children to school. At this time, KwaZulu/Natal appeared to have been the most stable region. Previously, a lot of the region's population migrated to work in the Transvaal (KwaZulu/Natal is an economically dependent region in the sense that it does not have any minerals or other natural resources). However, under the Group Areas Act of 1913, migrant workers from KwaZulu/Natal could not claim permanent residence in the Transvaal. For this reason, KwaZulu/Natal has always had a fairly homogeneous population with individuals who shared a common place of origin and a certain nationalism. After 1976, however, there was an increase in the number of immigrants to this region even if some came for only a temporary period. From then onward, the homogeneity of the region was challenged, and the definition of the Zulu nation took a different form. It was Inkatha that took up the position of defining and legitimizing the nation that exists within the geographic boundaries of KwaZulu/Natal.

Inkatha: A Brief History

Inkatha ka Zulu was founded in the 1920s by Solomon ka Dinizulu, son and heir to the last Zulu king. It was conceived as a cultural movement that would gain state recognition for the Zulu monarchy and preserve Zulu culture at a time when it seemed to be disintegrating in the face of the pressures from industrialization and urbanization. Inkatha is a Zulu word that refers to an object made and used by women to balance a load, usually firewood, on their heads. In rural societies, inkatha is made out of wet strands of grass, which are woven together to form a thick circular object; but it is common nowadays to find inkatha woven out of old material, usually cotton. The naming of this organization was intended to symbolise unity in the many groups of people that made up the Zulu nation. In this context the phrase Inkatha ka Zulu stands for the unity of the Zulu people.

By 1940 Inkatha ka Zulu had ceased to function. It was revived in 1975 as Inkatha Yenkululeko YeSizwe (Unity for the nation's freedom), and later Inkatha Freedom Party, by Chief Mangosuthu Buthelezi. While Inkatha Ka Zulu was solely committed to the preservation of the Zulu ethnic group as a cultural identity, Inkatha Yenkululeko YeSizwe extended its objectives to include black liberation within the wider South African context. Its main objective has been to hamper the Nationalist Party government's aims of breaking South Africa into black mini-nations. But in order to achieve this, Inkatha decided to mobilize on ethnic lines, a practice that contradicts its aim, and simultaneously helped disguise this aim from the central government. From its formation in 1975, leaders of Inkatha relied heavily on the power of chiefs in rural areas, even though these chiefs had to be convinced that the new movement was not going to marginalize them or dilute their powers.

Symbols

During its first eight years Inkatha was strengthened by ANC support for its political agenda. One powerful set of political symbols arose out of the image of Inkatha as the revived ANC. Inkatha colours (black, green, and gold), its political myth of origin and some leadership figures were drawn from aspects of ANC tradition, especially from the ANC's conservative branch in Natal before its banning. Another set of symbols was drawn from Zulu history. Inkatha's leaders presented their organization as a continuation of the ANC after a fifteen-year lull. Inkatha's secretary general, Oscar Dhlomo, stated that 'Inkatha was founded in response to the political vacuum that had been created when the African National Congress and Pan-Africanist Congress were banned' and it was formed 'on the principles of the founding fathers of the ANC' (Swart interview with Oscar Dhlomo, 1984). In a way, it is quite accurate to refer to a Zulu presence in the ANC. There were many Zulu-speaking leaders in the organization that came from the region of KwaZulu/Natal. But it is also true that they frequently showed a degree of Zulu prejudice and a tendency to form a regional faction. For instance, when the Zulu political leader John Dube, the first president of the ANC, was replaced in 1917, his response was to create a regional base that stood in conflict with the national African National Congress. His Natal Native Congress, a Natal version of the ANC, left a legacy of tension that was only resolved with the election of the Zulu Chief Albert Luthuli as president of the national ANC in 1952. This tension between the ANC and its Zulu members suggests that the Zulu presence has always been a controversial one, in part as a result of the position that the Zulus expected to occupy within the organization itself. However, Inkatha ignored these difficulties with the ANC tradition it presented. Instead, the political role of Albert Luthuli, president of the ANC at the time of its banning, and a Zulu chief (who, because of his participation in the ANC, was stripped of this function by the National Party government), was used as an essential link in the tradition created and presented by Inkatha.

The second set of symbols of legitimation that Inkatha uses arises from the pre-colonial history of the region and the manner in which capitalism penetrated the area of KwaZulu/Natal. In his presentation of history, Buthelezi argued that the Zulu nation had always been there. Its existence was not due to apartheid, but to the pre-colonial historical construction of the Zulu kingdom. This idea, which was being confirmed through restoration of the past under the leadership of Buthelezi, initially centred on legislating the existence of the Zulu Territorial Authority (ZTA), and later the KwaZulu Legislative Assembly (KLA). Buthelezi presented these as structures that could be used either to overthrow the apartheid system, or to reinforce the reawakening of the Zulu nation. It is therefore not surprising that Inkatha's initial positive appeal was to people who accepted a self-definition of being Zulu. Mare and Hamilton argue that this point indicates that Inkatha is an ethnic organization. On the other hand, however, this may also indicate that Buthelezi wished to prevent a repetition of the state intervention of 1960 by disguising Inkatha as a bantustan organization operating within the parameters of state ideology, so as to allow it the possibility of extending its operations to a national level at a later date. Indeed, this latter point makes more sense when Inkatha changed its constitution in 1977 to welcome all other African people into membership (albeit with little success on the ground). Furthermore, since the region of KwaZulu/Natal is the historic area in which most of the people who made up the Zulu kingdom were concentrated, most of the reasons for positive identification with what Inkatha stands for have been sought in this region.

Structures

During its early years Inkatha set up a solid structure that enabled it to carry out its agenda in a fairly organized way. Inkatha has a formal pyramidal structure, leading up from individual members, branches, and regions to various decision-making bodies and conferences. Two of Inkatha's bodies are worth examining in some detail: the National Council (NC), and the Youth Brigade. The NC will illuminate the relationship that Inkatha has with the KwaZulu government, and the Youth Brigade will illustrate the operation of Inkatha's structure using the example of Emandleni youth camp, with which I am familiar, having worked there in 1986 and 1987.

The NC was the policy-making organ with some three hundred members. It was composed of the central committee, the KwaZulu Legislative Assembly (KLA) members who were also members of Inkatha, four representatives of the regions, members of the brigades' executives, one representative from each affiliated organization, and the organization's administrative officials. Inkatha absorbed the KLA through the NC, so that it can be regarded as, in practice, 'the legislative arm of Inkatha' (Langner 1982, p. 71). The NC could, in fact, propose legislation to the Assembly. Schmahmann (1983, p. 285), commenting on the absorption, wrote that 'the potential for abuse by those who control the movement is ... great. Intermingling the Legislative Assembly with the National Council and the Cabinet with the Central Committee excludes the growth of effective opposition political parties.' What is clear from this is that at several levels, Inkatha was part and parcel of the bantustan (KwaZulu) administrative structure: all persons selected as candidates for parliamentary or local government were members of Inkatha; the chief minister of KwaZulu was also the president of Inkatha; and members of the KwaZulu Legislative Assembly served on the Inkatha National Council. In fact, it is safe to say that the leadership of KwaZulu and that of Inkatha were virtually the same.

While KwaZulu could not provide for all who live there through the KwaZulu government, Inkatha controlled enough resources to favour loyalists and punish opponents. Thus, it is safe to say that because of the overlap between Inkatha and KwaZulu government, in some cases, people were coerced to join in order to gain access to land, jobs, housing, pensions, and other resources. Teachers and civil servants were most vulnerable to Inkatha's pressure, since as employees of the government they had to pledge loyalty to Inkatha. Failure to belong to Inkatha could have resulted in the loss of material resources in a period of rural poverty. In towns, it might have lead to physical assaults.

The Youth Brigade created another dimension of Inkatha's structures. Studies such as Langner's have argued that the Youth Brigade was founded to counter the influence of more radical student organizations, especially in universities (although it is not clear as to how it was to do this). Generally speaking, Emandleni camp was born out of the national youth conference of 1981 in which a resolution to form youth corps was made. Emandleni camp and the other youth camps (usually referred to as corps) that followed were to absorb the thousands of young people who annually left school without any chance of employment.

Emandleni camp is located in the countryside, about ten miles outside Ulundi, KwaZulu's capital. While some people have suggested that the role that the youths play at Emandleni is similar to that of white youths in military service, I view Emandleni youths as performing the role that was performed by the *amabutho* regiments in pre-1879 Zululand. First, Emandleni camp is relatively self-sufficient. The youths grow food for the camp members, and the excess is sold at cheap rates to neighbouring Ulundi. The youths also build the camp's structures: roads, bridges and houses, and are sometimes taken out to other KwaZulu government projects. The camp receives funding from the KwaZulu government; most of this goes to paying personnel. At the end of their year's training the youths will go back to their respective communities and establish similar projects that encourage self-sufficiency.

The youths at Emandleni are also given intense military training, as was Shaka's *amabutho*. More time is spent on military training than on any other aspect in the camp, and kudos is given to those who survive this training without difficulties. And as with Shaka's regiments, the youths are divided into age groups, under the leadership of the most loyal member (selection procedures are complicated, but the leader has to show loyalty to the KwaZulu government). One difference between Shaka's regiments and those of Emandleni is that the camp regiments include women. Furthermore, while it was clear that Shaka's regiments were for external warfare, defence, and sometimes internal coercion, the reason for the military training at Emandleni initially was not clear. However, as the internal struggle between black groups intensified, particularly between Inkatha and the UDF/ANC, the reasons became more explicit. Emandleni youths have been used by Inkatha to fight its opponents in the struggle for power in KwaZulu/Natal.

During its first eight years of revival, Inkatha and, more specifically, Buthelezi, rose to power with the acquiescence of the ANC. Throughout the 1970s and early 1980s Buthelezi appealed for Nelson Mandela's release from prison. In fact, initially Inkatha gained the approval of a wide range of organizations and individuals, including independent unions, the ANC, and religious bodies. Furthermore, as a bantustan movement, Inkatha was protected from state action during its early years. However, these advantages became serious problems as the general mood in the country changed.

At the end of the 1970s Buthelezi's balancing act between a regional and Zulu mobilization, and an African nationalist movement changed. Inkatha's relationship with the ANC was ruptured, and Buthelezi's attempts to create an alternative political position under the leadership of the Zulu king failed.[8] The 1980s saw a drift away from any major concern with national politics and national political symbols. That current was defined by the youth groups, by the ANC with its strategies of armed struggle and economic sanctions, by the United Democratic Front (UDF, formed in 1983), by the Congress of South African Trade Unions (COSATU, launched in 1985), and by an organization that became known as the Mass Democratic Movement (MDM). For Inkatha, the 1980s were a period of regional consolidation, characterized by blatant ethnic political mobilization and a structural integration of the KwaZulu homeland and Natal provincial administration. Inkatha also drafted blueprints for regional reform through the Buthelezi Commission and negotiations referred to as the KwaZulu/Natal Indaba.[9] It was during this period that Inkatha worked to eliminate its opponents through violence and through control and distribution of jobs and houses. Moreover, the enemy for Inkatha involved not just political opponents such as the UDF/ANC, but included Zulus who rejected the version of a politicized ethnicity it propounded. Castigating and threatening these traitors to the Zulu cause became a common theme during the 1980s.

Inkatha and the United Democratic Front, 1980–1990

The decade of the 1980s saw interesting developments in KwaZulu/Natal. On the administrative side, increased legislative power was given to the KwaZulu government. Popular resistance forced the South African state to alter fundamentally the position originally envisaged for the homelands. Therefore KwaZulu became one of the homelands that successfully resisted moving into stage 3 of the Bantustan policy; that is, so-called independence. Reasons for refusing this third stage are not that clear, but it is possible to speculate that Inkatha did not want the Zulu people to lose their South African citizenship with the accompanying rights, as would have happened with an 'independent' KwaZulu. This would have been a retrogade step economically, since the region was highly dependent on the revenue it derived from regions such as Natal itself and the Transvaal. Therefore, instead of fighting for an independent KwaZulu, a greater measure of incorporation of the Bantustan into the bureaucratic structure of the state began. Discussions for a joint administration and legislature between the Natal Provincial Council and the KLA dominated the mid-1980s. These discussions became known as the KwaZulu/Natal Indaba (literally, KwaZulu/Natal story). As a result of such discussions, in 1987 KwaZulu realized its goal of taking police control in Durban's two major townships, KwaMashu and Umlazi. Furthermore, the KwaZulu police were given authority to stop and search any vehicle without a warrant and to seize any article deemed as evidence. People suspected of involvement in, or withholding information about theft, violence or illegal possession of firearms and ammunition could then be detained for ninety days.

Inkatha thus increased its control over the black population in the region. Mare and Hamilton argue that although up until 1983, ANC leadership had adapted a stance critical of Inkatha's actions (such as the destroying of a KwaMashu school), it had never openly broken its links with Inkatha. The ANC leadership was forced to be less open in its relations with Inkatha, because many of its more radical youths were critical of Inkatha's strategy of negotiation with the apartheid government. Moreover, Inkatha's intolerance of students' organizations further estranged the relationship between it and the students. It is unclear why the ANC did not simply cut ties with Inkatha. Perhaps the ANC did not want to be viewed as ostracizing the Zulu ethnic group but wanted rather to be seen as an inclusive organization that acknowledged ethnic differences. In any case, the low profile that the ANC held towards Inkatha was impaired with the rise of the United Democratic Front in 1984.

The formation of the UDF presented an immediate challenge to Inkatha's claim to an identity based on association with the ANC. The adaptation of the ANC's South African constitution, known as the Freedom Charter, by the UDF further isolated Inkatha from its basis of legitimacy as an inner wing of the ANC. Furthermore, the UDF's claim that it represented the political aspirations of the black population undermined Inkatha's claim to do so. The problem between the UDF and Inkatha was intensified in 1990 when the ANC was unbanned and the UDF dissolved.

The United Democratic Front: A Brief History

Delegates of all races representing over five hundred organizations came together to found the UDF in 1983. It was formed to coordinate opposition to the National Party government's constitutional reforms, and the proposed Tricameral Parliament. Generally speaking, although the government did implement this legislation in September 1984, the UDF succeeded in mobilizing widespread and concerted opposition to most of the reforms. Thus, the period of UDF's existence was one of escalating resistance to apartheid.

From its very inception the UDF was marked by divisions and tension resulting from, among other things, a lack of well-defined structures and objectives: the UDF did not have a constitution but instead adopted some vaguely defined working principles. The formal organizational contours of the UDF are easy to portray. At the national level the front was a federation of regional bodies, each of which was a front or umbrella structure for highly diverse affiliates ranged from students' groups to workers' groups to overtly political organizations. These existed independent of and remained formally separate from the UDF. The UDF was thus not a party; it never allowed for membership and did not have branches, but it had its own discrete structures at national, regional, and sub-regional levels. These structures organized campaigns, produced various kinds of information, helped build affiliates, channelled funds, and so on. How these different parts fitted together in practice was not clear when he states:

> The UDF was neither monolithic nor static: 'it' meant different things to different leaders or supporters, at different times and in different places. The perception of the 'whole' varied according to both the actual view from the vantage-point of the 'part' and the beliefs as to what the 'whole' should look like ... In one sense, there was no single 'UDF,' rather many different 'UDFs': an alliance, a party, a facade for the ANC, a civil rights movement, a national liberation movement, and so on. (Seeking 1994, p. 6)

This looseness and lack of definition made it possible for organizations with different opinions to work alongside each other. It also influenced the strategic choices made by its leaders: the UDF embraced any choices made to achieve its goals. Eventually these choices escalated the problem between the UDF's structures and affiliates, and between the UDF and other political movements in the country.

The criteria for affiliation to the UDF were far from restrictive, comprising only a commitment to the UDF's Declaration. This declaration proclaimed opposition to the Tricameral Parliament, which was later extended/interpreted by the UDF's secretary general as 'committing members to a non-racial, democratic and unitary South Africa, the particulars of which they are free to fill for themselves.'[10]

Inkatha's response to the formation of the UDF was to accuse it of being a surrogate of the ANC. Buthelezi described the UDF as 'Johnny-come-lately heroes' (Brewer 1986, p. 373), and the antagonism between the two organizations erupted into large-scale violence. The UDF posed a threat to Inkatha through undermining Inkatha's efforts to establish its hegemony over Natal's townships and, through the Congress of South Africa's Trade Unions (COSATU), threatened Inkatha's hegemony amongst the workers.

The UDF, COSATU, and Inkatha

As soon as it was set up in 1985 COSATU launched attacks on Buthelezi. The KwaZulu administration had initially gained considerable credibility in worker circles after the participation of Barmy Dladla, a senior Inkatha official, in the Trade Union Advisory Coordinating Council (TUACC) and in the 1973 Durban strikes. Buthelezi, however, took a different view and attacked the use of strikes by workers to solve specific grievances. Again, it is unclear why Buthelezi opposed workers' strikes, but it has been thought that he was playing an economic game, which he claimed was going to benefit the interests of KwaZulu and its people. That is, Buthelezi did not want to offend the white factory owners who were affected by these strikes since he was in the process of negotiating power-sharing between them and KwaZulu; such strikes were viewed as hindering the prosperity of these negotiations.

The leadership of Inkatha and the Federation of South African Trade Unions (FOSATU), the forerunner of COSATU, enjoyed a shaky relationship, the latter irritated that so many strikes were opposed by Inkatha. In spite of all this, many Zulu workers continued to be members of both Inkatha and FOSATU-affiliated unions. As long as the most significant and well-organized unions avoided overt political positions and alliances, a worker could belong to Inkatha and to a union without being disloyal to either. COSATU's sympathy for disinvestments – that is, its encouragement of foreign companies to leave the country – and its alignment with anti-Inkatha organizations, brought the divided loyalties of workers into focus. It also highlighted differences between Inkatha's response to workers' grievances and the way workers' unions addressed these grievances. On more than one occasion Inkatha appeared more interested in representing KwaZulu leadership interests than those of the workers. KwaZulu government had shares in most of the white-run businesses in the region and so it became more important for it to keep workers at work than to support their ideas of striking. In the 1984 sugar cane strike at Inkandla, for example, Inkatha sent in an impi to intimidate workers into going back to work. The UDF, on the other hand, appeared more willing to support the workers because most of the workers' grievances were in tune with its strategy of promoting ungovernability and of general defiance. UDF sympathy to the workers' plight meant that Inkatha was losing its constituency at an even faster rate. The result was more violence, with impis attacking all those suspected to be anti-Inkatha. The UDF and COSATU subsequently formed defence units in the townships.

The formation of COSATU changed the relationship that Inkatha had with the workers in more than one way. First, it shifted the centre of the organized working class from KwaZulu/Natal to the Transvaal, where COSATU made its headquarters. This made it possible for unionists to adopt a more provocative stance towards Inkatha without fear of reprisal since many workers active in the Transvaal were not KwaZulu government employees. Second, COSATU's claim to the ANC tradition undermined any political aspirations which Inkatha had hoped to achieve on the national level.

COSATU supported calls for economic sanctions and a socialist economic system in South Africa. Inkatha was against economic sanctions because it viewed them not just as punishing the apartheid state, but also penalizing ordinary people who lost their jobs. Thus, in opposition to COSATU, Inkatha inaugurated the United Workers' Union of South Africa (UWUSA), which pledged its support to Inkatha's political views, particularly those of investments and a free market economy. Violence erupted as Inkatha and the UDF fought for political control over the region, and the unbanning of the ANC further intensified this violence. In the following chapter, I describe the townships, the people in them, and how they navigated the controversial politics in the region. It is in these townships that Inkatha and ANC politics got played out, forcing individuals to create certain strategies for survival, and by so doing, to redefine and/or moderate already existing notions of Zuluness.

chapter 4

Townships

'Township' was the name given to areas created as a result of events at the end of the nineteenth and beginning of the twentieth centuries: the emancipation of slaves in 1833; the discovery of gold, diamonds, and other minerals; and the Land Acts of 1913 and 1936. The emancipation of slaves in 1833 meant that white farmers could no longer rely on a ready supply of forced labour. The development of mining and the growth of industry also led to the demand for cheap labour. Both situations led to a series of land acts which forced blacks into the state labour market. Under the Land Act of 1913 black people were zoned to reserves that made up only 14 per cent of the total land area of South Africa. Moreover, these reserves are located in the least fertile areas of the country. As a result, blacks were forcibly moved from agricultural land that they had previously owned and that was then apppropriated by white farmers. Those blacks leaving or evicted from white-owned land found refuge in the reserves and in towns, increasing the pressure on available resources in these places. In addition, the underdevelopment of the reserves played a significant role in forcing blacks to migrate from the rural areas to the nearest urban centre to look for work and a better life.

The migration from rural areas to the mines and factories forced municipalities to confront the problem of blacks living in white cities. Responses varied from region to region and from industry to industry. For example, in Durban, KwaZulu/Natal's largest city, the provision of permanent township areas for blacks was slow in coming, often approved reluctantly, and inadequately provided for, once approval had been given. Furthermore, thrifty city counsellors resented providing permanent housing for black inhabitants who at best were regarded as sojourners who contributed little or nothing to the paying of rates and taxes. As a result, large numbers of black rural migrants arriving in the city found themselves confronted with the problem of obtaining accommodation. Many turned to squatting,[1] either in backyards, in overcrowded slum tenements, or illegally on any open piece of land available. Between the years 1910 and 1913, for example, the size of Durban's black population increased from 16,489 to 20,203. Only 5,850 of this total were housed in municipal quarters (Minaar, 1992, p. 1). Up until 1958, therefore, when the first township was established, the government referred to black immigrant workers as slum dwellers, as shantytowns mushroomed around the city of Durban.

To resolve this problem, the apartheid government initiated housing projects for blacks, which were located in KwaZulu land but were administered by the Natal Provincial Administration. Thus, KwaMashu and Umlazi emerged as a result of the South African government's attempt to solve what it referred to as the 'black problem' (of housing). Both townships were initially established to rehouse the residents of Cato Manor, located west of the city centre and considered to be one of the worst slums. By the end of the 1950s Cato Manor accommodated over 120,000 people under appalling conditions which had developed in the absence of any intervention by the state authorities. Its residents were transferred to KwaMashu in 1958 and their shacks demolished. In 1965 Umlazi was opened for those Cato Manor residents that KwaMashu had not been able to house.

KwaMashu and Umlazi, on the eastern shore of South Africa, are the two largest townships in the KwaZulu/Natal. They are approximately twenty-five kilometres from the city centre, with KwaMashu located to the north and Umlazi to the south. At the time of conducting this study in 1992 it was difficult to estimate the number of residents in each township, because most residents were found in squatter areas, which were by law illegal areas. In 1972 both townships came under the ambit of Bantustan administration, that is, the KwaZulu Legislative Assembly (KLA). However, despite many promises from the South African government, until 1986 the KwaZulu police were denied control of these two townships, probably because of their proximity to the vital port of Durban and to the largest concentration of white inhabitants in the province. It is possible that the South African government was doubtful whether the newly formed KwaZulu police would be able to suppress political violence of these townships. The decision by the central government to finally hand over police control of Umlazi and KwaMashu was preceded by clashes which culminated in violence between UDF and Inkatha followers in 1985. Mare and Hamilton (1987, p. 215) argue that it was Inkatha's ability to suppress opposition during these clashes that finally convinced the apartheid government to put trust in KwaZulu police.

The integration of KwaMashu and Umlazi into KwaZulu was by no means a smooth process. In the early days KwaZulu authorities often met resistance from residents of these townships, often arising from resentment over the lack of resources such as schools, housing, and jobs under the KLA. Some residents were against having to join Inkatha in order to access these resources. However, during the period from 1975 to 1980 Inkatha enjoyed considerable popularity in the region and its prominence, together with state support, made it possible for KwaZulu to establish control over these two townships, and to set up institutional structures such as schools, hospitals, and police stations. By 1985, however, Inkatha's popularity had diminished. The birth of the UDF in 1983 challenged Inkatha's claim to be the inner wing of the ANC. The UDF also posed a threat to Inkatha's claim to be the largest representative of black people and the largest liberation movement in the country.

The Source of UDF and Inkatha Conflict in KwaMashu and Umlazi

Until 1985, Umlazi and KwaMashu townships were generally deemed to be quiescent and to have avoided the patterns of popular unrest and conflict elsewhere in South Africa. Although animosity had been brewing between UDF and Inkatha supporters, it had not reached the stage of a full-fledged violent confrontation. However, after the attack on the home of the mayor of Umlazi in June 1985, Inkatha leaders in Umlazi decided to establish defence units to combat politically motivated attacks on the homes of residents. Sabela, an Inkatha leader, said these units would liaise with the police in an effort to curb attacks. In July 1985 two Inkatha members' houses were burnt in Lamontville following three nights of violence. The UDF chairman in KwaZulu/Natal and Oscar Dhlomo, who was both Inkatha's secretary general and KwaZulu minister of education and culture, called for restraint and there were talks of holding a peace meeting between the UDF and Inkatha. But this never occurred, because on 1 August unidentified assailants gunned down Victoria Mxenge, a Durban attorney and an executive member of the UDF, in front of her Umlazi home.

The following day, the Azanian Students' Organisation (AZASO) and the Congress of South African Students (COSAS), both UDF affiliates, called for a week-long boycott of schools to observe a mourning period for Mxenge. The boycotts and marches that began on 5 August 1985 were initially composed of students, but they drew unemployed youths, looters, and opportunists in their wake. The targets of people's anger were the symbols of the apartheid system such as policemen and their houses, administrative and school buildings, but this soon extended to shops, businesses, and trading stores (Meer 1985, p. 2). Looting and arson occurred throughout the week in Umlazi and KwaMashu. By 7 August 1985 an estimated thousand Indians had fled Inanda (a Durban suburb which borders Umlazi and KwaMashu), to seek refuge in the Indian township of Phoenix after their homes had been attacked and looted. According to Sitas (1986, p. 109) a racial psychosis aggravated by the media's coverage was gripping both Inanda and Phoenix. Indeed, as Meer (1985, p. 46) points out, the media made much of the hostility of blacks towards Indians and failed to give due weight to the burning of black-owned shops in Inanda or to the fact that most of the people killed in the area were blacks.

It was at this stage that Inkatha vigilantes mobilized to protect businesses and property in the townships and to flush out and punish not only looters and criminals, but large numbers of students and UDF activists whom it believed instigated the riots. In the process, many innocent bystanders were hurt, killed, or left homeless. From 9 August busloads of organized Inkatha vigilantes known as amabutho, who had been organized from all over rural KwaZulu, arrived at KwaMashu and Inanda. The amabutho conducted house-to-house searches for victims, wielding sticks and shouting Inkatha slogans. Many UDF activists were merely forced to march, but others' fate was more severe, as demonstrated by the following terrifying but not uncommon excerpt from an affidavit by a man who lost his son during this period:

> before I reached KwaMashu station I saw a large crowd of 'amabutho' who told me to join them. They were armed with spears, bush-knives, knobkirries and sticks. I had no alternative but to join their group ... a portion of the group chased four young men who were standing in the road, amongst them my son ... three of them managed to escape. My son ... ran into my house which was close by and locked the door ... The warriors then stoned the windows and chopped down two doors. I went inside ... to attempt to prevent people from assaulting my son ... he told me that he and the other young men were merely ... watching the group of warriors pass by. I noticed

that my son was bleeding badly and it appeared that he had been stabbed all over his body. In my presence he was again stabbed and ... dragged from the house into the garden where the group stoned him and stabbed him and hit him on the head with bush knives. I attempted to intervene but it was useless and after a short time I noticed that my son was dead. (Black Sash Files, November 1985)

According to reports, many were forced to shout slogans such as, 'The UDF is a dog. It separates people.'[2]

The week of violence left political organizations, including Inkatha, with glaring gaps in their ability to control or direct events. The violence perpetrated by Inkatha's supporters raised questions about its strategy of non-violence and the ability of its leadership to control the actions of its supporters. Buthelezi's response was to distance the actions of the leadership from those of its followers. Similarly, this period of unrest showed that the UDF leadership was unable to prevent the progression of events from relatively peaceful school boycotts and students' demonstrations after Victoria Mxenge's death to the wide-scale rioting, looting, and arson that followed. UDF affiliates were not strong enough to protect their supporters from harassment and victimization by Inkatha supporters and in reorganizing and rebuilding UDF community organizations.

Inkatha was widely credited by the press with restoring order to Durban's townships in August of 1985, and Buthelezi won the title of peacemaker irrespective of the methods Inkatha supporters used to bring about this peace. Moreover, the amabutho were not the only perpetrators of violence after they took control of KwaMashu and Umlazi, but they certainly had an upper hand. By 10 August, with the help of the South African Defence Force (SADF), Inkatha had quelled the rioting and was engaged mainly in demonstrating its power by marching through the township streets.

Many viewed the August violence and the methods used by Inkatha supporters to oust opposition in KwaMashu and Umlazi as a new form of brutality. The unpredictability and randomness of attacks, coming as they were in the middle of the night and making no distinctions between targeted political activists and babies, also introduced a new dimension of fear. Overall, the explosion of violence in August 1985 allowed Inkatha to assert more vigorous control over KwaMashu and Umlazi and to make them 'no-go' areas for open organization or action by its opposition.

Inkatha, UDF, and Township Schools: The Politics of the 1990s

While Inkatha was able to make geographical gains in August 1985 in the townships of Umlazi and KwaMashu, it failed to contain the aspirations of young people in and townships surrounding the city of Durban. For this reason much of Inkatha's rhetoric and violence from 1985 onwards was aimed at students. While in the early 1980s Buthelezi had made an initial gesture of sympathizing with the reasons for school boycotts, by 1985 his position had changed. Since students continued to challenge and question education policies, administration, and curriculum, school boycotts in the townships challenged the authority of KwaZulu Department of Education and Culture, and were an indication that Inkatha had failed to appeal to significant and vocal numbers of young people in these townships. Others have also argued that Buthelezi's change of support for school boycotts was because of his awareness that young people were the mainstay of the UDF in KwaZulu townships.

UDF affiliates in KwaMashu and Umlazi found it hard to gain support from elderly community residents. Most of its supporters were students mobilized through the Azanian Students Organisation (AZASO) and the Congress of South African Students (COSAS).[3] It is most likely that some of the UDF policies did not appeal to elderly residents who had invested their entire lives and finances in the townships. For example, the UDF strategy of 'making South Africa ungovernable' involved creating chaos in the townships through destroying government property and boycotting government-owned stores, government-controlled means of transportation, and so on. Many residents lost their property, since there was very little effort by the UDF perpetrators to distinguish property owned by residents from that which was government-owned. Furthermore, the UDF policy of calling for economic sanctions against South Africa resulted in the closure of industries, and therefore in the loss of many jobs during a period of extreme poverty. Students, on the other hand, had little to lose and were attracted by the UDF slogan 'liberation now, education later' since they were already critical of the system of education that was available to them. Furthermore, there was an underlying perception that the UDF was something 'out there' rather than in the townships: its structures were said to be non-racial, while evidence indicated that black youth were the main protesters and that protests were concentrated in black townships. The UDF leadership did not reflect the majority of its followers; it was mainly made up of Indians, which resulted in it being viewed as being for Indians rather than for black people.[4]

The activities of Inkatha's youth brigades in the townships were not clear. Accounts by those who observed *amabutho* gangs indicated that these were by no means mainly comprised of 'youth,' however loose Inkatha's definition of youth may be. During school boycotts in the townships, Inkatha's Youth Brigade did not persuade other youths to conform to a disciplined behaviour similar to that exercised at Inkatha rallies. This might mean that Inkatha's youths were not dominant in township schools so that during times of school protests they followed UDF lead, or perhaps that they simply did not participate.

The rise of students' activities in KwaZulu/Natal and elsewhere came during the era of the UDF with its 1985 slogan 'liberation now, education later.' This slogan was a call for students to demonstrate their commitment to the liberation struggle by boycotting all apartheid structures, including school. Under COSAS, the schools surrounding Durban and Pietermaritzburg saw protest and boycotts over various grievances. Some schools that did not support this strategy initially stayed open, only to later close because of fear of reprisal from UDF supporters. Despite prosecution of youth leaders and activists by Inkatha, and the legal constraints placed on the organization of student bodies by the detention and banning of COSAS, from August 1985 onwards the resilience of student opposition to Inkatha was evident.

Protests and school boycotts by black students were having a disastrous effect. In December 1985, at a conference in Soweto, it was agreed that boycotting pupils, some of whom had not been going to school for over three years, should return to school on the condition that certain demands were met by the central government within three months. These demands included the lifting of the state of emergency, withdrawal of troops from townships, unbanning of COSAS, and the recognition of student representative councils. A National Education Crisis Committee (NECC) was formed, with representatives from eleven regions of South Africa.

At a meeting organized by the Regional Ad Hoc Committee in KwaZulu/Natal, it was agreed that students would go back to school at the end of January 1986, and that they would not pay school fees or money for books. In February the KwaZulu Department of Education and Culture denied that KwaZulu pupils were opposed to paying fees. However, by the end of March, Inkatha was clearly perturbed by evidence not only of numerous disturbances and boycotts within township schools in many parts of KwaZulu/Natal but also of growing solidarity among students, parents, and teachers. The 'back to school' slogan meant that students'

organizations which had been weakened by the almost two years of boycotts were then facilitating committees to work together to address the
crisis in the education system.

Ironically, the prospects of an organized national body, which not
only proposed to blur class and generation boundaries, but also suggested a return to classrooms to consolidate the liberation struggle,
appeared to Inkatha as a hijacking of its own platforms and constituencies. Inkatha's response to the NECC in KwaZulu/Natal was to criticize
and intimidate it. When on 6 April 1986 the NECC organized a conference at Congella Hall in Durban, Inkatha responded by bussing in impis
to attack delegates. As a result of this attack, two of the people bussed in
by Inkatha were killed. Inkatha was roundly condemned by the conference as an enemy of the people and as a 'fascist organisation in league
with the government' (*Natal Witness*, 4 April 1986). School boycotts,
which had been rife in KwaMashu before the conference because of
shortages or lack of promised books and stationery, were prolonged
despite the conference's call for a return to school. Students stated that
they feared reprisal from Inkatha after the deaths at the NECC conference. Buthelezi explained Inkatha's actions by arguing that the NECC
had scheduled the meeting as an attempt to make Congella a 'no-go'
area for him and that therefore the impis had acted out of anger in his
defence. However, the fact that the impis had been brought indicated
that the attack was not a spontaneous display of communal anger but
rather a planned action.

The control of one township or a part of a township by either UDF or
Inkatha was also symbolically marked. Townships are divided into
sections or units that are alphabetically and numerically marked (for
example, if one lives at Umlazi, the address might be Unit A, house
no. 677). During this struggle for control of the townships, groups
began to take over different sections and give them symbolic names. For
example, units with names like Moscow, symbolic of the communist revolution which led to the overthrow of capitalism in Russia, Zimbabwe,
symbolic of the Mugabe and Nkomo guerrilla warfare that led to the
overthrow of colonialism in Rhodesia, and Mozambique were all UDF-
controlled. On the other hand, names like India, symbolic of Gandhi's
peaceful revolution against British colonialism and therefore of
Inkatha's initial strategy of non-violence, were Inkatha-controlled. Similarly, symbolic names were given to supporters of each organization.
The UDF called Inkatha supporters *Otheleweni* or *oklova. Otheleweni*
refers to a barbaric way of fighting and entails a negative interpretation

of the military strategies employed by Shaka during the consolidation of the Zulu kingdom. *Oklova* means uneducated people. Inkatha referred to UDF supporters as *amaqabane,* meaning communists. However, it became a common practice for supporters to take up a label and assign to it a positive meaning. For example, the UDF took up the name *amaqabane* and used it to mean comrades. The important point, however, is that both the UDF and Inkatha were the key symbolic reference points in KwaZulu/Natal.

As the struggle for control over the townships and against apartheid in general continued, UDF strategies of speeding up liberation by making South Africa ungovernable made it vulnerable to state restrictions. Furthermore, while on the one hand the drastic conduct of many comrades (UDF/ANC supporters) of 'necklacing' and conducting 'kangaroo courts'[5] in the townships forced many into the hands of Inkatha, on the other hand, UDF activities appealed to many who were unemployed and to the youths who were unoccupied as a result of school boycotts. Thus, the UDF was not only a threat to the state but also to Inkatha since its existence meant competition for political influence especially in the region of KwaZulu/Natal. The restrictions that were placed over the UDF and other organizations at the end of 1986 gave an added advantage to Inkatha. Furthermore, as already stated, in mid-1986, the KLA had made an important political gain: control of police stations in Umlazi and KwaMashu.

These advantages for Buthelezi, Inkatha, and the KLA were short lived when, on 2 February 1990, President de Klerk transformed South African politics by unbanning organizations such as the ANC and lifting restrictions on the UDF. This meant the revival of formal competition for Inkatha's position in the country. The UDF had been able to inspire, politically educate, and mobilize large numbers of people into a broadly coherent struggle against apartheid. As a result, when the ANC was unbanned, it took over UDF structures and strategies in a way that enabled continuity in an already intense resistance against apartheid and its structures.

Criminal Elements and the Struggle

Political killings accounted for only a small fraction of the violence in South Africa during this era, and this was clearly the case in KwaMashu and to a lesser extent Umlazi. It has been estimated that purely criminal murders outnumbered politically motivated murders by five to one.

South Africa's murder rate accelerated to the point where it was reck-
oned to be ten times more than that of the United States. Unemployment surpasses 40 percent among black South Africans, reaching 90
per cent or more among the so-called lost generation of black youths.
The militancy of these youth during the 1980s township uprisings
scarcely equipped them to compete in an economy that had been
shrinking for most of that decade. More than ever before, black communities experienced acute housing shortages, lack of schools and transportation, the breakdown of families and of other traditional sources of
authority. Organized crime flourished, with shack lords running protection and gambling rackets and trafficking in drugs and guns. The blending of crime and politics became the order of the day, for political
groups used these shantytown lords to establish their presence in an
area. More than any township, KwaMashu illustrated the extreme the
anarchy that resulted because of the blending of crime with political
activity.

KwaMashu and Crime

From the late 1980s to about 1994, KwaMashu residents lived in fear of a
group known as *amasinyora,* an invented Zulu word used to refer to people who do bad deeds. Knowledge of the practices of amasinyora is
imperative because of the impact they had on the other groups in Kwa-
Mashu and Umlazi. It appears that little was done by the authorities to
stop the group's actions. What I document here, therefore, are different
narrations from various KwaMashu residents interviewed at the time of
the study about their understanding of this group and how its members
functioned.

The amasinyora were a group of youths involved in criminal acts
within KwaMashu. According to some residents, this group was originally a soccer group living in KwaMashu's K section. It used to be on
good terms with soccer groups in other sections who would organize
soccer games and many other social activities, formal or informal. It
seems as if there was a conflict between two soccer groups and the reasons for this conflict are not clear. Suddenly, these groups were no
longer talking, and were hunting each other like enemies.

Other informants suggested that the amasinyora emerged after the
unbanning of political parties in 1990, and it is claimed that the conflict
between the soccer groups was political. Proponents of this theory
argued that having the ANC officially recognized in the country pro-

vided challenges for Inkatha members, most of who were in the K section of KwaMashu, and that the conflict was a result of the K group
trying to force its neighbours and associates into being Inkatha. Yet
other people claimed that there never was any relationship between the
K section amasinyora and the rest of the soccer groups in the township,
and that amasinyora was an Inkatha formation with no history of ever
being a soccer club.

Witnessing the change of attitude towards it after the ANC was
unbanned, Inkatha had to devise ways to protect its territories or Kwa-
Zulu-controlled townships from ANC influence. It therefore created the
amasinyora in order to recruit more members. Unfortunately for
Inkatha, this new group used all kinds of techniques to scare people
away from joining the ANC. Eventually, the amasinyora was not only
involved in safeguarding Inkatha territory, but in criminal activities. As a
result of power given to it by Inkatha the group started regarding itself
as above the law, accountable to nobody, not even to Inkatha authorities. In turn, residents also viewed this group as possessing power,
beyond the hand of the law.

One wonders why Inkatha did not make amasinyora accountable for
their actions, which were clearly demeaning its political name. Perhaps
it was because the work of scaring residents away from joining the ANC
seems to have been very crucial to Inkatha. There is no evidence that
supports this explanation, and since both Inkatha and ANC members in
KwaMashu were equally terrified of amasinyora it appears that their
activities were without political boundaries. Interestingly, the participants involved in this study (one of whom lived in the K section of Kwa-
Mashu) argued that there was no direct link between Inkatha and
amasinyora. To these people, amasinyora were just a group of smart *tsotsis* (gangsters, hooligans, thieves, burglars), who exploited the loop-
holes in both the administrative and political structures. They agreed
that amasinyora and comrades (ANC members) did not see eye to eye,
but that the conflict was not political. These informants argued that
amasinyora were considered to be against comrades because comrades
were against criminal acts (even though evidence pointed otherwise).
Moreover, this did not necessarily mean that Inkatha was for criminal
acts, but that its ways of recruiting members were viewed as criminal.
Amasinyora were said to have had alliance with the police (and by implication with Inkatha) because the police did little to stop their activities
and at that time the political actions of Inkatha members could hardly
be distinguished from those of the police or the central state. Inkatha

had formalized its role in political repression through taking control of, and therefore, responsibility for, actions of KwaZulu police.

Despite the different explanations about the formation of amasinyora, a number of points were supported by all informants. First, amasinyora were a powerful group in the township, feared by all and often unchallenged. Second, the police did little to stop amasinyora's activities, who were therefore viewed as above the law. Third, there seems to have been a link, at least at the ideological level, between the practices of amasinyora and the beliefs and practices of the two prominent political organizations in the region, Inkatha and the ANC. This link might have been direct or indirect but all parties involved acknowledged its presence.

While the origins and affiliation of amasinyora were mysterious, their criminal acts were clear and terrifying. Their demands varied from people's cars to their wallets, clothes and sometimes their lives. Instances of rape were mentioned, but because of the stigmatization of rape victims within society, no women ever came forward. So what is known about rape and amasinyora is what they themselves said (amasinyora were openly boastful of their activities) and sometimes telling cries for help heard by passers-by at the places where the group operated. To demonstrate the hatred that people in general had developed for this group, I was repeatedly told this story: A group of amasinyora went to a beer store and demanded to be given a crate of beer to drink. Fearful of what might happen if he refused, the owner complied and the group sat down to drink, while the owner continued serving other customers. Halfway through their drinking, the amasinyora invited the beer store-owner to join them. The owner tried to escape the invitation by arguing that he was busy, upon which amasinyora responded by saying that his refusal was an indication that he did not like them, and further pointed out that there was nobody to be served at that particular time. Out of fear, the beer storeowner joined them. Two weeks later, the beer store-owner was found dead alongside the road. He had been killed not by amasinyora but by residents who had seen him drinking with them in the beer store. 'How dare he befriend such criminals?' the question was asked.

Umlazi and Crime

The criminal acts at Umlazi differed from those of KwaMashu in that they had minimal political overtones. The reasons for this are not clear.

Some people argued that Inkatha had succeeded to establish its authority in Umlazi to the point that residents who were not its supporters had two remaining options: leave the township, or be very quiet. Inkatha's control over this township was assisted by the fact that most of the Kwa-Zulu government structures were located there, and since Inkatha was the political wing of the KwaZulu government, it was difficult for other organizations to penetrate. As a result of this relatively stable political situation in Umlazi, institutions such as schools were able to operate without the political violence that would often result in their closing. It is for this reason that, despite their political beliefs, some parents from the neighbouring townships preferred to enrol their children in Umlazi schools. At least these schools guaranteed an education for their children, limited as that education was.

The presence of Inkatha in Umlazi, however, marginalized the existence of groups that chose to operate outside the auspices of any political organization. For example, during the course of this study, two of the key informants belonged to a youth group that had been started about six months prior to my arrival. This group had been established with the help of a resident, as a project for his honours degree at the Centre for Cultural Studies at the University of Natal. The group served different social interests for youths mainly from the A section of Umlazi. The dominant activities were music and drama, but the group would also meet during the week to help each other with schoolwork. Some days the group would meet just to talk to each other about their lives, thus offering support to each other. Two months after I had been involved with this group, I learnt that it had disbanded. On learning about the existence of this group, Inkatha officials had approached it, offering financial support on the condition that its members would agree to join Inkatha. Having refused this problematic financial offer, group members considered it best to disband in fear of being labelled anti-Inkatha, and by implication ANC, which might have resulted in the loss of their lives. Indeed, had the members agreed to join Inkatha, the group would have lost its autonomy, and would have had its goals changed to meet Inkatha's demands. In theory, all groups that aim to serve the 'needs of the society' however defined, had the right to seek financial support from the KLA administered township council. In practice, however, this support could only be achieved through groups' acknowledgment of Inkatha's authority over their destinies.

Any resistance to Inkatha authority in KwaMashu therefore resulted in violence, in the killing of hundreds of innocent people caught in the crossfire of the struggle for control over this township. Political motives spiralled into criminal violence, which also resulted in hundreds of deaths. But Inkatha's failure to exert authority in KwaMashu made it possible for residents to establish groups that operated without the threat from and fear of being forced into some political party. Some of these groups came under the auspices of the church, but most operated independently. At Umlazi, however, Inkatha's authority meant the suppression of many social groups (with the exception of soccer groups whose political strategies will be examined in chapter nine), and at the same time guaranteed the function of institutions such as schools, which were greatly valued in black communities. Coupled with the unavailability of social/entertainment structures, Inkatha's politics also made it impossible for Umlazi youth to organize, forcing them to look for other alternative communities in which to carry out their activities. In other words, besides staying at home or visiting friends, Umlazi youth found themselves having to leave the township in order to carry out activities that were valuable to them. For example, one of the participants in the study commuted to Lamontville to liaise and carry out the activities of Umkhonto, the ANC's military wing.[6] As far as Umlazi was concerned, this participant knew no politics and therefore had no political life.

In the following chapter, I discuss the changes in the political and social practices of groups as the struggle against apartheid intensified. How exactly did Inkatha's administrative and political control of the townships manifest itself in the everyday social and cultural practices of the people in these townships? And how did people respond to the interconnections between politics and everyday social practices? Specifically, I examine in depth the manner in which Zulu cultural practices, including language use, were understood and associated with the practices of Inkatha and/or ANC.

chapter 5

Setting Out the Tensions: Formal Politics, Cultural Practices, and the Definition of Zulu Identity

Six months ago, most of the deaths in South Africa were caused by police fire on rioters. Now more than half are due to black-on-black violence, mostly in clashes between left-wing Comrades and conservative vigilante groups known as Fathers. Radical black leaders allege that the Fathers are aided by police, but this is strongly denied. The Fathers say they are fighting against a takeover of black townships by teenagers who do not follow the African tradition of respect for elders.

World Press Review, August 1986

An underlying problem that faced individuals in KwaZulu/Natal was the complexity of criteria of identification and the way in which these criteria intersected with formal and interpersonal politics. In other words, the region was marked with tensions that resulted because of the intersection between institutionalized and conventionalized criteria of identity, and the way these criteria were problematically associated with the practices of political organizations, Inkatha and the ANC.

This chapter outlines four criteria of identification that individuals used to position themselves as Zulu or not Zulu, depending on space and context. It also examines the manner in which these criteria of identification may have been linked to the practices of political organizations, especially those of Inkatha and the ANC. This chapter further examines Zulu cultural practices, including the practice of *hlonipha* (literally, to respect) and of *ukukhonza* (literally, to worship). Operating alongside and often in conflict with these Zulu cultural practices were changes associated with industrialization and urbanization. The association of industrialization with the urban sectors, and with modernity and economic progress, made it possible for Zulu cultural practices to be associated with the rural areas, poverty and backwardness. A rural-urban or modern-backward dichotomy was thus created, which in itself added complexity to an already diverse situation. This chapter also analyses the manner in which Zulu cultural practices and those of industrialization/ modernization, were given meaning by political organization. This in turn made it difficult for individuals to engage in either set of practices without assuming or being linked to these organizations. This explains the core of the tension experienced, first, by individuals who defined themselves as Zulu but did not want to take up membership in any political organization, and second, by individuals who identified themselves as Zulu, who did not take up Inkatha membership, but who resorted to other political parties such as the ANC, which were in competition and conflict with Inkatha.

Institutionalized Definitions of Zulu Identity

Institutionalized definition of Zulu refers to that identity which was legitimized through the state legal system. Individuals needed this identity to gain access to certain kinds of state-controlled resources, including schools, housing, and jobs. Institutionalized definition of Zulu also refers to the manner in which this definition was recognized and legitimized by not only the state, but also by political organizations.

The Birthplace

The birthplace criterion is one that in pre-1879 Zululand tied individuals to specific homesteads and chiefdoms. The traditional homestead structure was co-opted by colonial administrators, resulting in continuity between migrants' families who remained in the region and the chiefs through whom the colonialists collected the hut tax. In its essence, this criterion requires one to have been born in KwaZulu/ Natal, or to have had parents born in the region and had maintained ties with the region.

Descent

Descent refers to the manner in which individuals traced their ancestry to the region, even if they were not born in KwaZulu/Natal. For instance, it was possible for individuals to use oral history and produce information that linked their ancestry to the region of KwaZulu/Natal, and if they desired, to re-establish ties and eventually settle with their tribes through the chiefs. Besides these individuals, Zulu children are brought up with information about their descent, and the roles their ancestors played in the Zulu wars of conquest and struggle against British colonialism. Thus, phrases like *uwuZulu Zu, uZulu woqobo* (you are Zulu Zu or you are a real Zulu), are commonly used in KwaZulu/Natal to distinguish those Zulu of historic origin from those who migrated into the area, especially after 1879.

For example, during my first month of data collection at KwaMashu, a friend, Khosi, drove me to see another friend, Dolana, who used to live in the same township. After knocking on her door for some time and receiving no response, I approached a group of people who were sitting outside the neighbouring house. I began the conversation with the usual Zulu salute and then asked if they knew where my friend and her family were or when they might be back? One man responded by stating that they could not give me the information unless they knew who I was and where I was from *ngoba* (because), he added, *'baningi abantu bokuhamba abafike babuze umuntu njengawe kanti bafuna ukumenzakalisa lowo muntu'* (there are a lot of outsiders who come looking for people just like you are doing, with the intention of doing them harm)[1] and the others nodded in agreement. I told them who I was and that I was from Melmoth. *'Kwesikabanike ke ndodakazi?'* (In whose area [chief] at Melmoth?) I was asked. *'Kwesika Mhawukeleni Mpungose'* (Mhawukeleni Mpungose's area), I responded, not knowing that the chief had died a few months before my return from Canada. *'Oh Usho losanda kushona? awu kwaba yindaba ebuhlungu-ke leyo'* (Oh you mean the one who died recently? That was a sad case) someone continued. *'Ubani kambe owathatha ubukhosi?'* (Who by the way took over the chieftainship?') This time, I had to think fast, *'Indodana yakhe'* (His son), I responded, merely drawing on my cultural knowledge of Zulu hereditary practices. *Kodwa lokhu yinto nje ongayifunda ngisho ephepheni. Awusho-ke ndodakazi, uwuzalo lwaphi?'* (But anybody can have this [information about the death of the chief] through newspapers. Tell us [our] daughter, whose descent are you?) Again I had to think fast, because by this time I had figured out that these people wanted to know if I could be trusted, and that this could only be done if I was a descendent of a Zulu person they had heard of in the past. I have very little knowledge of my father's line of descent beyond my grandfather, so I decided to recite my mother's line of descent. As I had anticipated, since my great-grandfather was a well-known man at the beginning of the twentieth century, some of the peo-ple in the group had heard of him and his offspring, including my mother. Upon discovering that I was Zulu by descent, because of my ability to clearly trace my past relatives to the region, I was given the information I needed: my friend had moved to one of the Durban sub-urbs, Redhill, about three months before my arrival. Prior to this move her house had been vandalized by amasinyora and everything in the house had been stolen. After this incident she made a decision to leave KwaMashu and her house was now being rented. I thanked the group and joined my friend in the car who, however, was not surprised that I was asked these questions.

Thus, being able to trace one's descent often exempted one from being capable of performing violent acts which were often associated with strangers, and non-status-Zulus. Even though evidence pointed otherwise, many still believed that status Zulus could not fight other status Zulus.

History

Zulu is the name (*isibongo*) of only one clan. The people themselves call their language *isiNtu* (human speech). Today, to call the language Zulu, though not a common African practice, is justifiable in as much as a suf-ficiently uniform language exists. In fact, isiNtu is used synonymously with Zulu to refer both to the language and the people's culture. It is also common nowadays to speak of the Zulus, meaning all the speakers of the language, and in addition implying that they are one people or, going still further, one political entity, although, this they have never been. Guy (1979) argues that even during the prime of the Zulu king-dom, one could distinguish (a) the Zulu nucleus of tribes closely bound and loyal to the Zulu royal house; (b) those whose ancestors held out against the Zulu power and neither fled nor subjected themselves, and (c) those who fled in time and never came under Zulu rule, and have no desire to be ruled by the house of Zulu to this day. Some from the lat-ter group led to the birth of the Ndebele nation in Zimbabwe, and the Shangane people in Mozambique.

What we now find in KwaZulu/Natal is a regrouping of Zulu-speaking people subdivided into well over three hundred tribes, including some dozens of the so-called *amaKholwa* (converts), mostly on mission reserves. The rule of the Zulu kings promoted the uniformity of custom and language we see today over large areas of the KwaZulu/Natal region. European rule and education, first by missionaries and later by the state, favoured this classification.

The tribes of Zulu-speakers are mostly known by the family or clan names (izibongo) of their chiefs. Tribal names do not necessarily reflect the actual composition of the tribes (just as the name Zulu did not and still does not reflect the actual composition of those people identified as Zulu). For example, while a tribe might be known as abakwaMpandza (Mpandza's people or Mpandza's descendants) there may be twenty or fifty different clan names represented within that tribe. What this actually means is that it was Mpandza who, at some historical period, consolidated that tribe and his descendants came to inherit the leadership role. Mpanza however, would be referred to as the 'father' of these people and be used as proof of the profundity of these people's Zulu identity. This was basically the method used to categorize people. Furthermore, the process of ukukhonza, 'passing,'[2] allowed for people coming from other parts of southern Africa to take up Zulu identity through, among other things, laying claim to a clan name. Integrating into the clan did not result in the loss of one's isibongo, which largely reflected the person's place of origin and time of integration. In precolonial society, the process of being integrated into Zulu society and keeping your isibongo did not present a problem, as long as one participated in the cultural practices of that clan and subsequently of the Zulu kingdom. In fact, Guy's (1979) definition of the Zulu as those who gave allegiance to the Zulu kings, who nurtured the land granted to them by the kings, and whose men served in the kingdom's army until 1879 is logical for this period.

In a general sense, history identified most Zulu people by the tribes to which they belonged. This also generally meant that through this grouping it became easy for people to identify different clan names under each tribe. If a person gave out a clan name that was not common to the KwaZulu/Natal region she was expected to demonstrate, when questioned, general knowledge of her tribe, including the name of her chief, and the other clan names found in the tribe. Those who failed to demonstrate such information were generally viewed as not of that tribe, and therefore not Zulu.

Language

Language was yet another criterion legitimized by the South African state and political organizations to construct and define Zulu identity.

But language on its own could not serve as criterion of identification, since Zulu was not just the language of KwaZulu/Natal but of other parts of southern Africa as well. In most instances, language, as a criterion of identification, was used in conjunction with other criteria, such as birthplace. For political organizations, it was the manner in which Zulu was used that carried more weight. For instance, it became important for Inkatha to mark those who spoke Zulu with an accent as foreigners, which it referred to as Johannesburg Zulu – that is, the ANC. For those who spoke the dialect of the region, other criteria of identification were used. All these criteria made it possible for the state, the ANC, and Inkatha to construct and legitimize different forms of Zulu identity.

State Definition

At the beginning of the twentieth century, alternative patterns of government, labour, and economic distribution and land occupation were established and were to be given extreme expression under apartheid. Apartheid brought about massive population removals, racial separation, political exclusion, labour exploitation and concomitant repression of the vast majority of the country's people. Under apartheid, a legal definition of Zulu was constructed. The South African Nationalist Party government instituted a legal structure that divided people along racial lines, and allocated these state-defined groups resources depending on the race they belonged to. Official segregation under apartheid also included geopolitical areas allocated along racial and linguistic lines. KwaZulu was one such geopolitical structure within the apartheid state, created as a home for those people defined by the Nationalist Party government linguistically and racially/ethnically as Zulu, thus forming Zulu nation. The legal definition of Zulu at this time referred to those black people who inhabited the region of KwaZulu/Natal and whose first language was Zulu.

Inkatha Definition

The creation of KwaZulu, however, added another dimension to this state-defined Zulu identity. It meant that being a black Zulu speaker and resident of KwaZulu/Natal was not enough for people to qualify as Zulus in the region. People also had to show allegiance to the KwaZulu homeland and to Inkatha for them to be identified as Zulus. Showing allegiance to KwaZulu and Inkatha involved, inter alia, participating in Inkatha political activities, as well as in Inkatha organized cultural events such as the celebration of Zulu ethnic symbols, including Shaka Day. This added criterion of identification was an important one because it became a prerequisite for individuals who wanted to access those economic resources controlled by KwaZulu homeland authority. The focus of Inkatha-defined Zulu identity was on participation in its activities.

ANC Definition

Operating alongside this Inkatha Zulu identity was the ANC version of a non-racial/ethnic democratic South Africa. Within this version, Inkatha's politicized ethnic nationalism was viewed as dangerous, a threat to the imagined non-racial South Africa. To the ANC, therefore, Zulu ethnicity became talked about as an imagined concept, a creation of Inkatha politics. Yet the belief that Zulu ethnicity was imagined did not mean that it was not socially real. Moreover, during this time, ethnicity involved visible local communities based on signals of dialect, kinship, status, religion and magical practices, and the more powerful forces of intimacy produced by fear of poverty and rural isolation. Also, economically, three and a half decades of state-based separate development had created ethnic-based networks of patronage and resource distribution, of coercion and control that were not to disappear with the arrival of democracy. A more pressing issue for the ANC, then, was how to deal with ethnic rights in the face of an imagined non-ethnic community.

Conventionalized Notions of Zulu

Conventionalized notions of being Zulu refer to the way individuals were labelled as Zulu because of the ways they engaged in Zulu cultural practices. To illustrate this definition, three practices in Zulu culture are examined: *hlonipha,* to respect, *imisebenzi,* traditional ceremonies, and *isibindi,* to be brave. These practices are important since they were the most recalled in formal and interpersonal politics as important criteria of identification. Furthermore, the association of these practices with formal organizations, especially Inkatha, necessitated that those who engaged in them deal with the consequences of such associations.

The Culture of Ukuhlonipha

In its broad sense, the Zulu term ukuhlonipha refers to any practice of respect. It can be divided into linguistic and performative practices. A common linguistic example of ukuhlonipha is *isihlonipho sabafazi* (women's language of respect), in which married women are taught how not to use the names of their male in-laws in their speech. To demonstrate this point, I will borrow an example from Finlayson (1995, p. 140) that demonstrates the constraints to which an English-speaking woman would be subjected in an attempt to conform to this linguistic custom.[3]

> Robert and Grace Green have three children – William, Joan and Margaret. William marries Mary and takes her home to his family. Here she is taught a new vocabulary by Joan, her sister-in-law, and where necessary is advised by Grace, her mother-in-law. This is because from now on she may never use the syllables occurring in her husband's family names, i.e. (simplistically) 'rob,' 'ert,' 'green,' 'will' and 'grace.' Thus, for the sentence 'Grace will not eat green yoghourt,' Mary would have to say something like, 'The older daughter of Smith refuses to eat grass-coloured yomix.'

One well-known example of this kind of ukuhlonipha as it applies to men involves Shaka who, after travelling a long distance without water, came to a well-watered place and wanted to name it *amanzi mnandi* (pleasant water). However, Shaka's mother was Nandi, and out of respect for her, he had to rename the place in order to avoid the *nandi* part of the qualificative. Hence he called the place *Amanzimtoti* after inventing the word *toti* to replace *nandi*. Similarly, Chief Buthelezi's grandfather, who was also king Cetswayo's deputy, was called Mnyamane Buthelezi. In Zulu, the colour black is *mnyama*. Out of respect for his grandfather, Buthelezi invented the name *mpintsolo* to substitute *mnyama,* and in his speeches, for phrases that would normally be expressed as *thina bantu abaMnyama* (we black people) he says, *thina bantu abampintsholo.*[4] It is important to state, however, that in general this syllabic avoidance by men is uncommon, and only in exceptional cases do men hlonipha.

What is referred to here as performative hlonipha relates more to behavioural practices and the manner in which these actions intersect with linguistic performances. This kind of ukuhlonipha is best described as avoidance, or to shun confrontation. It often applies to situations where verbal practices may shift from being respectful to confrontational and argumentative; and to practices where a young person has to let an older person know that she is wrong. Usually, in Zulu households, children are brought up with a strong emphasis on *ukuhlonipha abadala* (respect for adults) and on non-confrontational ways of disagreeing with adults. It is important to note that in Zulu there is no distinction between the concepts of elderliness, such as an elder sister (one year older than me), and that of adulthood, meaning a mature individual. Both are referred to as *badala* (adults). Thus, in Zulu, a six-year-old is an adult to a five-year-old; therefore, an element of respect is always expected from the five-year-old, even in cases where the six-year-old is wrong. If a conversation develops into an argument, it is expected that where two people of different ages are involved, the younger person will back off and the older person's statement will be the last. Being the last to speak does not necessarily mean that the older person is right, but is simply interpreted as hlonipha. In fact, what normally happens is that the younger person would remove herself from the scene, as a way of demonstrating her disagreement (performative hlonipha). Situations where the younger person argues with the adult are interpreted as disrespect (ukungahloniphi), no matter how correct the younger person may be.

A good example comes from an incident that occurred in my childhood when I was about ten years old. In the evenings, my older sister Sikhumbuzo and I took turns doing dishes after dinner and tidying the kitchen. One evening my sister told me to do the dishes. I refused and told her it was not my turn since I had washed them the previous day. She insisted that it was my turn, and because I did not want to give in, an argument started. My mother came in in the middle of this argument and demanded to know what was happening. I explained, and she also remembered that I had done the dishes the previous night, but instead of simply telling my sister to do the dishes, she told me *'awukhulumi kanjalo nodadewenu, geza izitsha lezi'* (you don't talk to your adult sister like that, do the dishes). I was upset, but did the dishes anyway. On the following two days, however, my sister did the dishes. I asked about this change of heart and she explained that my mother had spoken to her (during my absence, of course) about the incident and had told her that since she had cheated me, she had to pay me back by doing the dishes that whole week. The point worth noting here is not whether or not my sister was wrong, but that I had challenged and argued with her, an unacceptable practice in Zulu culture. Sikhumbuzo, wrong as she was, was an adult worthy of respect even though she was only a year older than myself. What I could have done was not argue with her and simply not do the dishes; she would have been the one to get into trouble for not doing the dishes anyway.

The Culture of Imisebenzi

Umsebenzi ('u'- singular and 'i'- plural) is a Zulu word that refers to any kind of work, and also to different kinds of traditional ceremonies, including religious ceremonies in which the families communicate and commune with their ancestors. One example is *isidikla,* a ceremony in which a boyfriend sends his relatives to officially acknowledge a pregnancy, and also to apologize to the girl's family since pregnancy was not supposed to occur before marriage. Although the details of the practice have been modified and redefined over time, the actual basis behind this practice is maintained. That is, the ceremony acts to officially bring together the two families and their ancestral spirits who watch over the infant when it is born. During such ceremonies, traditional Zulu beer is brewed, an animal is slaughtered, and Zulu meals are cooked as offerings to the ancestors. Only close relatives of the two families participate in such ceremonies, although nowadays it is common to include also friends of the two young people involved.

Other kinds of imisebenzi include marriage ceremonies in which the ancestors are officially notified of the departure of the bride and asked to watch over her, or a ceremony in which someone prepares a traditional gathering, usually a dinner, as a way of correcting an offence, and so on. Imisebenzi are basically viewed as a space for communicating with the ancestors as well as with the people one lives with.

The Culture of Isibindi

In its general meaning, isibindi refers to any practice of bravery or heroism. This practice is usually associated with the Zulu wars of conquest as well with struggles against British colonialism. The most common story of conquest is that of consolidation under Shaka, and the most common story of active resistance to colonialism is that of the war of 1879. The story of the Zulu war of 1879 has always been a fruitful ground for historians and a fascinating subject for those who are interested in the history of South Africa. Guy (1979) argues that this war 'led to a popular

speech and writing about the name "Zulu" to represent an idea of traditional African savagery, bravery, and barbarous nobility,' and to the
myth of the Zulu as the noblest of savages in European and American
imagination – an image which interestingly occurred only after the Zulu
independent power had been eroded. Yet this image has been highly
internalized amongst black South Africans; also governs people's practices and influences perceptions that people have of themselves and of
others.

Most Zulu children were brought up with this history and it is used to
encourage certain kinds of behaviour in them and to condemn others.
People used phrases like *'umZulu kahlulwa lutho'* (nothing can overcome
a Zulu) to legitimize their practices, and historic names such as Shaka
and Cetshwayo were continuously invoked by individuals in practices.

At the time of the study, this image of the Zulu as heroic people was
also associated with the practices of political organizations such as
Inkatha. To Inkatha, to be heroic meant that Zulu people demonstrated
their braveness through fighting and killing people considered enemies
of the organization. Such fighting contributed to the development of
the stereotypical savage Zulus who were mindless killers because of the
brutality involved in the death of the so-called enemies. This does not
mean that ANC based killings of, for example, necklacing were any less
savage, but for the Zulu, there was a history that was used to inform this
stereotype.

Zulu Culture and Formal Politics

Like the Zulu history and its symbols, Zulu cultural practices became
valuable resources for politicians to use in pursuing their goals. Politically, Inkatha was at the forefront in the practices that legitimized and
conventionalized the redefinition of ukuhlonipha. The structure of
Inkatha was such that people in positions of power were mainly chiefs
and their electives. These were the people viewed by Inkatha as deserving of hlonipha, and whose views could not be openly challenged by any
subordinates, be they subordinate in terms of age or status. The Inkatha
leadership, of especially in their policy of negotiating with the apartheid
government, was also above challenges, and those who questioned it
were reminded of this Zulu practice.

In addition to its stance on respect for authority in general, Inkatha,
as in ukuhlonipha, privileged the views of elderly people over those of
the youth, so that few in its top leadership came from the youth brigade.

In a nutshell, to Inkatha, the practice of hlonipha applied to youths first, who were subordinates mainly because of age, and then to those who did not have any status within its structures. Those people were to follow and not question what Inkatha planned, such as celebrating Shaka Day at designated Inkatha spaces.

Inkatha's emphasis on ukuhlonipha was in contrast to the teachings and the practices of the UDF/ANC. It is important to remember that UDF strategies of the 1980s focused on acts of defiance against the apartheid state and its structures, including KwaZulu. It is also important to remember that because of these strategies of defiance and ungovernability, the UDF was able to nurture youth's military interests. For example, the UDF promoted situations whereby youths were actively involved in destroying government property, stopping people who insisted on going to work during UDF/COSATU workers' strikes, and many others. In instances where youths stopped workers from going to work, many of the people stopped were adults, who, because of their age, deserved inhlonipho. Those youths who forced adults out of their cars and back to their homes, were often told by these adults *'anisahloniphi'* (you no longer respect [adults][5].]

Other Zulu practices associated with Inkatha were linked to rural areas. For example, Zulu imisebenzi are usually performed in the rural areas, and the ones performed in the townships are considered tokens of the actual ceremony. The process of ukuhlabela amadlozi, having a communion for and with the ancestors, is the most illustrative. In this practice all members of the family and their relatives are invited to the family's place of origin, which is also taken as the ancestoral home. Such a view persists because, even though the majority of the people work in urban centres, relations are maintained with the family still living in the rural areas, usually grandparents. The ceremony includes oracles, in which designated members of the family communicate with the ancestors, visits to the burial place, and music and dancing. Some people viewed such practices as associated with the devil, ignorance, and backwardness. Yet many Christians in KwaZulu/Natal incorporated such Zulu cultural practices into the Christian religion.

Inkatha itself engaged in imisebenzi as a way of legitimizing its practices. An event in 1986 when I worked for the department of the chief minister at Ulundi illustrates this. An Inkatha general meeting was organized by the Ulundi branch one afternoon, which all civil servants who worked for the KwaZulu headquarters in the parliament buildings were expected to attend. Apparently this branch lacked support from these civil servants, many of whom were registered but not practising Inkatha members. On this day, the organizers of the meeting decided to use amabutho from Emandleni camp to forcefully escort civil servants from the parliament building to the meeting, a distance of over seven kilometres. At the end of the workday we walked to the place where we normally took the buses to our homes only to find that there were no buses. These buses also belonged to the KwaZulu government and had been ordered by transport personnel to not show up. Even those people who lived in the nearby township and did not need to take buses were forced to walk to the meeting. In the end, we attended the meeting and, needless to say, there was a large turn-out.

Many civil servants were angered by this incident, and questioned Inkatha's practice of restricting freedom of choice. Chief Buthelezi was informed of this incident, and was advised by Inkatha's National Council to offer an apology to the civil servants on behalf of the organization. The apology took a form of *umsebenzi wokuxolisa*; that is, the Inkatha Ulundi branch organized a ceremonial dinner of apology. We stopped work at midday so we could participate in this umsebenzi, which was given at our workplace. As it is customary, this umsebenzi was marked with Zulu dishes and Zulu beer. Cows had been slaughtered, and Chief Buthelezi made a speech in which he officially apologized for the Inkatha organizers who had forced us to walk to the meeting and, at the same time, openly warned those considered opponents of punishment. In his speech Buthelezi also went on to explain the meaning of this umsebenzi and illustrated its meaning by using other historic incidents in which Zulu chiefs had done similar imisebenzi as a way of apologizing to whoever had been wrongly offended. The overriding message, however, was that once this umsebenzi was done, there were no other grievances anticipated and all civil servants were expected to accept the apology, irrespective of how they felt, for if they had refused to accept the apology, they would have been viewed as not only challenging Inkatha's practices, but Zulu culture itself.

During a traditional umsebenzi, both parties explain their points of view. The individual who has been offended usually asks for something material, known as *inhlawulo*, compensation, and because of the valuing of cattle in Zulu society it is common for the offended person to demand and be offered these as compensation. Therefore the dinner is not an apology on its own but provides space for negotiating about the conflict. It is also an indication that the offender admits to having done wrong and would like the issue resolved. However, in Chief Buthelezi's dinner, the practice was modified and redefined to suit the interest of Inkatha. At this dinner the voice of the offended civil servants was not heard; this space was not available for negotiating a solution, but for indirectly imposing authority. It appeared that the message was 'accept this apology or else...' and civil servants knew exactly what would have happened. It could also be interpreted that this modification was indicative of Inkatha's authoritaty over Zulu culture and of the power it held over us as civil servants.

Urban Cultures and Formal Politics

Alongside these Zulu customs there existed practices associated with urbanization and industrialization. What became important were the ways in which everyday urban practices were evaluated against Zulu cultural practices and were simultaneously given associations with political organizations. For example, ukungahloniphi, to disrespect, was basically viewed as an urban practice, not necessarily because this didn't happen in rural areas, but mainly because disrespectful practices were nourished during the UDF era, whose main base were the urbanized townships. The UDF youths questioned and verbally confronted not just authority figures such as teachers and politicians, but also ordinary adults in the streets. What practices were thought to be disrespectful? To Inkatha, it was the activities of the youths who engaged in the UDF strategies of defiance against the apartheid state and its structures, and who actively destroyed government property and forced adults out of their cars in attempts to prevent them from going to work during strikes. Other general practices of disrespect included the use of language, and the manner in which these uses were connected to the practices of political organizations.

Basically, there were two dominant languages in the townships, Zulu and Tsotsitaal. (Here, the use of English and Afrikaans is excluded mainly because these languages were associated with formal institutions such as schools.) Zulu was the language of the township, and although there were people whose first language was not Zulu, it was commonly expected that they learn and use it. There were, however, pockets of non-Zulu speakers in many squatter areas, whose origin is beyond the scope of this study. As a result of the homogeneous nature of the Kwa-Zulu region it was easy to identify those people whose first language was not Zulu and they were the first to be targeted by Inkatha as UDF.

Besides these non-Zulu speakers, first-language speakers of Zulu themselves often differentiated between the types of Zulu that people used. There was what was referred to as *isiZulu saseNkandla,* or the Zulu of Nkandla. This was associated with the more isolated rural areas like Nkandla, and sounded 'deeper' than the Zulu spoken in the townships. IsiZulu saseNkandla is distinguishable mainly in pitch, and sometimes in vocabulary. It is difficult to say whether or not individuals consciously used this rural pitch and vocabulary as a way of distinguishing themselves as real Zulu since often the use of this rural vocabulary was not to demonstrate the profundity of one's Zuluness, but was simply dependent on the speed with which individuals adopted the new lexicon that was being added to the Zulu language. For example, some of the key informants in the study pointed out to me on a number of occasions which I used rural vocabulary; I still said *yebo* instead of *ya* to indicate agreement, and *sawubona* instead of *kunjani* as a greeting.

My explanation of why I used these terms was that I had been left behind in these linguistic developments during my years in Canada, and therefore used these rural Zulu terms because of this gap. My mother disagreed and argued that words like *ya* and *kunjani* were not new in the townships. She pointed out that although I worked in the townships for years before leaving for Canada, I did not lose the deep Zulu accent that I grew up with in the semi-rural areas of Melmoth. She asserted that the relationship I had with this semi-urban area influenced the way I used language, and was an indication that those who did not grow up in the rural or semi-rural areas, and those who were disrespectful of such communities, were the most likely to adapt new varieties of language. While it is not really clear whether the use of one variety of Zulu over the other was a conscious effort, or because this was the variety that people were familiar with, the deeper the Zulu, the most likely it was that the speaker had association with the rural areas, and often, some association with Inkatha.

Tsotsitaal was associated with the urban areas mainly because it is an urban invention, used mostly by those who align themselves with the urban centres. The associations of Tsotsitaal are nevertheless wider than this division since they are tied up with age, gender, network, and ingroup language practices. In other words, young men who see themselves as belonging to the same social group mainly use Tsotsitaal. Tsotsitaal is not usually used in a conversation with adults because it is considered rude. It would indicate that the speakers viewed themselves as more urban and therefore better than the (rural) non-Tsotsitaal speaker. During this era, however, the use of Tsotsitaal also came to be associated with non-Zulu speakers and was interpreted to mean that the speakers did not know Zulu, were not Zulus, and therefore were most likely to be ANC.

Tsotsitaal also has its own varieties, and its grammatical construction varies between groups. For first-language speakers of Zulu, the Zulu grammatical structure and vocabulary is used, and for first-language speakers of Tswana, the Tswana vocabulary and its grammatical structure dominates their Tsotsitaal and so on. The Tsotsitaal in the townships of KwaMashu and Umlazi used mainly Zulu as its base, but since there were a number of Zulu varieties, this allowed for the existence of a variety of Tsotsitaals within the same township. Some of the groups who chose rural Zulu as the base for their Tsotsitaal were mainly influenced by the teachings of the Black Consciousness Movement (BCM) of the 1970s, which primarily argued that black people should restore their past and use it to understand and fight to the present. Therefore, to some of these groups the use of an 'uncontaminated' Zulu in their Tsotsitaal was symbolic of efforts towards this direction. Overall, those groups whose Tsotsitaal used rural Zulu were viewed by other social groups as socially conservative (with conservative meaning old-fashioned), but not backward or rural, because as stated, Tsotsitaal marked people off as urban, or modern.

Criteria of Identification, Cultural Practices, and Political Parties

How were these criteria of identification, urban and Zulu cultural practices, including language use, implemented in everyday lives. Who were the people affected most by such identity politics, and how did they negotiate the tension that resulted from the amalgamation and contestation of practices? Put differently, how were the boundaries and interconnections between urban and Zulu cultural practices managed, transcended, or negotiated?

All parties involved in this power struggle were in many ways affected by these criteria of identification. However, since Inkatha and its membership defined Zulu cultural practices, it is safe to say that Inkatha members were less affected by the Zulu culture criterion of identification than people in other political parties. Non-Zulu Inkatha were also affected by identity politics, but from what was known of Inkatha, it was clear that as long as these people engaged in Inkatha (and Zulu culture) practices, their ethnic identities did not become the focus. Furthermore, although Inkatha had changed its constitution to include non-Zulus, its membership was overwhelmingly Zulu.

People mostly affected by identity politics were Zulu-ANC members, who wanted to identify as Zulu in a politics where ANC members were identified as non-Zulu. The second group that was affected constituted of Zulu-ANC-modern individuals who were further isolated from the legitimized Inkatha meaning of Zulu by their linguistic practices. And a third group was that of Zulus and non-Zulus who did not align with any political organization. The following chapters examine each of these three groups and through the use of ethnographic material, outline how each group dealt with the conflicts in identity politics.

These chapters therefore, analyse some of the cultures that existed in the townships at the time of the study, and put forward factors that influenced personal choices made in the face of complex political practices. Within each group are discussions that illuminate the manner in which individuals in groups used different symbolic resources, especially Zulu history and language, to navigate township life, and to develop positive identities for themselves as members of society. Finally, although it was unclear how many of the youths belonged to such formally defined groups, according to students at the Centre for Cultural and Media Studies,[6] who conducted projects in these townships, it is estimated that these groups constituted over three-quarters of the youths in the townships; the other quarter was divided between Inkatha youths and those whom it was not clear what exactly they were doing.

chapter 6

Social/Cultural Groups: Tsatsatsa

The emergence of social/cultural groups such as *tsatsatsa*[1] at Umlazi has to be understood against the backdrop, first, of Inkatha control of this township which simultaneously embraced and isolated Zulus from each other; and second, the modification of UDF strategies of resistance against the apartheid state. Historically, tsatsatsa emerged at a crucial period for both the UDF and Inkatha. For Inkatha, this was the period from 1987 to 1989 during which it was forced to give up some geopolitical areas mainly because of the level of resistance it encountered from residents. This resistance was more felt in the townships that surround Durban and Pietermaritzburg because these areas were the last to be handed over from the provincial government to KwaZulu Government control. As a result, people were concerned about losing the economic rights they had had under the provincial government, and were further critical of their forced membership in Inkatha in order to have access to resources now controlled by the KwaZulu government. Nonetheless, Inkatha was able to take over control of most of these townships, including Umlazi, and to exert its political control by using guards to monitor and direct both the political activities and the social practices. Therefore, it became important that individuals who wanted to continue living at Umlazi, who nevertheless did not want to participate in Inkatha politics, find alternative and safe ways of doing a different kind of party politics. It also became important for those individuals who embraced Zulu cultural practices, including the use of language, to negotiate around the political associations that these Zulu cultural practices entailed.

The political formation of tsatsatsa discussed in this chapter was that of the UDF/ANC, yet these individuals lived at Umlazi. Given the level

of control that Inkatha had over this township, and the amount of violence that accompanied this control, how did these youths succeed in
doing ANC politics and continue to live in Umlazi? Did they engage in
Zulu cultural practices, and if they did, how did they negotiate the fact
that these practices were given legitimacy in Inkatha practices, and that
those who embraced them got labelled as Inkatha followers and not
ANC? This chapter addresses the complexity of criteria used to identify
individuals in the township, and the problems that faced people who
wanted to identify as ANC, Zulu, and 'cool,' in a period when none of
these categories were to inform or be informed by the practices of the
others.

The development of tsatsatsa also has to be understood in the context
of UDF and later ANC politics in this region. For the UDF, this was a
period in which the organization was under strict government restrictions, which made it difficult for the UDF to organize its activities. More
importantly, the UDF was in the process of revising its strategy of 'liberation now, education later.' Since by this time a lot of youths were unemployed, and were scarcely equipped to compete in South Africa's
economy. The previously discussed 'back to school' strategy pioneered
by the National Education Crises Committee (NECC) in 1987 encouraged students to both stop boycotting schools and to work instead
towards the creation of better education, through participating in
school structures and forming committees that were to work towards
this end. There were, however, problems that the NECC could not deal
with, such as overcrowding, high teacher-student ratios, and shortage of
books and stationery.

Thus, during this NECC era, the challenge was to devise a means of
keeping these schools open and not disrupted by political parties who
used them as platforms for mobilizing support. Accordingly, teachers or
admitting authorities screened their applicants. For example, those students who were known to have been at the forefront of the boycotts that
had led to the initial closure of schools in 1985 were not readmitted
because it was feared that they might mobilize again for similar practices. Moreover, it was difficult for students to transfer from one school
to the other because the new school demanded from the applicant a
transfer card from the last school attended, indicating things such as last
grade attended, results, and conduct. Transfer cards did not necessarily
guarantee admission, because some schools even went further and
would not admit students from schools whose students had been leading boycotts. In short, for one to be admitted to a school, it was impor-

tant to display good conduct by appearing not to be involved in any form of politics.

The Emergence of Tsatsatsa

The name tsatsatsa was invented by the youths because to them, this name sounded cool, and different from any other group names such as amasinyora, amampansula, which were also invented names that, however, used the Zulu inflectional affixes. For example, the Zulu affix 'nyo' (as in amasinyora) is mainly used to construct names that have associations with snake-like behaviour. Therefore, the name sinyora illuminates the nature of the practices of this group. The name tsatsatsa on the other hand, does not indicate any semantic relation or any grammatical information about the group itself. In this study, tsatsatsa is used to indicate a single group culture, and matsatsatsa refers to the individuals who made up the group. 'Matsatsatsa' is actually the term that group members used to refer to themselves. I suspect that the use of 'ma' to prefix *tsatsatsa* was borrowed from the Zulu way of referring to groups of people. For example, in Zulu, you do not talk about the Zulus, Swazis, or Vendas to indicate plurality of the people who make up these groups, but rather talk of amaZulu, amaSwazi, amaVenda respectively. Nonetheless, it is now common to find in the written form an 's,' as in English, used to indicate plurality. Also, the use of 'ma' to indicate the 'groupness' of people suggests an absence of a singular state of being. This is because 'ma' as a plural prefix is only used with uncountable nouns such as *amanzi*, water, *amasi*, yoghourt, *amafinyila*, mucus etc. ('a' = the). Thus, it is possible that they used 'ma'-*tsatsatsa* simply following the Zulu way of referring to a group of people.

Tsatsatsa were comprised of groups of boys and girls whose lives had been affected by the UDF/Inkatha conflict, which erupted into violence by 1985. Many of these individuals had lost their families and friends during this era, and were now living with relatives. The members of the tsatsatsa group, who participated in this study, had at one stage been involved with the UDF and some had been at the forefront in organizing UDF activities. At the time of the study, however, these tsatsatsa participants were now members or supporters of the ANC, and this was mainly because the ANC had taken over some of the UDF structures after its unbanning in 1990. It does appear, however, that by the time the UDF disbanded, some tsatsatsa participants had left the UDF mainly because they did not agree with some of its vigilante practices. The

unbanning of the ANC rescued those individuals who were already critical of some of the UDF practices but had no other political parties with
whom to associate themselves. (It is not clear, however, whether the formation of tsatsatsa served the political vacuum that individuals experienced after leaving the UDF but before joining the ANC since the latter
was still in exile.) During the UDF era most tsatsatsa participants had
changed schools during their secondary education, and some had even
dropped out of school for a number of years but later decided to go
back. All tsatsatsa participants had a strong commitment to obtaining a
high school diploma and going on to post-secondary education. Therefore, coming from broken families, participation in party politics, and a
strong commitment to education are three main features that characterized matsatsatsa. The following life histories highlight some of these
tsatsats characteristics:

Lunga Mlaba lived in unit V in Umlazi. He was born in Lamontville into
a family of three. He lost his mother at the age of six when she was
stabbed to death by gangsters who had come to rob their house. Lunga
and his two siblings witnessed the killing but were spared because it was
believed they couldn't identify the culprits. Since then, Lunga had lived
in Lamontville in the homes of four other relatives. For a short while
after his mother's death, Lunga's father looked after him and his siblings, but then he himself became sick and had to move to the KwaZulu
village of Bergville where he could live under the care of his own parents, Lunga's grandparents. Since then, Lunga had been under the care
of different relatives. A move from the care of one relative to another
came with a change of schools, though still in the townships. As a result
of the hardships that Lunga experienced, he began searching for reasons for his sufferings, and particularly reasons for the death of his
mother because he believed that if she was still alive he would have been
better off. At the age of sixteen, he first participated in UDF political
activities, which were organized through one of the schools he had
attended, and he has been active since then. Most of the schools he
attended were so politically active that they closed at least four times a
year as a result of political unrest. When, in 1989, his uncle told him he
could no longer afford to support him, he decided to go and live with
his maternal grandparents in Umlazi. It was then that he made an effort
to look for the most stable school in the township and finally decided on
Umganga High School, for this is the only high school that over the past
five years had not closed down because of political unrest.[2]

At the time of the study, Lunga had established relations with other tsatsatsa in the school and had taken part in organized ANC regional events such as demonstrations and meetings. Towards the end of data collection, Lunga and his friends were going to use the mid-year school holidays (June-July) to participate in ANC projects that taught black communities about voting. He was also concerned with passing his high school exams because he wanted to study electrical engineering in one of Durban's universities. Lunga also worked as a part-time packer at Pick'n Pay, one of the largest supermarkets in the region.

Lunga initially thought that the students at Umganga were very secretive about their political activities and loyalties and he had followed suit. Describing his first observation of the students' behaviour, Lunga stated:

'Nge risesi, ngangibona amaqenjana abantu bemile bexoxa, behleka, benza yonke lento. Uma ngithi ngiyasondela, bavele bathule kungathi bashaywe umbani. Uma ngisafika, nami ngafunda nje ukuzithulela ngingasho lutho uma ngifica abantu bexoxa. Ngelinye ilanga ngasondela kuleliqembu engase ngijwayele ukuzincikisa kulo. Kwakuyiqembu labafana elalijwayele ukuxoxa ngezinto eziningi ezingasho lutho njengezinto zesikole liphinde lidle namagwinya. Ngithe ngingazelele, omunye umfana wangibuza wathi 'mthaka, zishangani emzabalazweni?' Ngazabalaza ukumphendula, ngambuza ukuthi kuyena zishangani. Wangibheka ngokumangala – empeleni bonke babukeka bemangele. ... 'Usho ukuthi umi lapha nje awazi ukuthi siyini? Wuwewedwa-ke ongazi.' Ngokuphuma kwesikole, ngabuza omunye umfana ukuthi kanti ngempela zisha ngani emzabalazweni. Ngaqala kanjaloke ukwazi ukuthi kwenzekani kulesikole.

During break times I used to see groups of students standing, talking and laughing and doing all that. Usually, when I approached a group there would be silence as though its members had been struck by lightning. As a result I used to just stand around like everybody else and not say anything. So when I first came [to this school] I learnt not to talk much. Some days I joined a group of boys who were easy going and who spoke about all sorts of things especially about school events. I used to just hang around and share with them whatever goodies there were – usually bakes [something like doughnuts, but not exactly]. One day we were just standing when out of nowhere, someone asked me 'so what's with you in politics?'[3] I was reluctant to answer, so instead, I asked what was with him in the struggle. He was surprised; actually everybody in the group looked surprised. [He said] 'You mean you are standing here with us without knowing what we are? You are the only one who doesn't know.' At the end of the school day, I approached one of the boys from this group and asked him exactly what was [burning] in the struggle. This was the beginning of my understanding about politics in this school.)

Basically, Lunga and many other study informants argued that this school differed from others because of its ability to admit students with different political orientations. They stated that the school was neutral: that is, it was neither Inkatha nor ANC and its student and teacher populations were from more than these two political organizations. Furthermore, most informants stated that the school was able to embrace students of different political formations because they did not act as monitors or guards for any of the dominant political organizations. Also, it appeared that both students and teachers were familiar with the political orientation of many people in the school, but this was no big deal, as it was in other schools. A significant example of this knowledge is explained below.

One of the Standard Ten teachers, Zethu, who knew of my research at Greensburg High School, had asked me to pick up an application form for her son. On my way from Greensburg, I stopped by Umganga to drop off these forms. As we were talking, the bell rang and Zethu had to go to class. So as we were walking towards the door, Zethu saw a boy going towards the water tap, probably for a drink of water and she called out *'Awungisize lapha nduku emnyama'* (Help me out here black stick) so the boy turned around and came towards us. Zethu continued, *'awungiyele lapha kwa 10 ubatshele bakhiphe incwadi zeliterature, ngiyeza khona manje'* (could you go to the Standard 10 class and ask them to get ready their literature books – I will be over in a little while) and the boy left. I asked Zethu why she had used the phrase *Nduku emnyama* to refer to the boy. Previously, I had heard another teacher talking about a different student, and referring to him by this name. Zethu responded by saying *'Phela laba bayi PAC. Awoke ubanake nje ngisho begqhokile. Banalento yokufaka am t-shirt amnyama. Uma kuculwa kwenziwa imidlalo, abafuni lutho nje engesona isintu'* (It is because these are PAC. Try to notice what they wear. They have this habit of wearing black t-shirts underneath the white [school uniform] shirt [the black shirts usually showed whenever the white shirts were not fully buttoned]. Even in extra curricular activities, they do not want to be involved in anything that is not black [consciousness] oriented).

Zandile Nene lived in Unit A in Umlazi with three brothers and one sister. Her mother, who had brought up all five of them at Umlazi, died in

1991. Zandile had attended a number of different schools before finally settling at Umganga High. She dropped out of school at the age of fifteen and took a leading role in organizing the kind of UDF activities that were aimed at making South Africa ungovernable. It was during this time that Zandile got pregnant 'because we were immature, with little guidance from adults and too much time on our hands.' Because of her pregnancy, Zandile decided to redefine her goals and change her life. One of the decisions she took was to get an education that was to help her bring up her child in a more respectable way. Though late in applying for admission, she decided to approach the principal who, after she made many trips to the school, decided to enrol her. Before her mother's death, her mother cared for her baby until she came back from school and then she would take over. With the death of her mother, Zandile had to get help from neighbours and friends to care for her child and she seems to have been doing well. Zandile's main concern was to pass her matriculation examination and go to college. Very little of her past and social life was known to the school. This was a conscious effort on her part because if teachers and students knew about her life they would treat her differently. She gave Vukani (who is discussed below) as an example to illustrate this differential treatment based on one's past life. Apparently, because most students and teachers in the school knew that Vukani had been a member of Umkhonto (referred to as the MK) they treated him with suspicion and fear. On my first day of observing Zandile in her home, one of the teachers volunteered to drive me there because he was familiar with that section of Umlazi. Upon seeing Zandile holding her child, then eighteen months, his first words were *Bengingazi uyazi ukuthi unengane* (I didn't know you had a child). Because of her responsibility as a mother, Zandile had very little time to participate in outside activities, but she did not regret this. In her words, she had done her part in politics and it was time for her to move on. Moving on, however, did not mean a total disassociation from political activities, but compared with the rest of the tsatsatsa members, her involvement was minimal.

What made Lunga and Zandile, therefore, typical tsatsatsa is first, their past political involvement in the UDF and the manner in which this direct involvement affected their lives. Second, they both had a very strong sense of commitment to redirecting their lives for the better, and a recognition that this could mainly be achieved by getting support from people who were involved in the same practices, including ways of spending free time. Third, and more important, matsatsatsa continued to be involved in politics, despite the fact that some had suffered because of their political activism. Tsatsatsa informants believed that there was nothing wrong with politics, but, as Zandile put it, *'Okwenza ipolitiki ibembi yikuthi abantu baphenduka izilwane, bafune ukuphatha ngisho kungekho oluphathwayo. Yini – nje ongayiphatha lapha eMlazi, ngaphandle kwabantu abazibulawelwa yindlala?'* (What makes politics bad is that people turn and behave like animals because they want to rule even if there is nothing to rule. What is it that one can rule [over] here at Umlazi except ruling over hunger-striken people?) Fourth, economically, matsatsatsa did not depend on their families for support, but supported themselves with part-time jobs. Lunga had a part-time job, while Zandile made and brought baked goods to the school to sell to students and teachers. And finally, most matsatsatsa came from what was considered in the townships to be broken families. That is, for a variety of reasons, they did not live with their biological parents but lived with friends or relatives, whereas most of the other youths lived with at least one biological parent. Zandile, however, was an exception to this rule as she lived with her mother at the time of becoming tsatsatsa.

On the Margins of Tsatsatsa

Some people chose to operate at the margins of this group and sometimes on their own. In this book, these people are referred to as marginal, or as tsatsatsa-border participants. Usually, an individual who operated at the margins shared some but not all the values and beliefs of the group. He or she was usually accepted, but not as a full member of the group. This individual was not obliged to operate by the rules of the group, although in most cases, it was expected that she conform to these rules. In the townships, there were many reasons that made people want to be attached to a cultural group. For example, these groups acted as support structures for individuals by providing them with friendly relationships, which in some instances could lead to access to economic resources. Being attached to tsatsatsa gave one a chance of hearing about possible places for jobs, since most tsatsatsa had part-time jobs in the city. Since matsatsatsa had a reputation of being against criminal activities, store owners believed that any person they recommended would also be trustworthy. The following example demonstrates this point:

Ndabezitha, an informant operating on the margins of tsatsatsa, got a job in a bus depot as a bus washer because of his association with the group. Apparently, one of Lunga's bosses asked him to find a 'boy' who could work at his friend's bus depot. Lunga asked Zandile if she was interested, but she felt that she could not take this job because she needed more time to spend with her child. So on the next day Lunga sought advise from other tsatsatsa as to who might be a favourable candidate. Here is how some group members responded:

Sizwe: *Hayi! usumkhulu ndoda kulesitolo. Awusho, ukuqale kanjani-nje loMlungu?*
Wow! You are now really big in that store. How exactly did this white man begin [to ask you for this favour]?

Lunga: *Uthe ngingamtholela na umfansa onjengami ongasebenza edepo yomngani wakhe? Ngiphendule ngokudlala ngati usho ukuthini uma ethi umfana onjengami ngoba uyazi ukuthi angilona iwele? Uphendule wathi usho umfana ofana nami, okhuluma nohlonipha njengami nalabangani bami abahlale befika bezongibona. Sigcine sivumelene ukuthi lowo muntu ngofika naye ngomsombuluko.*
He asked if I could get him a boy who is like me who can work at his friend's depot. I jokingly responded by asking him what he meant by a person who is like me because he knows I am not a twin. He stated that he meant someone like me, who speak and is respectful like me and the friends who usually visit me [on workdays]. At the end we agreed that I will bring someone with me on Monday.

Sizwe: *Cha umkhulu ndoda. Ubani nje ongalunga?*
No man, you are big. Who do you think is suitable?

Lunga: *Ngicabange uZandile, kodwa uthe akukhomuntu ozosala nengane*
I thought of Zandile, but she said that she has to take care of her child.

Thulile: *Angayiletha kimi ngemigqibelo ayilande ntambama.*
She can bring her to me on Saturday mornings and pick her up in the afternoons.

Muzi: *Uhlala kude wena. Futhi-ke enzenjani mhla usebenza?*
You live far. Also, what will she do on those days when you have to work?

Thulile: *Uqinisile (Ngokunqikaza) – Mhlawumbe u Vukani uyafuna nje umsebenzi.*
That is true (hesitantly) – Maybe Vukani does want a job (Vukani was another tsatsatsa-border informant and is discussed below).

Sizwe, Lunga, Muzi: *Cha bo bo ukudlala ngomlilo*
No, no, no. Do not play with fire.

Nombuso: *Yini ningamfuni uVukani*
How come you don't think Vukani is fine?

Sizwe: *Siyazi phela ukuthi wena umthanda kabi. Ungasilokothi umtshele. Uya-bona, UVukani akananhliziyo futhi akezwani namaBhunu. Uma nje angahle axabane nalomlungu esemsebenzela, angamlahla phansi ngenhlamvu.*
We know that you like him a lot. So don't sell us out by telling him. You see, Vukani doesn't have a heart, and he doesn't like Boers. So if it happens that he gets into conflict with the owner of the depot, he will just shoot him dead.

In the end, it was decided that Ndabezitha, an individual who also operated at the margins of tsatsatsa, was the suitable candidate. After being informed by Lunga about this possibility, Ndabezitha enthusiastically took up the job offer.

Individuals also wanted to be associated with a particular cultural group in order to be judged by their cultural behaviour and not by their political affiliation, which in most cases was not even known. That is, there were certain practices that groups emphasized in the townships as a way of giving themselves a character. The above example indicates that respect for adult authority and specific ways of talking were some of the dominant features generally used to define individuals. Groups such as tsatsatsa, who were aware of these practices – partly because of their Zulu heritage and partly because of their knowledge of where to deploy these practices – capitalized on them to their advantage. The value given to these social practices tended to overshadow participation in political activities.

For example, in an interview with Lunga, I asked him if he thought his boss knew of his political involvement with the ANC.

Lunga: *Hawu sisi Nombuso, usho ukuthi awukazi ukuthi abantu abadala nabelungu bacabanga ukuthi ipolitiki eyabantu abangalaleli? Uma ngibheka nje lomlungu ungibona ngiyiNkatha.*
But sisi Nombuso, you mean you still don't know that elderly and white people think that politics is only practised by those youths who have no respect [for adults]? When I think of it, this white man sees me as an Inkatha member.

Nombuso: *Kukuphatha kanjani ukuthi loMlungu ukubona uyiNkatha?*
How does it make you feel that this white man views you as Inkatha?, I asked him.
Akungihluphi mina lokho. Kwesinye isikhathi kukhona izinto okufanele ungazishayimkhuba ukuze ufike lapho uqonde khona.

That doesn't really bother me. Sometimes there are things you have to ignore in order to get where you want to be at.

What Lunga was also saying was that respect for adult authority was not just traditional Zulu practice, but was critically intertwined with the political ideologies of Inkatha. Furthermore, Lunga's statements support the view that big capitalists such as business owners favoured Inkatha's pro-capitalists stance and its moderate approach to democratic changes rather than the approach of political groups such as the ANC and PAC.

Vukani Ndaba operated at the margins of tsatsatsa, but people in his school did not refer to him as tsatsatsa, but as a member of the Umkhonto (MK). Vukani was born in Lamontville and lived there until 1985. At that time, he decided to be actively involved in UDF activities because of the mystery surrounding his father's death: he had been stabbed nine times in a conflict believed to have been between UDF and Inkatha supporters. While Vukani did not know much at that time of the differences between these two organizations, he decided to join the UDF because of its alliance with the ANC. Vukani stated that the ANC concept of the armed struggle appealed to him because he was looking for ways to participate actively against apartheid. Inkatha did not offer anything similar but had instead embarked on peaceful negotiations with the state. Furthermore, a lot of the youths in his school (Mafumbuka High School) were in favour of the UDF. From this period onwards, Vukani lived a politically active life, often participating in UDF activities that resulted in the closure of many schools. In 1984, for example, Vukani did not write his standard six final exams because of the riots and class boycotts. As a result of the school closure, the following year he found himself repeating the same grade at a different school because he had been expelled from Mafumbuka. As the struggle between the UDF and Inkatha intensified, and as his activism grew, Vukani was forced to leave the country for safety reasons, and in exile he joined Umkhonto. He returned to Umlazi four years later when he believed the situation in the country had changed and when he was almost certain that nobody would remember him. Upon his return he went to live with his father's brother at unit G in Umlazi. Vukani chose to attend Umganga High School because he attended this school before going into exile, and had caused no political turmoil there. He believed that the school was more accepting of students' practices than any of the other schools he had gone to before.

At the time of the study Vukani's family turned a blind eye to all his activities. He interpreted this to mean that they did not care about him. He said that when he left for exile, for instance, they never looked for him, and when he returned they didn't ask him where he had been or why he had returned. However, in the light of Inkatha's activities in Umlazi to oust opposition, it is possible that Vukani's family were merely using this blindness as a defence against intimidation. If they were asked about Vukani, they could say that they did not know anything about him or his activities but that they were obligated by tradition to keep him since he was an orphan. Vukani also argued that the fact that his family did not talk to him about politics indicated that they were ignorant about the subject, especially since they did not participate in any political activities (which in Umlazi would have been Inkatha activities). Yet again, it is possible that this lack of involvement may have been more because they did not want to draw attention to themselves and be asked to account for Vukani's activities. It may also be that they did not support Inkatha politics; however, unlike Vukani, they had no other avenues to practise what they believed. Vukani's family situation illustrates some of the confusion and ambiguity that resulted in families because of the interconnection of formal politics with everyday practices.

At the time of the study Vukani was still actively involved with Umkhonto and the ANC. Nevertheless, most of his activism took place in Lamontville, and this made it possible for him to be viewed as a retired Umkhonto person in Umlazi. Like tsatsatsa, Vukani was mostly concerned with passing his matriculation since he, like most youths, believed that education was the tool towards social mobility. Vukani hardly spoke about his experiences in exile but towards the end of data collection, I got a chance to talk to him about some of his experiences. Following is an extract from the interview in which Vukani spoke about his experiences in exile and the impact of these experiences in his life.

Nombuso: *Wathola kunjani e-exile?*
How was exile for you?
Vukani: *Ngingathi nje kukhona izinto ezinhle nezimbi engazithola khona. Okubi nje kokuqala ukuthi ngangingajwayele impilo yokuhlukubezwa. Uyazi lapha uhlukubezwa izinto eziningi othi uma uzibheka uzibuze ukuthi ingempela thina bantu abamnyama senzani ukuze sihlushwe kangaka. Into yokuqala nje eyangihluphayo wukugula. Ngaphathwa izifo eziningi kakhulukazi imalaria. Uyazi nje nawe ukuthi ibhoke kanjani kulawamazwe ngob ayashisa.*

I partially admire my life in exile because it had its own advantages, although there were many disadvantages. One of the biggest disadvantages was that I was not used to rough life. Youths here complain about poverty and all that – these are things that when you look at exile life, you find them minimal. In exile we went through many frustrating things that forced me to ask what it is that we as black people did to deserve such suffering. One of the things I had to endure was sickness, especially malaria. You know how malaria is common in those very hot countries.

Nombuso: *Maphi amazwe -Ingempela, weta wawukuphi nendawo?*
Which countries – where exactly were you?

Vukani: *Ngaqala e-Angola, ngase ngidlulela e-Mazimbu*
I started in Angola, and then went on to Mazimbu (Tanzania)

Nombuso: *Yini enye yezinto ongayikhumbula owayifunda lapho?*
What is it that you can say you learnt from exile?

Vukani: *Uyazi kulukhuni ngempela ukusho. Ungangithathi kabi uma ungizwa ngisho kanje. Uyazi laphana ngafunda ukuzonda amaBhunu ngendlela engalungile. Sasithi uma sizibuza ukuthi sihlupheka kangaka-nje kungani-sigula, silamba, silwa, sihamba iziganga kungani, sibone nje ukuthi kungenxa yamaBhunu. Kunamhlanje ayikapheli leyonzondo. Ngike ngihlale ngizibuze ukuthi impilo yami iyakuphi ingempela. Awubheke nje isikole- sengimdala ukuthi ngingabe ngisafunda ustandadi 10. Uyazi ukuthi ngineminyaka emingaki? Ngineminyaka ewu 26. Kodwa ayikho into engingayenza. Uma ngifuna ukuqhubeka kufanele ngidlule khona. Into eyenza ngibe semuva kanje yi exile- namaBhunu. Into engingayithandi ngohambo lwami ku e-xilwe ukuthi ngisoleka njalo ebantwini. Uyazi nje nawe ukuthi abantu bangibheka kanjani. Ungathi ngiyisilwane esithile.*

You know it's difficult to say. Don't take what I am going to say negatively. There [in exile] I learnt to hate Boers dangerously. Whenever we asked ourselves reasons for our sufferings – hunger, sicknesses, war, travelling in wildernesses, and all that – we used to conclude that it was because of the Boers. Up until today, that hatred still dominates my thinking. Sometimes I sit and ask myself about where my life is going. Just look at schooling. I am too old to be doing standard 10. Do you know how old I am? I am twenty-six years old. But there is nothing I can do. I have to do this in order to move forward. All this is because of exile, and the Boers. What I also don't like about the effects of exile is that I am always under suspicion. You also have seen the way people view me. It's like I am some animal or something.

When Vukani first arrived from exile and rejoined Umganga High School, students, teachers, and administration personnel treated him suspiciously. The students were afraid of associating with him because they did not know much about him, how his life might have changed because of the experience of exile and the MK. For unclear reasons, Vukani did not do anything to ease people's suspicions and in fact added to them by keeping to himself. One of his teachers, Zethu, suggested that Vukani liked to portray himself that way because it gave him power over most people in the school, and that he strategically used this power to get what he wanted: *'awuboni nje uma efika ethi kuwe "misi ngicela ukuthi ngisheshe ngihambe esikoleni namhlanje ngoba kukhona izinto okufanele ngizenze," Uvele umvumele. Awumbuzi njengezinye izingane ukuthi ingempela yini lento emphuthumisayo eyenza ashiye isikole. Othisha abaningi bayamsaba ngoba bacabanga ukuthi uma bembuza uzocabanga ukuthi bangena izindaba zakhe, bese ebenzakalisa.'* (Just look, when he comes to you [as a teacher] and says 'Miss, is it fine if I leave school early today because there are some things I need to do?,' you don't ask about the nature of those things as you would with other students. Most teachers fear to ask because they think Vukani will think they are prying into his business and then he will revolt against them [shoot them]). In class, Vukani was equally reserved and, as one of his teachers said, he did not laugh even if a joke was told.

About three months into the school term, an incident happened that helped change students' and some teachers' attitude towards him. The principal of the school was going around checking what students were doing during their study time, which was the last period of the day. He found Vukani's class making a lot of noise and not studying at all. He then went on to punish the whole class. When it was Vukani's turn to be punished, he refused and argued that he had not been making any noise. He then turned around to some matsatsatsa in the class and pointing at them, he asked the principal to verify his story with them. The matsatsatsa confirmed that Vukani had not been making any noise. The principal in turn responded by saying that the matsatsatsa's response was influenced by fear of what Vukani would do to them if they responded otherwise. Vukani then challenged the principal to go to the class teacher and ask her if he ever spoke in class. In the end, Vukani was the only student not punished, and this left some level of envy with his classmates because he had done the impossible: challenged the school principal. This incident also removed a kind of stereotypical belief that was associated with Vukani and the MK in general. That is, the MK was known more for its military actions than anything else, therefore, because Vukani hardly spoke, a lot of people argued that he wasn't a man of words but of (MK) action. What in fact Vukani did during this incident was to negotiate his way out of punishment by using words, not action.

More importantly, however, this incident showed matsatsatsa that Vukani knew who they were. He had indirectly acknowledged their existence and the power they had in the classroom since he had specifically turned to them for support. This kind of acknowledgment helped form friendship between Vukani and matsatsatsa, which eventually contributed to a change in the perceptions that students and teachers had of Vukani. Although some teachers were still suspicious of him, by the time my study began, he was treated like all other students. Vukani's association with a group of students that was highly popular in the school worked to his advantage. At the least, it made other students think that he was approachable.

Vukani, however, was never fully considered a tsatsatsa and was referred to by his matsatsatsa schoolmates and teachers alike, as 'that MK guy.' Although Vukani shared some of the political beliefs of *tsatsatsa* (all matsatsatsa were members of the ANC) he never bought into their cultural practices. Therefore, it is safe to refer to Vukani as an individual operating at the margins or borders of tsatsatsa. Outside the school, however, Vukani did not have any friends, and preferred not to talk much about what he did at home. This I suspect was because he feared that once his friends knew that he was still involved with the MK, they would not want to be too closely associated with him. In some instances, however, Vukani did participate in some *tsatsatsa* activities over the weekends, such as watching a movie at an entertainment place known as 'The Wheel.'

The fact that Vukani was identified as an MK member did not present a problem between him, his *tsatsatsa* friends and his class in general. He acted as a critic, pointing out to the group its strengths and flaws. One valuable criticism was that this particular *tsatsatsa* group devalued people who did not adopt *'izinto zabo ezifana nokugqhoka amabhulukwe athile. Bakuthatha ingathi awazi lutho'* (their things – like dressing in a certain kind of jeans. They treat you like you do not know anything), and that *'mina bangamukela ngoba bebona nginosizo'* (they only accepted me because they discovered I could be of value to them). At the same time Vukani praised those practices that tsatsatsa stood for like condemning mischief, advocating discipline, and encouraging the philosophy of black consciousness: *'Konke lokho ngakufunda kumkhonto'* (all of that I learnt from the MK). Although the dress code accusation made by Vukani was strongly denied, the group did work on it and by the end of the study, the group had more members.

Tsatsatsa Social and Political Practices

Tsatsatsa social practices were most often compared to and indeed understood in relation to the social practices of *mampansula*.[4] Mpansula is a long-established culture that dates back to the 1970s, while at the time of data collection, tsatsatsa culture was still emerging, dating to the beginning of the 1990s. In fact, it is safe to state that at the time of the study, to be mpansula was somehow outdated and was considered by *matsatsatsa* as old-fashioned. Mpansula presented a version of what it meant to be a black youth in the 1970s, but this version had been challenged by other groups such as *tsatsatsa*, and no longer enjoyed the status it had in the 1970s.

The distinguishing characteristics between mampansula and *matsatsatsa* centred on political ideologies that govern the groups' ways of socializing and participating politics. The governing philosophy of tsatsatsa was that of the ANC, which put emphasis on the integration of races and their cultures as a way of dealing with the changes in society. This philosophy influenced the socio-cultural practices of matsatsatsa which included for example, physical appearance, ways of spending free time, and so on. Matsatsatsa were said to listen to what was referred to as cool music such as jazz and some hip-hop, kept their hair short, and engaged in what was considered by a lot of people in the townships unusual recreational activities such as modelling and weight-lifting. Such practices indicated a desire on the part of tsatsatsa to surpass racial categories, which manifested themselves even in sports. Moreover, tsatsatsa recreational activities were marked by the presence of other races, particularly white people. Also, matsatsatsa were careful about their physical appearance especially the way they dressed, and ensured that it was acceptable to society. In fact matsatsatsa were usually dressed in what was considered fashionable at that time.

The philosophy of mampansula, on the other hand, was that of Black Consciousness based on Steve Biko's teachings of the 1970s. Mampansula emphasized the revitalization of black history and its cultures as a way of dealing with changes in society. Pre-colonial practices were viewed as communal in orientation; that is, Africans were economically dependent on each other, and shared most of what they had. Mampan-sula argued that the revitalization of these practices would instil in youths a sense of pride. Who they were was portrayed, for example, in dress and talk. Mampansula listened to rasta (reggae) music, and grew dreadlocks because such practices were defined as black culture. There was also an element of struggle and defiance against certain kinds of state-controlled social practices found in mpansula. The state to control of who and how marijuana was used was not accepted by mampansula, who argued that pre-colonial societies owned and used dagga (mari-juana)[5] and viewed it as a healing rather than a poisonous grass. So it was common to find groups of mpansula youths smoking dagga partly as an act of defiance against the state, and partly as a social habit.

Another characteristic that distinguished mpansula was social space. While it was common to find matsatsatsa in predominantly white areas forming social relations with people of different races, and to find them involved in white-oriented leisure activities such as weight-lifting, mam-pansula social practices were predominantly black-oriented. In a nut-shell, the differences between mpansula and tsatsatsa were black space vis-à-vis pluralism and ways of retreating from dominant (white-defined) society vis-à-vis ways of entering mainstream society. It is important to note that the contrast between these two groups was not necessarily the past versus the present, rather two different stances towards the present. It is correct to conclude that the differences between the two is that mampansula (re)presented one version of a non-rural, hip, sophisti-cated black person that was expressed in politics through the activities of the PAC and the BCM; matsatsatsa, on the other hand, (re)presented an alternative world view of what it meant to be a black person (male or female), who was influenced by the ANC ideology of a non-racial South Africa.

What further characterized tsatsatsa from other groups in the town-ships was a strong sense of purity, a desire to stay away from crime. These criminal activities may have been politically motivated, such as forcing people to stay away from work, or economically oriented, like stealing food. To this extent, their peers sometimes referred to matsat-satsa as *abangcwele*, the holy ones. Most tsatsatsa participants came from a poor background, but most of them assisted their families by getting part-time jobs. Through their work, tsatsatsa participants were able to learn more about and sometimes participate in white culture – to go, for example, to places where the young white boys with whom they worked spent their time. Lunga, for example, worked as a packer at Pick and

Pay, and made friends with one of the supervisors, a white youth called Nick who was almost the same age as himself. As Lunga and Nick got to know more about each other, Lunga learnt about an athletic club to which Nick belonged. Lunga had always been interested in weight-lifting, but had never been able to do it because of lack of sports centres in the townships. After making his interest known, Nick agreed to take Lunga to the club.[6] When Lunga became a member of the club he introduced other tsatsatsa members also interested in weight-lifting.

That Participation in white-defined social areas was not coincidental, as might be suggested by Lunga's case, but was in fact sought by matsatsa-tsa. Sizwe, for example, played in a jazz band to which he was introduced by a white co-worker. Thulile hung out with a white girl nicknamed Zee and got to be introduced to other white girls in the group. This kind of friendship had not always been smooth for Thulile who, by her own admission, found it tiring and boring because, as she put it, *'abenzi lutho. bahlale nje bevakashelana emakubo bazixoxele izindaba. Anginalutho enginga-luxoxa nabo. Ngifuna ukwenza izinto ezifana nokubuka izitolo'* (they don't do anything but just visit each other's homes and talk. I don't have anything to talk about with them. I want to go out and do stuff like window-shopping).

Thulile often helped her aunt (who is also her guardian) with some of her duties in a white-owned boutique over the weekends. Thulile did not get paid by the owner but by her aunt, since it was her duties that she did. For this reason, Thulile did not work every weekend; her going to the boutique depended on the amount of housework she had. The owner of the boutique had a daughter, Zee, who had similar work condi-tions as Thulile. Thulile mentioned this white teenager to her tsatsatsa friends who immediately encouraged her to establish a friendship with Zee (which was consequently going to result in a possible friendship with the whole group). However, Thulile was not interested and had in fact turned down Zee's invitation to go to a lunch-hour concert at the city square. Finally, not being able to withstand the pressure from her friends, Thulile became friends with Zee. Despite its boring nature, she maintained her friendship with Zee so as to keep smooth her relation-ship with tsatsatsa. Thulile was highly dependent on matsatsatsa for sup-port, and talked of her friends as her family. To explain this dependency, Thulile stated: *'Anginamuntu phela lamhlabeni ngaphandle kwabo. Bangabantu abayaziyo impilo yami. U-anti uyasebenza futhi unezinto eziningi ezihlale zisenqondweni yakhe. Angifuni ukumhlupha.'* (I do not have anybody and these are my friends who understand my life. I can talk and be with them at any time. My aunt is always working. She has a lot of things in her mind and I don't want to worry her).

Matsatsatsa did not participate in township events such as soccer, or watching movies in a community hall, but spent their free time in the then newly opened multiracial amusement or recreational places such as the Wheel, a huge, casino-like amusement place with movie theatres, restaurants, shops, and games. It is in the heart of Durban, by the beachfront, and away from the townships. People of all races go there to spend time, to meet with each other, and to just hang out as most teenagers do. Such places were very attractive to matsatsatsa possibly because they provide opportunity for wider/international interaction and since these places represented dominant society values.

The fact that matsatsatsa distanced themselves from social activities of the townships was in part motivated by the desire to stay uncorrupted. Often community-organized events were disrupted by criminal and political thuggery. Some people attended local townships events not because they were interested in soccer or a movie, but because they wanted to track down political enemies. Although soccer groups were supposed to be neutral (and this will be discussed in chapter 8), their existence made it possible for people to disguise their agendas and gain popularity as soccer players. It then became easy for popular players to recruit for certain political organizations. Even weddings and funerals were not immune to politics; indeed, they were often dangerous events characterized by cross-political violence.

Matsatsatsa were strongly influenced by the ANC vision of a non-racial democratic South Africa, but this vision came with the baggage of elitism; it meant being able to participate white-dominated places that were considered elitist. The fact that matsatsatsa were interested in weightlifting, for example, illuminates the desire to improve their status, since the sport, like golf and tennis, was considered white and, by implication, elitist. Matsatsatsa travelled for an hour to lift weights rather than jog around the township as other residents did. This was despite the fact that jogging was considered a safe activity in the townships, especially since people did it in groups. Usually these groups were named by the times at which they jogged: the 5 am group; or 5 pm group and so on. Asking one non-tsatsatsa participant why he thought tsatsatsa did not like jogging he said, *'Bacabanga ukuthi yinto yoZulu, buka bangenza ngisho eyabo i club'* (They think it's a Zulu thing [meaning backward]. Look, they can even start their own jogging club).

Specific Representations about Identity

Matsatsatsa also made specific statements that illuminate the ways that these youths viewed themselves in relation to Zulu identity and political activities in the township. They viewed themselves as Zulu, and used Zulu history to define and legitimise their practices as Zulu in ideology. For example, history as a criterion was used through the calling up of historic names as illustrated by the following example.

At the time of data collection, the South African Teachers' Union (SATU), an ANC affiliate, called for a teachers' strike to protest salaries and general working conditions. At Umganga High School, in the first week of protest, some students who were in the final grade were concerned about missing classes; other students saw this as sort of a holiday, a break from teacher authority. Some classes went on as usual, however, because some teachers did not participate in this strike, either because they were Inkatha, therefore belonged to a different teacher organization, or because they simply did not agree with the concept of strikes. Students who were at the last grade took turns teaching each other and negotiated, together with the principal, with those teachers who did not participate in the strike, to help them with some of the subjects.

In one of the conversations I had with matsatsatsa they expressed concern about the strike and the way it was going to hinder their ability to do well in the final examination. Present in this conversation were, myself, Muzi, Sizwe, Lunga, Vukani, and Thulile.

Nombuso: *Siniphethe kanjani lesiteleka?*
How is the strike affecting you?

Vukani: *Hayi mina ngithi ziqhudelene Nkombose kababa. Kade sasiteleka basi-bone kungathi asiphili emakhanda. Ake bazabalaze nabo bezwe ukuthi kun-jani.*
I say let them fight each other Nkombose kababa.[7] We [students] have long been struggling on our own and they [teachers] have been looking at us as though we are crazy. Let them struggle and feel how it is.

Lunga: *Noma kunjalo, yithi esizofa ekugcineni. Sengithi nje kungcono kulokhu ngoba noma ngingafeyila, akungenxa yami.*
Even if that's the case, we are the ones who will eventually suffer. I sometimes console myself by thinking that even if I fail this year, at least it won't be my fault.

Muzi: *Mina ngisovalweni. Ngithi uma ngicabanga iMaths, kuthi mangikhale. Ngizibona kulonyaka ozayo ngiphinda iclass sengimdala kangaka.*

As for me, I am afraid. Whenever I think of maths, I feel like crying. I picture myself repeating the same class next year, old as I am.

Sizwe: *Awu mina ngeke ingehlule. Angihlulwa yinto engakhulumi. Ngimfunge uCetshwayo avuke, ngizophasa lonyaka.*

Not me, I won't fail maths. I have never been defeated by anything that doesn't talk.[8] I swear in the name of Cetshwayo, I will pass this year (active translation: Cetshwayo will rise from the dead, if I do not pass this year).

Thulile: *Kusho ukuthi eyangonyaka odlule i-Maths yayinomlomo, yikho nje wayifeyila?*

Does this mean that last year's maths could speak and that's why you failed it? (We all laughed.)

Sizwe: *Ngiyanibona nje nina nicabanga ukuthi ngiyadlala. NgiwuZulu mina, angihlulwa lutho. Noma ngingayifeyila maths, kodwa ngizophasa lonyaka.*

I see. You think I am joking. I *am Zulu nothing defeats me.* Even if I fail maths, I will not fail (the entire exam) [my emphasis].

Sizwe's statements indicate that to swear in the name of Cetshwayo is to vow to do the right, impossible, heroic, and valued thing. Yet the victory won in 1879 was short-lived as the British won the battle of Ulundi and exiled Cetshwayo. But tsatsatsa participants do not talk about this battle because it is of no significance to them, and after all, as they reminded me, *'leyompi eyalelandela i-Sandlwana yayekwa ngoba uZulu ethembiswa izwe, hayi ngoba ehluleka'* (the peace that followed Ulundi was only attained by promising the Zulu people that they would retain possession of their land if they laid down their arms).

Tsatsatsa also spoke about their birthplaces to define themselves as Zulu or not Zulu. For example, in classroom discussions, when directly asked if they are Zulu they unanimously used their birthplace to identify themselves. In the other informal discussions they shifted tacitly to other criteria of identity or to a different identity. In one of our classroom discussions about the Zulu language, I asked why it was that Zulu people did not learn Sotho even when they worked in places such as Johannesburg where Sotho and Tswana dominated. The discussion started in English, but later developed in Zulu. Vukani was first to respond to this question (this discussion was recorded and the English language mistakes are those of the speakers):

Vukani: Zulus don't want to learn it because they think they are big.

Muzi: Not that they think, *sibakhule vele. Asifuni ukukhuluma njengamazi-zimbane*
Not that they think, we are real big. We don't want to speak like mazi-zimbane (a term that implies that someone is not real Zulu/human or humane in a Zulu way).
Some people in the class laugh.

Vukani: *uyabona, abantu abafananani abahambe beshaya abantu ngezagila ngoba nithi bangamazizimbane.*
You see, its people like you who go around beating people up with knobkerries because you say they are mazizimbane.

Nombuso: *Awusitshele Zethu. AmaZulu ababizelani abantu ngamazizimbane?*
Tell us, Zethu, why do Zulu people call non-Zulus *amazizimbane?* (I directed this question to her because she was among those who had laughed at Muzi's statement.)

Zethu: *Phendula Muzi. Wuwe loqale lendaba yamazizimbane.*
Respond Muzi. You are the one who started this whole mazizimbane issue.

Muzi: (ecabanga) *Hayi angazi. Yinto nje yoZulu leyo. Mina abazali bami baqhamuka eSwazini. Angizazi ezinye izinto zoZulu.*
[Thoughtfully] I don't really know. That's just something that's for Zulus. I don't know because my parents migrated from Swaziland. So I don't know some Zulu things.
(But Muzi, who is tsatsatsa, had earlier identified himself as Zulu because, as he said, 'I speak Zulu'.)

Nhlanhla: *Awusho Mbongi Zulu omkhulu*
Tell us Mbongi, the (real) Zulu.
(Mbongi was well known in the school because of his ability to recite the praise songs of the Zulu kings from Shaka to the present king. He became popular during the school arts week where students chose projects to present to the entire school. In this class, the students had decided to perform the Zulu drama 'ukufa kukaShaka' (the death of Shaka) which was also part of their syllabus. Mbongi had assumed the role of Shaka's praise singer known in Zulu as *imbongi*).

Mbongi: *Hayi nami angizazi izinto zoZulu ngoba umawami owaseMalawi. Kusho ukuthi ngiwumZulu nganxanye ngiwumMalawi.*
No, I do not know Zulu things because my mother is Malawian. This means I am partly Malawian and partly Zulu.

In earlier discussions, some of these youths had identified themselves as Zulu because of their knowledge of the Zulu language, even though some later mentioned that at home they used a different language, usually that of the place of the parents' origin. Some were also known as Zulu because of their behaviour, such as Mbongi in the above example. However, in discussions that were critical of Zulu social practices, these young people categorically refused to be identified as Zulu, as indicated by the above example. In fact, at one stage of discussing symbols in politics, the discussion ended with all participants having systematically denied their Zulu heritage, a heritage that in other contexts was the pride of most.

Another available criterion of identification was descent, which made it possible for tsatsatsa to view themselves not just as Zulu, but Zulu Zu or Zulu of historic origin. For example, Lunga told us how his great-grandfather had participated in the wars that led to the Zulu people's takeover control of the land around Bergville, which borders Lesotho and South Africa in the northeast. He therefore considered himself as 'Inzalo yamaqhawe' (a product of heroes) because of his ancestors' involvement in these wars of conquest. But like all other criteria, descent also had its own complexities. An interesting case is that of the tsatsatsa-border participant nicknamed Ndabezitha (one of the words of praise and respect used to acknowledge loyalty to Zulu royalty). This was a name given to him by his classmates because he had been in the habit of demanding respect for himself as royalty since his great-grandfather was Sibiya, Shaka's chief minister. Because the events that had resulted in the nickname were actually humorous, Ndabezitha didn't mind the nickname and in fact, liked it so much that he marked all his schoolbooks 'Thetha NDABEZITHA Sibiya.' In another session we shared ideas about how other groups might feel about the use of Zulu as a national language, especially in the light of the then ongoing Zulu-Xhosa conflict, which characterized the Transvaal at that time. Some participants stated that they had felt uncomfortable using Zulu in the Transvaal because the language singled them out as Zulus and therefore Inkatha, and made them open to attack by non-Zulu speakers. 'Why is this so?' I asked.

Lunga: *angithi uGatsha (Buthelezi) ufuna sonke sibewoZulu sithathe amawisa siyolwa nabantu bakithi ukuze sitshengise ukuthi singamaqhawe*
It's all because of Gatsha who wants us to be Zulu. He wants us to take up knobkerries and go and fight our own people to show that we are brave.

Sizwe: *Uthini Ndabezitha? Uthi ungakhuluma nje nabakini ebukhosini bay-iyeke lento?*
What do you say, Ndabezitha. Do you think you can approach your relative in royalty to stop this? (We all laughed).

Ndabezitha responded by telling us that in actual fact, he was not royalty, and that he actually was not Zulu because he had learnt that Sibiya's father was a Bushman, therefore there was no way in which Sibiya could have been Shaka's chief minister 'because we all know that the Zulu had minimum contact with the Bushmen.'

What we also knew but did not talk about was that many of Shaka's chief ministers and advisers were eminent commoners who had come to the fore through their exceptional military ability rather than through their royal birth. In this context, Ndabezitha disassociated himself from Zulu identity and also attempted to move away from the use of Zulu in his attempts to explain why he could not be considered royalty, or even Zulu for that matter. It is important to point out, however, that such a shift in language use, as demonstrated by Ndabezitha, was not a common practice with the informants I worked with in this study or in the region in general. This was so, mainly because the conflict that existed was between Zulu-speakers, therefore, the use of Zulu was not always demarcative. Usually, informants were most likely to move away from Zulu identity by using an alternative criterion of identification such as birthplace, but would still maintain the use of the Zulu language.

Put together however, the things that matsatsatsa did and those that they said made it possible for them to be ANC people in the Inkatha-controlled township of Umlazi. By appearing to be responsible youths, devoted to schooling and other valued practices such as having a job, they gained a positive reputation that even Inkatha vigilantes acknowledged. Most importantly, tsatsatsa used symbolic resources such as the Zulu language and history as a way of defining who they were. The use of these symbols made them appear to be like Inkatha, or rather, not very different from the Zulu people who participated in Inkatha politics.

These three criteria of identification: birthplace, descent, and history, though accepted in a certain context, were all surpassed by a single predominant formula of group membership: language. Language became a complex criterion because all parties involved in the region were Zulu speakers. In the following chapter the complex role of language is examined

chapter 7

Tsatsatsa Language, Cultural Practices, and the Politics of Identity

Language and Social Practices in Formal Domains

Umganga High School

Seven of the ten key participants in the study were students at Umganga High School and six of these seven students were tsatsatsa. One was church-based and the remaining two operated at the margins of tsatsatsa. Umganga needs to be understood against the background of Inkatha control of Umlazi. Like most schools in KwaZulu townships, Umganga was accountable to the KwaZulu Department of Education and Culture (KDEC) and often had to account for the actions of its students and teachers. The principal and his deputies acted as links between the school and the KDEC and were responsible for relating and implementing departmental policies at the school. The relationship that Umganga had with the KDEC was a tense one, often marked with threats from KwaZulu officials to the school authorities. The main problem was that Umganga continued to question, ignore, or resist a number of orders that came from the KDEC. For example, during the time of collecting data the South African Teachers Union (SATU), an ANC affiliate, called for a countrywide teacher boycott as a way of addressing their grievances. The KDEC opposed this boycott, ordered all teachers in KwaZulu schools to go back to work, and argued that all grievances were to be channelled through the Natal African Teachers Union (NATU), an Inkatha affiliate (all teachers working under the KDEC were by KwaZulu law NATU members).

At Umganga, those teachers who were SATU members boycotted school and on one afternoon attended a citywide meeting held at

Umlazi city hall. Some local KDEC officials went to the meeting with the aim of getting the names of all teachers from KwaZulu schools and to send this list to the headquarters at Ulundi. The teachers refused to give out their names, so all principals were later ordered to submit to Ulundi a list of all those teachers who were not in schools on the day of the meeting and who had not been in schools during the week of the boycott. The reason given was that since these teachers were not at work when expected to be, their salaries had to be adjusted. The principal at Umganga did not agree with these orders, and simply ignored them. A letter was then sent by the KDEC asking him to explain his actions and also warning him of possible harsh consequences that could be taken if he did not comply. He also ignored this letter, arguing that the KDEC expected him to act as *igundane* (a rat) sniffing out teacher politics for Inkatha. During the boycott, the principal had called a meeting to talk to those teachers who came to school and asked them for suggestions on how to deal with those classes without teachers. In the end, it was decided that classes be combined, just to ensure that teaching went on and that students' hope to succeed did not dwindle.

The principal's way of dealing with the strike and with KDEC orders does not mean that there were no problems among the teaching staff in the school. Conflicts did arise during this period of teacher boycott, mainly concerned with issues of teacher responsibility, loyalty, and so on. Where Lunganga differed from other schools, however, was in the willingness of teachers to discuss issues, irrespective of political affiliation. Indeed, this did not mirror the broader practices of Inkatha and the ANC, whose willingness to carry on negotiations with the National Party government did not bring a willingness to talk among themselves as black groups. The overriding image of political groups at that time was that of the black-on-black violence and inability to talk among themselves. Nonetheless, ordinary people that belonged to these groups were doing the opposite; that is, they negotiated issues in order to be able to live and work with each other.

Defying orders from the KDEC was interpreted by the KwaZulu government and Inkatha to mean that the individuals involved were anti-Inkatha and hence anti-Zulu. It would be wrong, however, to suggest that teachers or even the students in this school were anti-Zulu. Indeed, some of the teachers upheld Zulu culture even though they were not members of Inkatha. This is well illustrated by the incident discussed in chapter 2 when a teacher disciplined a student for referring to Chief Buthelezi without the proper referenced title. Even though the teacher was known as ANC, her actions suggests that she still upheld the Zulu culture of hlonipha and expected that all Zulu students, despite their political orientation, would hlonipha.

Perhaps the most distinguishing feature at Umganga was the cordial relationship between students and teachers. As many teachers pointed out, this was one of the highest achievements of the National Education Crisis Committee (NECC) committees. Although Umganga authorities never admitted to having been influenced by the suggestions made by the NECC, the teacher-student-parent committees that existed in the school were started during the era of the NECC, with its back-to-school strategy of 1988. These committees helped channel information be-tween groups of students and teachers and looked for ways of resolving conflict. Although in the initial interviews a lot of students stated that they went to Umganga because of its political neutrality, this did not mean that students did not participate in political activities. As explained in the previous chapter, neutrality actually meant that everybody accepted and respected people's choice of political affilliation. Some individuals like matsatsatsa were respected because of the organizations they belonged to, and also because of the way they carried out their political activism, and some like Vukani were feared because they were considered too radical, since they had participated in what most students referred to as guerrilla warfare. It is not clear, however, how Inkatha students fitted into this school, since most were not active and did not talk about their activities publicly.[1] That is, irrespective of my ANC political affiliation, I had reason to believe that Inkatha youths in this school did not talk much about or act out their politics. PAC supporters were, like those of the ANC, very active in the school, especially since they were very vocal about the philosophy of Black Consciousness. During the school's theatre day, for example, PAC students put on a fashion show and paraded different old African outfits from all over Southern Africa. The name of the show itself, *IAf-rika eMnyama* (Black Africa), was symbolic of the philosophy of Black Consciousness.

Umganga also differed from other schools in the townships because it refused to declare itself either ANC or Inkatha. The make-up of both the student and teacher populations at Umganga ranged from Inkatha supporters to PAC to ANC. The philosophy of the school was that of political inclusion and the acceptance of differences related mainly to political orientation. At the centre of institutions, therefore, existed a problem of political and socio-cultural identities. Often, the two were synonymous and dictated how individuals viewed themselves and others around them.

Language Practices in the School

As in many black schools, Umganga had an English-only policy. Zulu was forbidden in the classroom as well as in the playgrounds. It was argued by Umganga officials that the use of English in the school was important because four of the six subjects that students needed to pass their matric examination were in English, and that therefore practice makes perfect. This English-only policy, however, was difficult to implement. Participants, when asked what languages they used in the school, cited Zulu and English or Zulu and Afrikaans. This was not surprising because the school was solely constituted of first-language speakers, or Zulu (ZLI), including the teachers. Zulu was used not just by the students, but also by the teachers in their classrooms. This includes the use of Zulu by teachers teaching what was known as English language and comprehension. At Umganga, two classrooms were of interest to this study. One was a Standard 10 class, which included all tsatsatsa participants involved in this study. The other was a Standard 9 class which had in it one individual belonging to a church group (Ngubo) from KwaMashu. In this section, the focus is on the Standard 10 classroom, and a discussion about the Standard 9 class is developed in chapter 9, in which the church as a social space is discussed.

In the Standard 10 classroom, there seems to have been a great attempt to use only the official languages of the school, especially in the presence of adult authority. This could have been motivated by tsatsatsa practice of doing what was right, which included respect for classroom and school policy in general. It could also have been motivated by the need to do well in the final examination which, to a greater extent, demonstrated command of the English language. This final examination determined whether students could obtain either postsecondary education or jobs, since the language of schooling was also linked to the language of work. Further, it is possible that this practice of staying within the official language of the school was influenced by the political orientation of the students in this class. Most, if not all the students in the classroom were members or supporters of the ANC. Although at this time the ANC had adopted a policy that called for the equalisation of all the languages in the country, its own practices indicated a strong attraction towards the use of English. All ANC meetings, rallies, and demonstrations which these students participated in took place in English. It is therefore possible that a link existed between what went on in these ANC activities and students' language practices in the classroom.

In this Standard 10 class therefore, all learning took place in English. (Afrikaans was not used for instruction but operated informally between students. Also, Afrikaans, like Zulu, was taught as a subject). Teachers and students did their best to help each other towards this goal. In the discussions I had with tsatsatsa and their classmates, two distinct moments of contradictory Zulu language use emerged. The first moment indexes the manner in which people positively positioned themselves and were positioned by others positively because of their use and knowledge of Zulu as compared to English. The second moment indexes the ways in which others situated individuals negatively because of their use of Zulu as opposed to the use of English.

A Positive View of Zulu Language Use in Relation to English and Afrikaans

During the first week of data collection, I was hitch-hiking[2] and was given a lift to the city centre by a stranger, an Indian man driving through the city to Richards Bay. In our discussion about the changes that were taking place, this man mentioned that he thought Zulu should be the national language of South Africa.[3] What was more interesting was not his choice of Zulu per se, but rather the fact that issues of language choice were no longer just a concern of policy-makers alone, but also of ordinary people in the streets.

This positive view of the use of Zulu was also demonstrated in the formal discussions I had with tsatsatsa and their classmates. In group discussions, participants unanimously said Zulu when asked 'which language do you think should be the national language of the country?' The reasons for this choice varied, but all rested on a positive interpretation of the language. Of the twenty-two participants involved in the discussions, fifteen stated that because the language is spoken by 'great' people who fought and conquered during Shaka times (an exact translation would be 'big' but the Zulu word they used means both great and many) and also because the Zulu are a brave nation who fought the British without any guns. Of these fifteen participants, six were the tsatsatsa key informants. Five of the participants argued that Zulu is easy to learn; that the other Bantu languages in the country borrow a lot from Zulu; and two of the participants said they chose Zulu because it is the language of the majority of the population.

To take this issue further, I asked, 'If you were to choose between English and Afrikaans for a national language, which one would you choose?' Twelve of the twenty-two participants chose Afrikaans and gave the following reasons: Afrikaans is easy to learn because its grammatical structure is like that of Zulu; Afrikaans is indigenous to South Africa, therefore, unlike English, where the British dictate to us which forms are correct and which forms are wrong; with Afrikaans 'we will be the only ones telling everybody what is correct and wrong Afrikaans'; because the Afrikaners are the ones who control the places where they work and therefore it is important to know their language. One of the participants explained that he had a brother who had been educated in KwaZulu/Natal, and had a bachelor's degree in electrical engineering but could not find a job in the Transvaal because he did not have good Afrikaans. Eight of the participants chose English because it is an international language (reflecting the ANC's political rhetoric of the time). Two of the participants refused to choose.

These responses equate to the use of Zulu with a positive interpretation of history and culture of bravery and resistance against some forms of domination. In fact it is possible to argue that Zulu, especially as used by tsatsatsa in social spaces, was often a symbol of power, used to resist cultural modes of domination such as language. To expand this point, I will examine a discussion I had with tsatsatsa and their classmates. This example involves an ANC rally at the city centre which tsatsatsa and some of their classmates attended. Because some of the students did not know, or rather were not sure of, my political orientation before this rally, in the next class discussion that we had, we spent some time talking about events at the rally. Prior to this discussion, I had observed that during ANC events such as meetings and demonstrations, tsatsatsa would use Zulu in the presence of their white friends who supported their cause. This I thought was odd especially in the light of the ANC rhetoric of the use of English in such situations. I asked reasons for this persistence in the use of Zulu even when they had a non-Zulu speaker in their presence: 'Don't you think you ought to be a little bit inclusive?' I asked. Vukani said: 'When I use Zulu with other black people I feel free and understood, but when I am with whites, I feel proud. It makes me proud to see white people struggle to learn our language because then it shows me that they too have a lot that they don't know.' At one level, Vukani's statement means that there was a space in which his use of Zulu put him in a position of knowing, therefore, of power. At another level this statement could be taken to mean that there was a level in which black people used Zulu to indicate a shared culture or even solidarity symbolized by the words 'free' and 'understood.' In this political space, Zulu allowed certain practices of power and subordination to coexist without necessarily causing conflict among members involved. However, this coexistence was made possible because of implied rules of communication that existed within this social space; that is, whites had to agree to be spoken to in Zulu in order to participate within this space.

Another encounter I had with Vukani that demonstrates this even more clearly was my complaint to him that he was making me feel old by continuously calling me sisi Nombuso while we belonged to the same age group (in Zulu 'sisi' is the prefix used to show respect, usually for one's status acquired through age, marriage, and so on). His response was *'awukahle wena sisi' Nombuso, ake sikhulume isiZulu ke manje'* (wait a minute sisi Nombuso, let's now talk Zulu). We had been speaking Zulu all along. As a Zulu person, my understanding of Vukani's statement was that he was actually saying: let us draw from our shared culture of how Zulu people address those they respect.

A similar incident occurred when one day I misread the timetable and arrived at the beginning of a period which I thought was for me to use for discussion. Upon entering the classroom the students pointed out that this was not my period, but for biology, and that the period that had just ended was the one I was supposed to have used. Someone suggested that I arrange to use this biology period, and to trade one of my future discussion times with biology. I thought this was a good idea, and was on my way out to negotiate this with the biology teacher when someone else pointed out that the biology teacher was a very difficult strict-to-the-rules-person, and that he probably would not agree to this suggestion since he was on his way to the class anyway (we could see him through the windows walking towards the class). Everybody agreed, but Sizwe suggested that perhaps he would agree if *'ukhulume naye isiZulu kahle'* (I spoke in Zulu nicely with him), again the rest agreed. With this suggestion, I left to negotiate with the biology teacher and he agreed. On my return, the class wanted to know what I had said and I responded by saying *'ngikhulume naye isiZulu njengoba nishilo'* (I spoke Zulu nicely with him as you suggested) and they laughed. My understanding of their suggestion was that I had to employ a specific (shared) Zulu method of request in order to get what I wanted, a method that I would not have known if I was not Zulu. I did exactly that.

It is difficult to state exactly what I said that convinced the teacher to trade his class period with me. But I remember walking towards him thinking about what Sizwe had said and how I was going to put it into practice. I knew that in the conversation, I had to make him feel respected and in a position of power, with the right to debate, refuse, or accept the proposal. I also knew that I had to do this in no other language than Zulu despite the fact that English was the language of the school. Had I used English, I would have somehow taken a position of power associated with the use of English in many situations. Relating back to the class the biology class teacher's exact words of agreement: *'cha ubekekahle nkosazane, kulungile'* (You presented your case well nkosazane,[4] it's ok); one of the students stated *'cha uyasazi isiZulu'* (no, you really know Zulu). In all these three examples, it appeared as if Zulu was used to refer to both the language, and to the implementation of cultural practices that the language entailed.

The use of Zulu to indicate a shared culture and solidarity was not only expressed in participants' actual statements about language use, but got enacted in classroom discussions as in the following example. This discussion aimed at teasing out public opinion about the use of English in the township, that is, in informal domains. The following discussion is documented in its original form and the language mistakes in it are those of the speakers, not the author.

Category 1[5]

Let's talk about speaking Zulu. How does this make us feel?
(a) I feel confident because I can express everything that I want to and explain it clearly.
(b) I feel free when I am with blacks but if I am with whites *ngizizwa ngiziqhenya* (I feel proud). White people say they like our language because of our clicks. *Uyazi nje nawe – abo 'xha' nabo 'gqha'* (you also know, the 'xhas' and the 'qhas').
(c) *Ngizizwa nginogqhozi* (I feel enthusiastic).
(d) *Ngizizwa nginofuqufuqu. Ake sikhulume sizwane-ke manje. Ngizizwa ngijabule.* Kodwa with English people – uyazi nje nawe, they say a lot of things. (I feel enthusiastic. Let's now talk and hear each other. I feel happy. But with English people – you also know, they say a lot of things).

Category 2
Let us talk about how we feel when we use English whether in the classroom or outside.

(a) I feel unspeakable – I can't explain this. Sometimes I feel good,
    sometimes bad because I can't express myself. ('Unspeakable' here
    means one's inability to express oneself – a direct Zulu translation).
(b) I am shy when I am in the classroom because I think my English is
    not good, but not when I am outside.
(c) I feel happy, but not like I speak Zulu because I can't explain some-
    thing that I want to express in English simply.
(d) I feel proud because it's the language that is spoken by the whites
    and I feel like I'm the same as the whites.

Nombuso: What kinds of thing do people say when someone uses
English?

With this question, the discussion moved on to how the public or township views those who use English. While this was a somehow long and
unstructured conversation – the sense that students often voiced their
ideas without necessarily linking them to what the previous person had
said – it revealed some of the underlying township attitudes regarding
the use of English outside formal institutions.

(a) If you use English, people say you phone yourself – uyazifonela,
    uyazitshela.[6] They say you put your feather in your hat.
(b) I have a sister who is at multiracial school. She is seven years old. At
    home we always speak to her in English. She is no longer under-
    stand much Zulu. I don't know why though we speak to her in
    English. We just do.
(c) We – when I am at home we always use Zulu. I don't want to put
    myself in the pain of biting my tongue. We just use Zulu.

This discussion deserves two levels of analysis: at the pattern of language use and its meaning; and the actual meaning of these students'
statements. Looking first at the pattern of language use, the responses
in category 1 indicate a positive moment in the use of Zulu and this is
reflected by the integration of the Zulu language in an English structured discussion. In fact, what starts with the inception of a short Zulu
phrase in (b) is taken and expanded by the next student into a short
sentence (c), and finally a declaration for the use of Zulu in response
(d). The responses in category 2 suggest some qualification about the
Zulu-English distinction in that the conversation goes back to English,
with Zulu used only to explain concepts that students thought could not

be understood by the researcher. These responses indicate that, while these students did attempt to stay and use the language of education, in some cases there is a shift in practice. This shift occurs, as indicated by the responses in category 1, in instances where students have to voice out ideas that positively link their practices to the Zulu language. Furthermore, this shift could be understood as occurring because of an attempt by the students to express solidarity, or rather a shared understood culture indicated by phrases such as 'let's now talk and hear one another,' and 'you also know.'

This discussion demonstrates three things. The first point raised by the statements in category 1 relates to the issue of power derived from the use of Zulu by Zulu speakers in the presence of non-Zulu speakers, specifically whites. Statements in this category also demonstrate that Zulu was sometimes inclusive in practice – that is, it brought speakers of the same linguistic background to the same level. The second issue, derived from the statements in category 2, is that students had mixed feelings about the use of English in the classroom. Some felt positive when expressing themselves because they felt they were the 'same as whites' and, given South Africa's racial history, this implied that they had power; others did not feel good because of their inability to express themselves correctly. These mixed feelings inform us about the value of English in formal institutions like the school: those who used it felt powerful, while those who were unsure about their knowledge of it felt subordinated. The third issue is that of the contradictory nature of languages, in this case English, and the way these contradictions were played out in everyday practices. For instance, while it is clear from this discussion that the use of English outside the school was not a common practice, and was in fact viewed with scrutiny, this use of English, problematic as it was, also gave the speakers some position of power. The meaning given to languages in everyday practices was often symbolic of power relations between and within racial groups.

A Negative View of Zulu Language Use

The second moment in the use of the Zulu language was its association with ignorance or illiteracy. For example, tsatsatsa informants were very vocal and adamant in their use of Zulu, and were not enthusiastic about the political rhetoric for English. The only time they spoke English was in the classroom where the situation required it of them. One afternoon I was in a school bus that went all over Umlazi dropping off some childlren and picking up others in different units in the township. This was to be the first time I overheard matsatsatsa speaking to each other and to a few other friends in the bus in English. They were talking about all kinds of things, ranging from schoolwork to things they were going to do over the weekend. At one time they discussed an English composition homework entitled 'The person I would like to meet.' Apparently Vukani had written that he would like to meet Bill Clinton and talk to him about the war that the Americans were supporting in Angola,[7] upon which someone responded *'uyikhomanisi langempela'* (you are a true [real] communist). It is worth noting that the use of Zulu here lightened the statement, to avoid misinterpretation, as Vukani's radical political stance was usually a source of conflict. Besides this statement, and a few Zulu words now and then, all conversations in the bus went on in English. After listening for a while, I decided to ask for an explanation and got the following response from Sizwe: 'children from multiracial schools – you see they don't want to speak with us. They have shoulders.[8] If we speak with them in Zulu they reply in English to show us that we don't know much. They say *singoZulu* (we are Zulu). So most of the times we speak in English to show them that we know.' The use of Zulu in this example refers to a specific practice of ignorance.

Within this positioning of the use of Zulu, the language also takes its meaning from associations with the practices of Inkatha. To develop this point, I will re-examine the discussions I had with tsatsatsa and their classmates regarding their choice of Zulu as a national language especially in the light of the then ongoing Zulu-Xhosa conflict in the Transvaal at the time. In this discussion some participants indicated that the use of Zulu in the Transvaal singled them out as Zulus, and therefore as Inkatha, and made them open to attack by non-Zulu speakers.

I later synthesised this discussion about the use of Zulu in the Transvaal with a friend and colleague, Nhlanhla Nkosi. He mentioned that in the Transvaal, the use of Zulu also distinguishes the young from the old. To demonstrate his point, he narrated his experiences in two different vans that he used to get from Johannesburg to Soweto and from Soweto to the city centre. In the first van were twelve other passengers and he talked to some of them. During these conversations, Nhlanhla was identifiable as a Zulu from KwaZulu/Natal, therefore Inkatha, because he spoke Zulu differently from the rest of the passengers who spoke Johannesburg Zulu. At the end of the trip, one passenger announced to the driver that *'uzongena enkingeni uma ezoletha amaShaka laSoweto'* (he would get into trouble if he brought the Shakas to Soweto (*amaShaka* is a derogatory name sometimes used to refer to Zulus by non-Zulus)). The van driver apologized and drove on to wherever he was going. On his next trip from Soweto to the city centre Nhlanhla ensured that in conversations with other passengers he used tsotsitaal, which it difficult for an audience to tell the speaker's place of origin. Indeed in KwaZulu/ Natal itself, the use of tsotsitaal often identified speakers as foreigners; in other words, non-Zulus and therefore ANC. In Johannesburg, on the other hand, tsotsitaal mostly distinguished the rural from the urban. On this particular trip, Nhlanhla was nonetheless identifiable first as a Roman Catholic priest and second, as a person in his mid-forties, because of the priest uniform and his middle-aged looks. While he was talking to two passengers, another passenger interrupted and asked, *'umuntu omdala onjani lo, owumfundisi nokwenza njengawe okhuluma kanje?'* (What kind of an elderly person who is a priest for that matter who speaks [tsotsitaal] as you do?).

So while the use of Zulu often placed people as Inkatha, as demonstrated in Nhlanhla's first trip, resorting to other varieties of language was often not the best solution; for these varieties marked one as being urban rather than country, an important distinction which, however, carried other consequences. As stated, country people were held to be responsible individuals who still carried on valued African practices, while those believed to be urban (and used tsotsitaal) were generally viewed to have abandoned these practices because of corruption by urbanization and industrialization. Nhlanhla's example and those of tsatsatsa discussed earlier, also point to the fact that Zulu, tsotsitaal, and English had multiple associations that were much broader than associations with Inkatha and the ANC and went beyond the boundaries of KwaZulu/Natal.

Language and Social Practices in Informal Domains

Private, Informal Group Gatherings

A common tsatsatsa way of spending free time was to visit each other's homes, mainly on weekends. They would play cards, watch television, study, eat together, or just talk about current events. In five of the seven gatherings in which I took part, Vukani was not there. This was partly because Vukani preferred to keep to himself and partly because the others did not extend an invitation to him because often his views differed from those of the tsatsatsa core circle, and, as Muzi pointed out, *'uthatha impilo kalukhuni uVukani'* (Vukani takes life too seriously). In a nutshell, Muzi's statement translated to something like, 'Vukani is not fun to be with.' These gatherings were in most cases unplanned and so it was unusual for all members to be part of a gathering. In most cases however, Muzi, Thulile, and Sizwe formed the core of these gatherings and, depending on job and childcare responsibilities, Lunga and Zandile would attend.

An interesting discussion occurred at one of these gatherings, centred on tsatsatsa dress code and general physical appearance. Vukani had pointed out during the week before this weekend gathering that matsatsatsa liked to look rich and therefore better than other ordinary people. He also said that this practice contradicted the ANC aim of equality amongst all South Africans because *'abantu abathi balwela ulingano becabanga ukuthi kungcono babengcono kunabanye, ayikho into engalunga'* (if people who claim to be fighting for equality [like you matsatsatsa] still think in terms of looking better than others, then nothing will ever change). (After this criticism, Sizwe and Lunga distanced themselves from Vukani for some time). Vukani's criticism had been based on the fact that matsatsatsa liked to wear gold chains that were, according to him, an unnecessary expense. During this informal gathering, I reintroduced this topic and it sparked off an interesting discussion.

In general, Thulile agreed with Vukani, and spoke about other practices that went against the ideologies that tsatsatsa stood for. For example, she mentioned that Sizwe and Lunga continuously dictated to her what she should look like, and yet they spoke about gender equity. Lunga at this juncture became defensive and reminded Thulile of the things he had done that indicated that he was for women's lib. He recounted some things which included how they (tsatsatsa men) never asked her to cook for the group if the gathering took place in her home but instead cooked together with her, how he had approached Zandile for a job while his boss had asked him to look for a boy, and so on. Concluding his defence, Lunga asked Thulile if she really agreed with Vukani's idea that they wanted to look better than other people. Thulile stated that she agreed with Vukani when he said that their dress code contradicted the whole notion of equality. Sizwe then jumped in and stated *'wo wena ufuna sibukeke siwoZulu njengoVukani'* (Oh you want us to look Zulu just like Vukani). Thulile asked for clarification. Sizwe responded, *'Cabanga: uma uthatha uVukani umkhumule ibhulukwe, umfake ibheshu, umphathise iwisa, awutholi uZulu Zu?'* (Think about it: if you take off Vukani's pair of trousers, put him in an *ibheshu* [a traditional dress for men made out of cow skin], and give him a knobkerrie, don't you get a true Zulu [Zulu Zu]?) We all laughed.

Vukani was derogatorily said to be Zulu Zu, a phrase that matsatsatsa usually used positively to define themselves. It is difficult to actually say what it was with Vukani that made Sizwe come to such a conclusion, which suggested that to be Zulu is biologically/physically inherent since, if put in traditional gear, some individuals were likely to look more Zulu than others. It is possible that matsatsatsa interpreted Vukani's criticism to mean that he was old-fashioned, backward, categories that were negatively associated with being Zulu. It is also possible that in this episode, being Zulu referred to those people who challenged matsatsatsa, such as Vukani. This means that a possibility exists that labelling Vukani as Zulu Zu negatively was not necessarily because he was backward, but because he was in most cases critical of, or in opposition to, the practices of inner-core tsatsatsa. Such conversations, however, could have only occurred in an informal setting, and in the presence of people who shared the same views.[9]

Public Group Outings

The language of tsatsatsa was Zulu. In informal and formal discussions that I had with matsatsatsa, they were very articulate in the use of Zulu as their language of communication. On one occasion Sizwe and Vukani were in the vicinity of the area in which I worked, and decided to drop by my office to see if I was there. On entering the department, they had to go past the secretary who was a white English speaker to find out the location of my office. After exchanging greetings with me, they commented, 'sesifike saba amaNgisi phela lapha sikubuza' (we have just been English [people] over there asking for you). To tsatsatsa there was often no difference between speaking a language and becoming that language. For example, on some of the occasions tsatsatsa teased Thulile about how she had pretended not to hear them when they called out for her in a music concert that she had attended with Zee, her white girlfriend. Muzi teased her, 'abengasizwa yini esewumLungu nje' (How could she have heard us as she was being white [by walking and speaking with a white person]). Another space where using English was often interpreted as becoming English was at the white-dominated sports centre that Lunga frequented. On some occasions, Lunga would ask Sizwe to accompany him there and in most cases Sizwe agreed because he was also interested in weight-lifting. On one occasion, Sizwe refused and stated, '*into ehluphayo laphana ukuthi umuntu ufike abe wumlungu ekhulu-mana nesiNgisi. Ungathi ngeke ngilunge impela*' (The problem with that place is that we become Englishmen speaking English. I can't be like that today). Since this club was dominated by white people, often Sizwe and Lunga found themselves having to socialize in English, a practice that they avoided because they did not like nor felt comfortable in.

Being or becoming a language user varied among languages. A person was most likely to 'become' Zulu (wuZulu) by merely using Zulu, and white (uMlungu) by using English. However, this did not apply to the use of Afrikaans. Of the twelve participants who chose Afrikaans as a national language, four came from the six tsatsatsa participants in the study. Their reason was an economic one. Indeed in the playground where there was no authority figure, tsatsatsa participants used Zulu and Afrikaans while many others would use Zulu alone, or Zulu and, if need be, English. Tsatsatsa participants made conscious efforts to practise Afrikaans because one of them (Sizwe) had not been promoted at his work because he did not speak good Afrikaans to the customers. But in their use of Afrikaans, matsatsatsa did not see themselves as Afrikaners in the way as they viewed themselves English whenever they used the English language. Vukani, however, was against the reasons behind tsatsatsa use of Afrikaans and referred to it as an 'unhealthy hidden agenda.' He argued that giving the Afrikaners what they wanted – learning their language – was equivalent to submitting to their rule; it was like submitting to defeat. But when asked by Sizwe what his way out would be in such situations, Vukani did not have a solution, only that he would rather leave that job if he had been by-passed like that.

In some of their outings, tsatsatsa had to monitor the way they spoke to each other, depending on what they were saying and also on the people around them. For example, to call someone Zulu got different interpretations that were dependent on the context under which the statement was uttered. Also, to categorize and negatively refer to one as Zulu did not present a problem at all if uttered by a speaker belonging to the same group. Tsatsatsa participants, for example, used this same phrase while talking to each other. On one occasion, I accompanied Vukani, Sizwe, and Zandile to the theatre to watch the movie *Malcolm X*. At the end of the day we took the bus back to Umlazi and continued our discussion about the movie. At the beginning of the movie, there is a part where the unconverted Malcolm X uses a hair product to perm his hair, which had to be washed out as soon as it started to burn. At the time of Malcolm's arrest, police found him with his head in the toilet

bowl trying to wash out the chemical from his hair because he had discovered too late that there was no water in the building. We were laughing and joking about this scene when Sizwe wanted to know what it was
that Malcolm X had put on his hair that made him go so crazy (I suspect
that the reason Sizwe did not know about this hair product was because
tsatsatsa was against the use of chemical products that changed the physical look of black people). Zandile responded to Sizwe's question by saying *'awukahle wena Sizwe ukuba wuZulu'* (Stop being Zulu/[backward,
ignorant], Sizwe). Sizwe did not respond to Zandile's comment but simply insisted on a response to his question. *'Ubani ozochazela loZulu'* (Who
is going to explain to this Zulu?) Zandile joked. Vukani explained to
Sizwe about the chemical, but ended his explanation by saying *'uyezwa-ke
Zulu?'* (Is it clear now Zulu? [backward or ignorant one?]) An elderly
woman sitting on the seat in front of us, next to Zandile (the three of us
were in the back seat), who obviously had been following the conversation, turned around and asked, *'awukahle mntanami, yini engalunganga
ekubeni wuZulu?'* (Wait a minute my child, what's wrong with being
Zulu?). The conversation ended.

Within this context, the use of 'wuZulu' means exactly the same thing
as 'NgoZulu' used by the multiracial school goers in the bus ('wu' is the
singular, 'ngo' the plural). But such uses within groups were accepted.
Put together, then, the school bus and the movie examples express a
certain interpretation and explain the manner in which this interpretation was linked to conventional stylistic connotations. These examples
also speak to the variation between intragroup and intergroup interaction. That is, conversations that took place between groups, such as matsatsatsa and the multiracial school students, differed from those that
occurred within matsatsatsa as a group. It is the knowledge of cultural
spaces, the ability to employ conversational tools that were always important at this stage. Such conversational tools were, nevertheless, expres-
sions of the symbolic power between the languages Zulu and English,
and sometimes between the speakers involved in interaction. For
instance, in the bus, the use of English was an indicator of the status
associated with it as a language of education and commerce. Zulu, on
the other hand, was given a subordinate position there. This analysis
also introduces us to the new class of elites that was being formed even
before the democratic process was implemented. Yet tsatsatsa practice
in the bus, of demonstrating that they too were educated, also indicates
that the practice of using English to construct relations of power and
subordination within groups did not go unchallenged.

That tsatsatsa use Zulu, however, did not stop members from regarding negatively people who used the very same Zulu language. I mentioned before that tsatsatsa was usually compared with mpansula and that while there were not many differentiating characteristics, language and specifically the Zulu language was a clear distinguishing feature. One of the responses I was given by Lunga concerning differences between tsatsatsa and mpansula was that *'amampansula angoZulu'* (mampansula are Zulu/[backward/conservative]). This time the use of this phrase was ambiguous to me so I asked for clarification. I was given linguistic examples that elucidated what the group was saying. For example, I was told that the language of mampansula is tsotsi, but that tsotsi is dominated by Zulu, and not just Zulu, but 'old' Zulu. Lunga also gave me another example: *'amampansula athi leli elikaBhodwe noMthaniya'*: mampansula refer to KwaZulu/Natal as the land of Bhodwe and Mthaniya – names used by Zulu people during the Shepstone era. Again, this is an example of how Zulu was given different interpretations, dependent on context, place, and the people involved. For instance, while Lunga and Sizwe took pride in the use of the Zulu language, they were critical of its use by mampansula, and also of the variety of Zulu that mampansula chose to adopt.

Such practices within social groups further indicated the differences between groups, especially those marked by political ideologies. As noted in the Malcolm X example, tsatsatsa was against the use of chemical products that change the physical look of black people, even at the same time proclaiming to be in favour of 'adapting to modern times.' This anti-chemical practice was borrowed more from the teachings of the BCM than from those of the ANC, yet tsatsatsa never acknowledged that there were similarities between it and mpansula. The manner in which mpansula used Zulu was in a way similar to the way tsatsatsa did not use chemical products. That is, both practices were motivated by a desire to stay within the old way of doing things. Put differently, both tsatsatsa and mpansula shared a common interest which centred on the desire to maintain that which is African and uncontaminated by modern practice. To mpansula, this was expressed in the desire to preserve the Zulu language and to tsatsatsa, it was safeguarding the 'African body.' However, these groups did not acknowledge these similarities, and those that did were stigmatized. Pushed further, this analysis could be applied to the differences and hostility that existed between political parties (in this case, the ANC and the PAC), which refused to look at the similarities among themselves but instead focused on the differences which were used as sources for conflict.

Individual Practices

Tsatsatsa participants were also involved in a number of places where they participated as individuals without the presence of other matsatsatsa. Such spaces included the homes, workplaces, and sometimes recreational activities. In order to get a sense of what matsatsatsa did as individuals, an examination of Lunga's practices illuminates the tension between Zulu culture and modern practices and further demonstrates the contradictions in associating social practices with those of political organizations.

Lunga

Lunga was just beginning to build a family life for himself. At the time of the study, Lunga had started living with his grandparents, his late mother's parents. He shared a four-room township house with seven other family members – an uncle, two aunts, two cousins, and the two grandparents. Lunga and his two aunts were the ones with jobs and it was their incomes that supported the family. Lunga's grandfather was a retired baker and his grandmother used to work as a domestic for a white family. His uncle was unemployed and his two cousins attended secondary school.

Lunga had certain tasks in the home, which he did after school and on weekends. During the week, the vegetable garden was Lunga's main responsibility. He and his uncle were also responsible for the general cleanliness of the house. On Friday afternoons and Saturday mornings until 1 o'clock, Lunga went to work at Pick'n Pay. On some Saturday afternoons, he had to meet with one or both of his aunts (all three of them worked in the city centre) and assist with grocery shopping, and with carrying the groceries home. During those afternoons when there was no grocery shopping to be done or when his aunts thought they could manage on their own, Lunga stayed in the city and went to a sports club to lift weights. Sunday afternoons he went to a movie at the Wheel or just hung out there with friends.

Work

Lunga's job was physically demanding because he had to pack groceries onto a cart, push them out to the customer's car, and unload them from the cart into the car. At the time of this study Lunga had been working at this place for almost eighteen months and had thus established relations with some of the customers who were regulars in the shop. During the times that I went to observe Lunga, I would just stand at the end of the shop and keep a distance between him and the cashier because I did not want to create a situation where one of them would feel that I was policing them. I observed the interactions between Lunga and the customers and also between him and the people he worked with. Generally, it was difficult to hear what was said in these interactions, but sometimes I would hear a few things. When the store was not busy, I would chat with Lunga, and as I got used to the people he worked with, I also had conversations with them. These discussions were only of a general nature, about where we lived, our families, jobs, and finances, and sometimes about the then anticipated elections.

Many of the cashiers that Lunga worked with were women, and most were older than him. So it was usual for Lunga to spend some of his time at work fulfilling the cashiers' requests, which were not part of his job, but as he was younger than they were, he was not in a position to object. These requests came not only from the cashier whose customers Lunga was to pack for, but from other cashiers as well. For example, one day I overheard a cashier calling out to Lunga, 'Awungisize lapha ndodana ungicelele ushintshi lapha ehovisi uma usuqedile' (Help me here my son; when you finish please go get some coins for me from the office). Another time I overheard another cashier saying 'Usize ndodana ungiphosele lencwadi esigxhotsheni ngelantshi yakho' (Don't forget my son to go and post this letter for me during your lunch hour). On some occasions I heard Lunga's cashier protesting on his behalf, telling another cashier that he should ask his own second packer to go get coins for her, and added 'ungathi ngoba lomfana uyahlonipha bese nimgqhilaza' (just because this boy is respectful does not mean you should enslave him). The other cashier agreed that they were actually too demanding of Lunga.

In general, Lunga was viewed as a respectful, reliable, and trustworthy individual by his co-workers as well as his bosses. During an interview, I asked Lunga why he never protested the way the other cashiers overworked him or even refused to do what they asked even though it was not part of his job. He responded by saying, 'Empeleni ukuthi ngiyazi ukuthi bangithuma ngoba bengethemba. Futhi bangithatha njengengane yabo. Uyabona ukuba nalababanye abafana bayahlonipha ngabe bayabathuma. Akungoba befuna ukungigqhilaza. Angijwayele ukwenqaba kanti lababanye abahloniphi. Bavele babatshele nje ukuthi abazenzele bona. Abasazi IsiZulu.'

(In reality it is because I know that they ask me to do things for them because they trust me, and they treat me like their own children. The other boys I work with usually tell them to go do these things for themselves. I think that's disrespectful. So I know that they ask me to do things for them not because they are being unfair. It's because the others don't know Zulu [culture]).

During this same interview I also asked him about something that I had observed during the times I visited him: that most of the customers he established relations with were whites, despite the fact that the shop had customers from all races. When I asked the reason he said:

Lunga: *Uyabona sisi Nombuso, abelungu bayakwazi ukukubonga ngemali. Noma bazi ukuthi umsebenzi wakho lona bayakwazi ukuthi unezidingo. Kanti oZulu laba bavele bathi 'siyabonga mntanami' kube kuphela. Kubona abangiboni ngiwumsebenzi. Bangibona njengengane yabo abayithumayo.*
You see sisi Nombuso white people know how to appreciate your efforts with money. (This doesn't translate very well.) Even though they know that this is my job they realize that I have needs. Zulus on the other hand just say 'thank you my child' and that's all. To them I am like their child and not an employee.

Nombuso: *Mhlawumbe yingoba bengenayo imali....*
Maybe they don't have the money ... (Lunga jumped in before I could finish the statement.)

Lunga: *Awu kahle wena sisi Nombuso, ukhona umuntu ongenayo u 50cents?*
Wait sisi Nombuso, do you know a person who doesn't have 50 cents?

Nombuso: *Kulungileke mhlawumbe yingoba kungelona usiko ukwenzenjalo.*
I agree with you there, but maybe it's because it's not cultural [in Zulu] to do so.

Lunga: *Ukuthi akulona usiko akusho ukuthi asingacabangelani.*
That this is not in our culture does not mean we should not be understanding of each other's situation.

Nombuso: *Benzenjani kulabafana bamaNdiya osebenza nabo?*
What do they do to the other Indian boys [packers] you work with?

Lunga: *Angazi. Angikaze nginake. Into engiyaziyo ukuthi siyesibange abelungu sonke ngoba siyazi ukuthi sizothola imali. Yikhonje kusemqoka ukuthi nginabami engizwana nabo.*
I don't know. I haven't noticed. What I know is that we [packers] usually compete for white customers because we know we will get some money. That is why it's important that I have established relations with specific customers.

What appeared to be contradictions in Lunga's attitude was actually a result of the blending of two social practices: one based on European ways of doing things such as to tip; and the other based on Zulu social practices of hlonipha. It is clear that his women co-workers viewed Lunga as indodana, a son, and that he understood and embraced this position. In Zulu, mothers have authority over their sons, and can give them orders that they expect to be carried out without questions. Lunga complied with this practice even if it sometimes put him at a disadvantage, that is, being overworked. In instances where the authority that mothers exert over their sons is overused, it is not the son that complains, but other adult members of the family. In Lunga's case, it was his cashier who came to his defence by playing the role of an adult member of the 'cashier family.'

A complexity emerged when Zulu cultural practices intersected with practices of wage labour. It is unclear why exactly black people did not tip Lunga, or if they tipped packers at all. It is possible that to them, Lunga was doing something that he would do anyway (he would assist carry their purchase because of the Zulu tradition of hlonipha abadala, respect for adults). What added complication to this already diverse practice was that, since the shop specialized in household things, most of its customers were adults. When the shop was busy and there were not enough second packers, priority was given to older people because of the Zulu tradition of hlonipha. This practice then presented Lunga's job as 'helping' the adults rather than just doing a job. Lunga's analysis of the two situations also indicates the ambiguity faced by individuals trying to negotiate between Zulu cultural practices and those of urbanization and commerce. On the one hand, he appeared to be suggesting that this was done because black customers viewed him as *mntanami*, their child, a practice that he understood and accepted when enacted by the cashiers; on the other hand, he seemed to have been saying that this was done because of a failure to see things beyond cultural practices. Lunga's situation demonstrates the challenges placed on Zulu cultural practices by politics, labour conditions, and western customs. Lunga's difficulties also illuminate the problems individuals encountered in attempts to reconcile old Zulu ways with new ways of being that were shaped by western practices.

Sports
Lunga belonged to a sports club to which he was introduced by a friend and boss, Nick. Usually Lunga and Nick went to the club

together, or sometimes made arrangements to meet there. As a member of the club, Lunga could bring a guest once a month to use the sports facilities. Lunga had been a member of the club for about a year and he was a familiar face to most people who frequented the place. This sports centre was, however, dominated by white people, and from my observations I would estimate that over 90 percent of the people who went there were white. My introduction to the club and its members was as Lunga's friend, and I was able to use some of the facilities whenever I was there without having to pay a membership fee. In most cases I went there just to hang out and talk with Lunga, but in some instances I participated in aerobic classes while waiting for Lunga to finish what he was doing. Besides the times I participated in aerobic classes, I was never in the club for more than an hour at a time; hanging out, watching mainly men lift weights in a sports centre was not the best adventure.

From my observations, Lunga seemed to have good relations with other club members and all communication took place in English. This happened even if other tsatsatsa members like Sizwe joined Lunga. When I asked Lunga why he and Sizwe did not use Zulu in the club, he told me that they didn't want to alienate the people around them. Nick and Lunga also communicated in English, just as they did at Pick'n Pay. All my visits to this sports centre were prearranged with Lunga, because I could not enter the club unless I was a member or a guest of a member. Sometimes I would go there with Lunga, and in some cases, would arrange to meet with him there. On those time when we did not go together, we arranged that Lunga wait for me at the reception desk just to ensure that I did not have problems getting in.

On one occasion, I went in to find Lunga and Nick at the reception desk teasing each other about who was stronger, and basing their judgment on how much weight they could lift. The receptionist appeared to have been part of this interchange given the attention she was paying to them. So when I entered, Lunga explained to me what all this teasing was about:

Lunga: Actually we lifted the same weight. But I say I am stronger because I did not struggle either, I just lifted it once.
Nick: I didn't struggle too. I just lifted it.
Receptionist: Actually I can believe Lunga [that he lifted it without difficulty] because, do you know Matthew?
We all nodded. (Matthew was the white weight trainer of the centre.)

Receptionist: The other day I asked him to lift for me one of those buckets [points at a bucket] full of water and to fill the water bottle in the weight room. He couldn't. Usually, I ask Agnes [Agnes was the black woman cleaner] and she does it with no difficulty.

Lunga usually maintained his cool and did not easily get worked up, but on this day, he couldn't. He was so angry he couldn't speak. He finally walked out the door and left us looking at each other. I quickly followed and we went to take the bus back to Umlazi. Later, the event was retold to other tsatsatsa some of whom already knew about it because they had spoken to Lunga before this particular day. On this occasion, Lunga explained that he was enraged by the fact that the receptionist was implying that all black people are just strong and good for lifting up things. He was more annoyed by the receptionist's insensitivity towards Agnes's position: he lifted weights because it was fun, while Agnes lifted that bucket because it was work. Lunga argued that by making a comparison between him and Agnes, the receptionist demonstrated her failure to understand Agnes's plight.

Lunga: *Babezomqasha na ukuba wayethe akakwazi ukuqukula amabhakede. Kwesinye isikhathi ngike ngizibuze ukuthi ngiyelani laphana.*
Would they have employed her if she had said she could not lift buckets? Sometimes I ask myself why I go to such places.
Vukani: *Ingempela nina niyelani?*
In reality, why do you all go there?
Sizwe: (forcefully): *Ngoba siyathanda.*
Because we like to.
Nombuso: *Manje awumtshelangangani ukuthi ucabangani ngalento ayishoyo?*
So why didn't you tell her about what you felt about her statement?
Lunga: *Uyazi kwesinye isikhathi kubangathi uchitha isikhathi. Uqalakanjani nje ukuchaza into enje?*
You know sometimes it seems like a waste of time [to explain this because they don't understand]. How do you begin to explain such things anyway?
Vukani: *Kungoba niyesaba. Nincenga ukuthi uma nibatshela nizongangena lapha ekilabhini.*
It is because you fear that they won't allow you back into the club if you challenge them.
(There was a minute of silence and then Thulile spoke.)

Thulile: *Abelungu bavamile ukwenza njalo. Nalapha kusebenza khona uanti, ngiyengibone nje ukuthi cha abameabangeli.*
It is common for white people to do such things. Even at my aunt's work place, I often observe how inconsiderate they are to her ...

Thulile then went on to relate some of her observations of the way her aunt's boss treated her. In the end, however, the conversation came back to Vukani's question: why did tsatsatsa keep going to places where they felt subordinated and powerless? The response was that they liked lifting weights and that they felt they had the right to go there if they wanted to. The underlying question related to the changes that were emerging in social practices. Black people were penetrating into spaces that were originally designed for whites, even though as individuals tsatsatsa sometimes felt powerless to change the nature of these practices, as a group there were things that they were able to do to change the character of the spaces in which they participated.

Language and Other Criteria of Identification

I started by describing the contradictions inherent in defining Zulu identity in KwaZulu/Natal. These definitions came from political organisations such as Inkatha and the ANC, the South African state, and ordinary people. To political organizations, Zulu identity centred on political practices, which came down to supporting one political ideology or the other. Those who supported Inkatha, for example, were expected to talk, dress, and participate in activities that supported Inkatha's ideological practices. Similarly, those who supported the ANC were expected to dress differently, or even talk differently from Inkatha supporters.

Inkatha's emphasis on an autonomous Zulu nation within the South African state had to be legitimized by presenting the Zulu people as internally homogeneous, in contrast to the rest of other black people in the country. Yet within this Zulu group existed differences that could not be ignored. Such differences were a combination of cultural and political practices that challenged Inkatha's methods of representation viewed as undemocratic and autocratic. For the ANC, pluralistic politics became a problem that resulted from the recognition of historic symbols that were used to legitimize the Zulu group. If the ANC acknowledged these symbols as it did, then its practice of pluralistic politics in KwaZulu/Natal was in itself controversial.

Tsatsatsa participants dealt with this controversy through acting out contradictions in identity politics. First, tsatsatsa participants constructed their identities by valuing historic symbols that were mainly associated with Inkatha politics. In cases where these symbols conflicted with the interests of individuals, tsatsatsa simply shifted to other criteria of identification, such as birthplace, which then positioned them as not Zulu. Denying that one was Zulu was nevertheless done in instances where being Zulu positioned one problematically.

Second, besides Zulu history and the symbols associated with it, tsatsatsa were well grounded in Zulu cultural tradition, particularly the tradition of respect for the elders. Lunga's relationship with older female co-workers demonstrates that matsatsatsa still adhered to this practice even though it was sometimes to their disadvantaged. This behaviour contradicted the view that was associated with youths at this time who were seen as showing disrespect not only to the elderly, but also to different symbols of authority. In the *Malcolm X* bus incident, tsatsatsa participants respected the old woman by not talking back to her, thus, enacting performative hlonipha. A typical youth response of the time would have been to tell her to mind her own business.

Third, tsatsatsa participants did not buy into the ANC terminology of 'South Africans' as a way of nationally/ethnically identifying individuals, but continued to refer to themselves as Zulus. In fact, had they referred to themselves as South Africans as the ANC expected them to, they would have been easy to pick up as non-Zulu, therefore, ANC, and by implication, anti-Inkatha.

Fourth, the language choice of tsatsatsa was mostly Zulu. This distinguished tsatsatsa from other youths who used other languages, especially tsotsitaal, to indicate that they were not Zulu, which to them meant rural, backward, or ignorant – all labels that were negatively associated with Inkatha. By using Zulu in key situations, especially in the township of Umlazi, tsatsatsa did not distinguish themselves as different from but, rather, similar to the rest of the other Zulu (Inkatha) people in the township. Furthermore, the way in which tsatsatsa used Zulu demonstrates that despite its associations with being backward, ignorant and being Inkatha, there were many ways in which Zulu was used positively. Tsatsatsa used Zulu to express solidarity, to carry out in-group conversations, and to ask for favours. This use of Zulu demonstrates the contradictions in institutionalized practices of language use, including Afrikaans and English. For example, the ANC had introduced the use of English in its meetings, rallies and demonstrations. Yet in these same political rallies, tsatsatsa used Zulu in the presence of their white friends because a rally was a space that gave them power which could only be enacted through the use of the Zulu language. Schools also had long declared English as the language of education; yet it was clear, for example, that to obtain a favour, one had to ask for it in Zulu. What language and other criteria of identification did was to enable tsatsatsa to legitimize their Zulu identities in different ways. The calling up of a criterion was, however, dependent on the content of what was discussed, the space in which it was discussed, and the people involved in the discussion.

Yet it is important to acknowledge those practices that distinguished tsatsatsa as a group. For instance, Inkatha organized celebrations for Dingane's Day at the time of data collection. Matsatsatsa did not go to this event, which was scheduled to take place at King's Park, Durban's largest soccer stadium. Instead, matsatsatsa invited me to come with them to listen to a group of white singers, led by a white woman, C.J. Powers, but known in Zulu as Thandeka (loved one), because this group 'sang Zulu songs that documented Zulu history and struggles.' By refusing to attend the celebration at King's Park stadium, matsatsatsa were defying Inkatha law. It is, however, not clear how defiant tsatsatsa were because they celebrated this event anyway, even though it was at a different space. In fact, it could be argued that at this point tsaksatsa were doing ethnic politics, because of the reasons they gave for going to listen to Thandeka. It is the ambiguity in practices, both in the township and outside the townships that allowed tsatsatsa to live in Umlazi without being viewed by Inkatha as 'the enemy.'

chapter 8

Social Groups: Soccer

Like tsatsatsa, soccer groups need to be understood within the context of the political turmoil that engulfed the townships in the late 1980s and the beginning of the 1990s. The individuals who made up the soccer groups that are the subjects of this study were, like those in tsatsatsa, attempting to deal with hardships characteristic of this period. Also, these individuals used soccer as an activity that presented them as responsible members of the community. There were, however, significant characteristics that made the soccer groups different from tsatsatsa and other groups. One feature that distinguished these groups was the fact that soccer is a leisure activity.

Writing on the notion of leisure time, Turner states that because leisure presupposes 'work,' a non-work or even anti-work phase, it is imbued with two kinds of freedom: 'freedom-from' and 'freedom-to.' Freedom from means that leisure-time 'represents *freedom from* a whole heap of institutional obligations prescribed by the basic forms of social, particularly technology and bureaucratic, organisation.' Freedom from also implies taking time off from 'forced chronologically regulated rhythms of factory and office and a chance to recuperate and enjoy natural biological rhythms again' (1982, 36–7). The second kind of freedom that leisure time enables, 'freedom to,' allows individuals to generate 'new symbolic worlds of entertainment, sport, games, diversion of all kinds. It is, furthermore, *freedom to* transcend social structural limitation, freedom to *play* ...' (p. 37, emphasis in the original). Turner goes on to argue that whilst sport can be hard and be governed by rules and routines that might be even more harsh than those of the work situation, the fact that individuals choose to participate in sport makes games such as soccer a part of an individual's freedom of his/her personal growth. Sport's optional nature makes it enabling. Turner further argues that individuals who participate in leisure activities are not committed by material needs, moral or legal obligation. Instead, leisure activities are chosen because of expected fun and enjoyment and therefore sport is unmotivated by gain and does not have any ideological purpose.

It is this framework that needs to be kept in mind when analysing the nature of soccer as a social space in the township of Umlazi. This chapter discusses the manner in which soccer as a leisure activity enabled certain kinds of social processes to be enacted both communicatively, that is verbally, and performatively. Communicative practices refer to mainly verbal/linguistic behaviour, and performative practices are those that were, in most cases, acted out with minimum or no verbal/linguistic behaviour involved. This chapter describes how something as common as a soccer game was essential to individuals in creating their identities. It describes how soccer enabled individuals to create a space *from* institutional obligations such as those imposed by political organizations and also how it offered, to use Turner's concept, a space *to* transcend social structural limitations through the formation of this space itself as a symbolic world of entertainment. Unlike Turner, however, in this chapter sport is viewed as possessing both utilitarian and ideological purpose. The soccer groups in this study had underlying ideological purposes, and it can be argued that without these purposes these groups would not have existed. The political state of KwaZulu/Natal, which was characterized by intense violence, together with the poverty in the townships and other equally disturbing social features, did not permit a random pursuit of activities, leisure or work, formal or informal. Yet despite structural constraints these soccer groups were able to generate a symbolic world in which they could enact, for example, Zulu practices, even though these were problematically associated with Inkatha. As with tsatsatsa, language played an important role and often ordained the manner in which certain events were enacted verbally and performatively.

Soccer Groups: Their Formation

Soccer is a very popular sport in South Africa's black communities. Small children grow up kicking the ball on the streets, playgrounds, or on any available open space. In the townships, weekends are filled with soccer games, when teams from different units challenge each other.

Soccer groups range from the local, composed of residents of a community, be it a township or a village, to the provincial and the national. Soccer games attract a large number of spectators at all levels. Provincial soccer groups also attract a large number of supporters and financial investors, and often hold social events such as beauty pageants. The groups that concern us here are the local ones that operated in the townships at the time of this study. These groups did not receive any financial backing from the city council nor did they host any social events. In rare cases players moved up to play in provincial teams but most players remained at the local level. The purpose of local soccer groups was mainly for fun and to entertain residents during free time at weekends.

In the late 1980s, during the period of conflict between the UDF and Inkatha, soccer groups were co-opted into political activities in quite interesting ways. Political organizations were aware of the potential of soccer groups to attract a large number of supporters, and they used them to mobilize political support in the townships. The KwaMashu case discussed in chapter four provides an example of co-option of soccer groups by a political organization. To go back a little, KwaMashu soccer groups had been in existence long before the formation of the UDF in 1983. These groups were not associated with Inkatha, which had existed in the region since 1975, but when Inkatha and the UDF started competing for political control over the townships, both organizations looked toward these soccer groups as potential vehicles for recruiting members.

From talking with residents of KwaMashu, it appears that this was more Inkatha's strategy than the UDF's. These residents argued that Inkatha was in a better position to buy-off players because of the funds it received from the KwaZulu government. The soccer players Inkatha recruited were then expected to recruit for Inkatha in the rest of the townships. It caused conflict between different soccer groups in Kwa-Mashu, because some did not want to be involved with Inkatha (or any other organization for that matter). It also caused problems between the newly recruited Inkatha soccer players and many of the rest of the township residents who resented the fact that they were now being forced into joining Inkatha, which meant spending the little amount of money they had on membership fees, participating in Inkatha conferences, and so on. As the players met with resistance, they started using vigilante practices and forcing people to join Inkatha. As time went on, these soccer vigilantes not only recruited members for Inkatha but also

got involved in criminal activities. Later, some members of the now
Inkatha vigilantes formed the group that became known as amasinyora
discussed in chapter five. The end result was that many township soccer
groups disbanded, and local-level soccer was halted in many of the townships around Durban.

The soccer groups in this study, therefore, began years after the formation of amasinyora. However, the imposition of the state of emergency in 1989 restricted the activities of most political organizations
like the UDF, which in turn meant that the on-going violence between
the UDF and Inkatha was reduced. It was at this time that some residents decided to revive soccer for recreation and entertainment. The
formation of soccer groups, especially at Umlazi, was partly an attempt
to divert youth interest from politics, and partly to provide alternatives
for those who were not necessarily interested in party politics. The tendency to participate in party politics out of sheer boredom accelerated
during the UDF era which witnessed the closure of schools, high rates
of unemployment, and so on. The soccer groups whose members participated in this study were developed from an idea of two men, Langa
and Nyanga, who operated with no help from the city council since
they had refused to operate under the umbrella of Inkatha. (I never
understood how it was that these groups were able to function while
others who had refused to pledge loyalty to Inkatha were forced to disband; perhaps they were viewed as not posing any meaningful threat to
Inkatha.)

Soccer groups were more community-based, operating under a broad
structure in which youths of a similar age group were put together to
form a team. At the time of the study there were over twenty teams, all
playing in the only playground in the township, which belonged to one
of the high schools, Menzi. The overriding principle was to get away
from politics; thus the philosophy of these soccer groups was to not
bring politics to the playground.

Akhona Dladla, nicknamed Sugar, serves as an example of the kind of
individual involved in the soccer groups. Sugar lived in Umlazi with his
mother and stepfather. His mother was a nurse and worked at Manzini,
one of Durban's hospital that serviced the black population. His stepfather owned a hairdressing salon in one of the townships. Two years
before the study, Sugar had lived with his grandmother in Sebokeng, a
Johannesburg township. He moved to Umlazi because of the ANC-
Inkatha conflict that was then proliferating in the Transvaal province.

To his mother, Umlazi had reached a relatively peaceful stage resulting from Inkatha's control of the township. Upon his arrival, Sugar and his mother looked for a kind of school that was going to provide him with the best kind of education, outside the township and therefore immune to the political unrest found in the townships. They found one, Greensburg High School: a model A boarding school, with 90 per cent white population and about twenty kilometres outside Umlazi. Sugar's parents preferred that he commute instead of staying in the hostels; it was cheaper that way. Sugar had made a name for himself as a soccer player in the township and spent most of his out-of-school-time in the playground. Soccer as a sport appealed to Sugar as an alternative option to political activities. Having witnessed the conflicts in the Transvaal, Sugar did not want political events to affect his life.

What distinguished Sugar from *matsatsatsa* was his non-participatory stance in formal politics. Sugar also came from what was considered a stable family, residing with at least one biological parent in the household. Usually, in such households, the parents influenced the social activities of their children, and in many ways their choice of, and behaviour in, formal politics. Also, Sugar's economic situation differed from that of *matsatsatsa* in that his parents were financially responsible for his well being, therefore, he did not have to get a part-time job in order to make ends meet. Indeed, when Sugar was asked why he didn't socialize with *matsatsatsa*, he responded by saying, *'Angisona isichaka'* (I am not poor). Thus, Sugar's reason for joining soccer was initially to have a way of spending his free time, not necessarily to look for social and political support as matsatsatsa. However, later this soccer group ended up being more than just an escape from political activities; instead, it helped Sugar understand his experiences of schooling in a white-dominated institution.

Negotiating Identities

As stated, in KwaZulu/Natal, Inkatha had instituted a hegemonic political Zulu culture, which legitimized certain kinds of social practices and devalued others. These practices were used to articulate the struggle against the apartheid state but, more importantly, in the late 1980s and early 1990s they delineated who was Zulu and who was not. In this soccer space, important rules existed that helped negotiate the problems that emerged as a result of the intersection between formal politics and interpersonal politics.

The Code of Silence

One of the rules that operated within this soccer space was the code of silence. Individuals did not talk about who they were, neither did they talk about social activities that occurred outside the playground if it was suspected that such talk would eventually lead to discussions about politics. This code of silence allowed those who might have been involved in political activities to play soccer without fear of being questioned by the other players. However, there were events that could have allowed a discussion around what was going on in the political sphere. For example, it is usual in South Africa for weekends and public holidays to hold soccer games and competitions. Yet during holidays designated for observing Zulu historic events, such as Shaka Day, only activities that marked this event were considered by Inkatha as legitimate. The result was that soccer games were not scheduled on these days. Before the struggle between black groups erupted into violence, those people who did not want to participate in the public celebration of such events would often spend this time off work at a soccer game. This was true of both rural and urban communities. In the 1990s, however, those individuals who did not participate in these celebrations, that were usually organized by Inkatha, had no option but to stay home.

The soccer groups in this study observed such holidays. Nonetheless, because of this code of silence, it was never clear whether they did not schedule games or team practices for such holidays was because they were out celebrating this historic day, or because they did not want to put themselves in a dangerous position of being considered anti-Inkatha. Individuals hardly spoke to each other about events with political overtones. Conversations about political events were censored, and in instances where they emerged, the conversation ended as soon as possible.

For example, on one Saturday afternoon the goalie of the 'under 16' team did not show up to a friendly game against the 'under 14 team.' When he showed up the following Wednesday afternoon, the regular practice day, Langa asked him about his unexplained absence. The goalie explained that his friend's cousin had died and he had accompanied his friend to the funeral. Langa was sympathetic and asked about the cause of death. By this time, five or so other players had gathered around. The goalie replied that the boy had been killed in an Inkatha-ANC conflict in Lamontville. He added this statement by saying *Izinja zoZulu* (Zulu dogs). Another player asked how the killing had occurred, still keeping the terminology of 'Zulu dogs.' At this stage, Langa jumped in and demanded that the practice begin.

Two ambiguities emerge from this example. In the first place, both these players were Zulu, at least by state definition and by descent criterion of identification. However, there appeared an identity shift that was influenced by the non-verbalized political position of these players. It is clear that these players did not consider themselves Zulu at this time; those in the conflict who were on the side of Inkatha got labelled as Zulu dogs, capable of inhuman action; and by inference, those who, like the dead boy, were on the side of the ANC, could not be given the label of Zulu, but rather took a different ethnic label, Xhosa or most likely remained non-ethnic. To these players, the label Zulu became something out there, associated with violent accounts, but not necessarily with them. This means that the ethnic label Zulu was situated in experience rather than having a fixed meaning as the state presented it. Furthermore, the ethnic form of differentiation, situational as it was, was always at play when conflict between political parties erupted.

The second ambiguity is found in Langa's actions. Some players argued (outside the playground, of course) that his move to stop the conversation emanated from his inability to deal with insults directed to the Zulu people; they therefore interpreted this as indication that he was an Inkatha supporter. On the other hand, Langa himself argued that his primary mission was to ensure that no politically motivated conflict occurred in the playground since this would have affected the existence of this space. Censoring conversations that could have resulted in unhealthy political overtones became a strategic way of dealing with controversial political subjects.

Construction of Soccer as a Secure Zulu Space

Another rule that governed the soccer space was centred around valuing Zulu cultural practices, since here most practices were done with a shared understanding that everyone in this space was Zulu. This was so despite the fact that some players like Sugar were of different ethnic heritage. For example, phrases like, 'in Zulu things aren't done that way,' 'we will trounce you like we trounced the Boers [Afrikaners] at Ncome,' 'no that's not Zulu,' and so on, were common phrases that were used and accepted by the players. Teams in competition with each other always used symbolic references to historic wars in which Zulus defeated their colonial opponents. Yet it was never clear whether such references implied a strong attachment to clearly-defined Zulu identity, or whether individuals generally drew on Zulu symbols because they were a readily available resource.

One of the events that happened in this space that speaks to the way Zulu culture and tradition were valued was a trip to the monuments at Dingane's kraal, which were reconstructed to retell the story of the conflict between the Zulu and the Afrikaners. This trip was organized by the two coaches in conjunction with team leaders, and those players who financially could not afford to go were subsidized by those who could. Although I did not participate in the trip, through conversations later I know that the players came back with vivid images of how the Boers massacred the Zulus by employing a laager made from their ox carts. Later, I asked the coaches why it was important that they took a trip to this monumental site. Langa, who observed the code of silence to the letter, responded by saying that it was intended to keep the players busy. When I asked why they did not take players to the beach, for example, he responded by just looking at me. The other coach, Nyanga, responded by stating that it was important for the players to have knowledge of Zulu history. When I asked why this knowledge was important, his response was that it was just simply important.

Despite this tendency to keep silent about political events, or those that would focus on the problems of the association of Zulu culture and Inkatha, there clearly existed a defined manner of doing things within soccer which tended to be 'traditional.' Traditional refers to the way in which people who defined themselves as Zulu, believed, worshipped, and behaved prior to, or even during, the political conflict between groups. This involved, among other things, the manner in which people spoke to each other, dealt with conflict, and also managed relations between individuals within different aspects of life, including family, sport, and other spaces.

Within this soccer culture, hlonipha abadala (respect for adults) was always observed, and soccer players did not conform to the practice of the 1990s in which youth challenged and confronted adults. However, in some instances, a trend of rebellion, or rather challenge to adult authority often surfaced, but it was acted out rather than spoken. For example, since this was the only space available to soccer players, there was always competition between teams for practise time. A trend began to take shape when a team made up of workers between the ages twenty-five and thirty would come and order the youth teams to end their game or to cut short their practice. As the soccer field operated on first-come, first-served basis the youths did not like this and asked the coach to talk to this team. But often the coach was not there, and they would still be bossed off the field whenever the adults appeared. A simple and effective way of resolving this issue would have been for the youth to stand ground and tell the workers off. This, however, many players agreed was too confrontational, *bazositshela ukuthi izingane azikhulumi kanjalo nabantu abadala* (they will remind us that Zulu youngsters don't talk to adults like that), one player concluded. After long deliberations, one player, Lolo, came with a suggestion: *asibakhombise ukuthi lento abayenzayo ayilunganga ngokubabizela eshashalazini* (let's *show* them that they are wrong and challenge them to a game) (my emphasis). In the end it was agreed that the 'under 16' team, the eldest of these teams, would challenge the team of workers to a game. Whoever won was to have unchallenged access to the field for a period of a month. The coach, who, like myself, thought this impractical since these workers were experienced players, agreed to present this proposal to the workers who also, laughingly, agreed. The 'under 16' team won the game.

Another example involves a conversation between myself and Lolo, in the presence of Sugar and the coach Nyanga. I had noticed that whenever there was a meeting, or a need for a meeting, someone would go around the playground informing the players about it. In some cases, when the meeting was of special importance, players who wanted the meeting would discuss it with one or both of the coaches before informing the rest of the players. I had noticed also that the Zulu term used for these meetings was not the common term umhlangano, but rather, the traditional term isigcawu. Generally speaking, umhlangano is a meeting, and isigcawu is an area in traditional societies where the community comes together to talk about important issues, to celebrate certain occasions such as weddings, to prosecute those people who had committed crimes in the society, to perform rituals such the ceremony of the eating of the first fruit, and so on. Thus, isigcawu embraces both space and event, while umhlangano refers only to meetings. On one occasion I asked Lolo why he had used isigcawu instead of umhlangano and he jokingly responded by saying *awukahle ukushaya sengathi isiZulu awusazi* (don't pretend you do not know Zulu). On this particular day, he came with Sugar to inform me that there was a meeting, and the conversation went like this:

Lolo: *sesizoya esigcawini uma beqeda labafana abaphakathi.*
We are going to the isigcawu once this team finishes.

Nombuso: *siyabonga. Awusho futhi, wathi kungani uthi kusesigcawini ungasho ukuthi kusemhlanganweni laphana?*
We thank you. Tell me again, why do you call the place *esigcawini* instead of *emhlanganweni?*
Lolo: *Angithi wathi uyasazi isiZulu wena manje ungibuzelani futhi?*
But didn't you say you know Zulu, why then are you asking me again?
Nombuso: *Ukuthi ngifuna ukwazi ukuthi ukwazi kwami kuliqiniso kangaka-nani.*
It's just because I want to be sure that we have the same knowledge.
Lolo: (Looks at me, opens his mouth, hesitates, and walks away).
Sugar: (follows Lolo, but walks slower than him, and then turns around and says):
Ungamnaki lo. Ukuthi nje akafuni ukwenziwa uZulu.
Don't mind him. It's just that he doesn't want to be made Zulu.

Both examples demonstrate that certain kinds of behaviours were always motivated by a desire to stay within Zulu cultural practices, even though being Zulu as a label was always according to a particular circumstance. In the first example, the young soccer teams wanted to tell the team of workers that what they were doing was not acceptable, but nonetheless saw it important to do so in a non-confrontational way – performative hlonipha. The second example also indicates Lolo's act of hlonipha towards me. My reading of his action was that he didn't want to respond to the question, since he thought I was annoyingly asking him something to which I knew the answer.[1] However, instead of telling me to go to hell, he decided to simply walk away and leave me to work out the meaning of his actions. It is also possible that Lolo interpreted my question as a test of his Zulu cultural knowledge. Yet another interpretation might be that Lolo did not respond to the question because I was asking him to do something that was not done in this space: talk about Zulu culture and other politically related topics. Sugar's statement, which could be interpreted as both an apology on behalf of, and an explanation for his friend's actions, is communicative hlonipha, in that it attempts to eliminate some ambiguity surrounding his friend's actions. All these possible explanations demonstrate that the multiplicity of meanings, the ambiguity of people's actions, partly added to the security of this space. In other words, the code of silence and hlonipha, used either separately or together, worked to create an ambiguity in practices that ultimately made soccer a safe space.
While performative hlonipha often happened because of some dis-

agreement that took place in verbal communication, there were times when the youths chose to use language as a means of challenging adults, as well as expressing their views of how things were, or should have been. That is, there were cases in which youths by their speech challenged the Zulu practice of ukuhlonipha abadala. Yet even the use of language itself, controversial as it was, indirectly suggested a valuing of Zulu culture, as indicated by the following language-based example.

As stated, language was highly reflective in KwaZulu/Natal, marking Inkatha members from ANC members and, by connotation, Zulu from Xhosa respectively. Although this was not a criterion that was used when people were asked directly if they were Zulu, it is one that emerged constantly in discussions about the social and political situation in the region and in South Africa as a whole. Language, the Zulu language in particular as an identity criterion, centred around one's manner of speaking it as well as in the moments which one chose to use it. Moreover, in KwaZulu/Natal, it is easy to identify those for whom Zulu is the first language (ZL1) from those for whom it is not (ZL2). Usually, ZL2 speakers were migrants from other parts of the country or even from neighbouring countries. Because Zulu is dominant in the area, newcomers were usually the ones who learn the language of the region; however, in most cases, their first language influences their Zulu. As a result, it is easy to identify, by just listening to the speaker, whether that person is of Zulu, Xhosa, Sotho, Tswana, or Mpondo heritage.

An unusual but illustrative example is an exchange that occurred between two ZL2 speakers of Tswana heritage, one an ANC representative called Zamo, and the other the soccer player, Sugar. (The ANC representative was introduced as a community organizer, so no one was aware of his true identity until the end of the meeting. I only learned about his ANC identity when I bumped into him at an ANC meeting to which a different participant invited me.) Sugar had migrated to Umlazi from Sebokeng in the Transvaal two years before this study commenced. The ANC representative, on the other hand, had just come into the region from Soweto (also in the Transvaal) to invite members of Sugar's soccer team to Soweto to play against a team 'of similar origins and principles.' But from 1992 onwards, Soweto and indeed the whole Transvaal province, witnessed outbreaks of ANC/Inkatha conflicts, which resulted in the well-documented hostel killings. Zamo spoke English to the group, I suspect because he didn't know much Zulu, but Sugar addressed Zamo (and the group) in Zulu:

Sugar: *Ho yonke lento eyenzeka emahositela sazi ngani ukuthi labantu ngeke babone abanye nje oZulu bese besihlasela?*
Given what's happening in the hostels, how do we know that this other team and people around won't see just another bunch of Zulu people and attack us?

Zamo: They won't. We have spoken to the group in Soweto just like I am speaking to you ... But I don't think *you* should worry because nobody can identify you that way (meaning, as Zulu).

Sugar: *Ngiwuyena.*
But I am.

Zamo: You are not. Listen to you (listen to the way you speak Zulu).

Sugar: *Akusho lutho lokho, wonke umuntu la ungibona nginjengaye.*
That doesn't matter, everybody sees me here as the same.

Zamo (in Tswana): *Ha lona taba batho kaofela ba mponake le ke moZulu*
Maybe, but in future, you will be asked, where did you come from? / how are you Zulu?

Sugar: (looks at Zamo, and keeps quiet).

It is ironic that an invitation that had been aimed at promoting inter-group relations and narrowing down group conflict, ethnic or other-wise, ended up doing the direct opposite. By telling Sugar that he was not identifiable as Zulu within a group of ZL1 speakers, Zamo singled him out of a group that he cherished, and Sugar's attempts at holding on to his Zulu identity finally got annihilated when he realized that, in fact, the category of descent did single him out as non-Zulu. It is, how-ever, unclear how alienated Sugar was in this incident because his final action of keeping quiet could be interpreted as performative hlonipha. That is, it is possible that Sugar simply kept quiet not because he felt alienated, but mainly because he wanted Zamo to figure out for himself the meaning of his silence. Put differently, it is possible that Sugar was in actual fact saying to Zamo, 'If you want to think that way, go ahead, but I don't agree. At the same time I don't want to argue with you because you are an adult.'

If, however, we eliminate this latter possible interpretation (of hlo-nipha), it is possible to argue that in this example, language did two things. First, by changing from English to the use of Tswana, Zamo was able to claim Sugar away from his Zulu friends to his ethnic Tswana identity through reminding him of the importance of birthplace and descent as criteria of identification. Second, Sugar's use of Zulu positioned him as one of the group. That is, within the group, Sugar was accepted as Zulu, even though he spoke Zulu with a Tswana accent, because of the moments he chose to use Zulu in a situation where for him, Tswana (also spoken by Zamo) or English would have been equally appropriate. It appears within this case that Sugar was accepted performatively as Zulu; that his use of Zulu allowed him to participate and be part of a group that would have otherwise excluded him. That his peers did not identify Sugar as Tswana was demonstrated to me the first time I went to observe him. When I was finally able to locate him, it was through someone who said *Usho lo ongasazi kahle isiZulu* (you mean the one who doesn't know Zulu very well). A typical rhetoric of the time would have been 'you mean that Tswana,' since ethnicity had been greatly elaborated in both popular and political Zulu or South African tradition. There is more to be learned from this example than language choice and group solidarity. It also speaks to the contradictions that faced individuals who attempted to cross over ethnic and linguistic boundaries and to the controversial nature of the use of (Zulu) language as both exclusive and inclusive.

The negotiation of identities within soccer could be said to have relied on two important functions. First was the complexity of what being Zulu really meant. This ambiguity enabled individuals to engage in certain performances and also to disassociate themselves from others. All practices, however, fell under the ambiguous category of Zulu. Individuals agreed to participate in functions that positioned them positively as Zulu, even if these practices might have been challenging authorized notions of Zuluness. At the same time, people were quick to disassociate themselves from the label Zulu if, according to 'group standards,' it carried with it unacceptable practices. What I refer to as group standards was also unclear, resulting from the censorship of political conversations in this space. The negotiation of identities then, related a lot to the way in which individuals agreed not to clarify or talk about what was meant by the label Zulu, especially its political connotations.

Individuals were also able to negotiate their identities through drawing on their linguistic repertoires, which made it possible for them to form intimate relations across the ethnic boundary, as demonstrated by Sugar's example. Nonetheless, even those who successfully crossed over this boundary, were at times forced to contend with difficulties in which culture and politics intertwined.

Language Use and Symbolic Power

Most studies that investigate language use in South Africa focus on the actions of policy-makers and language planners (see, for example, Cluver 1992; Weinstein 1980). Language planners in South Africa traditionally focused on three kinds of data: studies of language attitudes; the number of speakers for each language, and the status and level of development of various languages. During the transitional period during which this study was conducted, language attitudes were evolving as political changes were introduced and an envisioned democratic state was fast approaching. There were probably changes in other social spheres, such as in language use, but this could not be confirmed by any data at that time. I have already demonstrated, for instance, that tsatsatsa practices and attitudes towards the learning and use of Afrikaans, and its choice as a national language of South Africa, contradicted the ANC and international notion that youths held negative attitudes towards this language. In this section, I further develop the controversial yet undocumented use of Afrikaans in informal domains during this period, and argue that this use verified existing power relations within and between groups, as well as attitude changes towards this language. Soccer groups were no exception to this controversial practice.

Cluver documents the manner in which the Afrikaans-speaking group monopolized political power and determined that their language would be an important cultural resource. The development of Afrikaner symbols as South Africa's official national symbols was done through language planning, which confirmed the reality of racial separation into ethno-linguistic groups. Cluver (1992, p. 106) cites the years 1806 to 1976 as those which witnessed different attempts to standardize, elaborate, and spread Afrikaans. These attempts were enacted with the exclusion of black groups, and against the backdrop of continued liberation struggles. The victory of Afrikaans as the official language took form when the Nationalist Party came to power in 1948. The Afrikaners formed the basis of this party, whose identity was forged through the promotion of the Afrikaans speakers as belonging to a distinct ethnic group.

By 1992 Afrikaans, along with English, had long enjoyed the status of a national language. By this time also, both Afrikaans and English had become the language through which black South Africans had to earn their living, since most of the work opportunities were either in white areas or were controlled by whites. The history of the Boers as owners of most farmland in the region gave them a powerful base from which to exercise power. However, because of its association with apartheid and its loathed policies of oppression, together with its association with the Afrikaans-speaking government's brutal repression of the 1976 students' uprisings, Afrikaans did not enjoy the same status as English. Afrikaans, as a language, came to be associated with command and domination. Similarly, individuals who wanted to demonstrate their power over others often drew on this symbolic value of Afrikaans. In the soccer groups, Afrikaans was used to issue instructions and commands such as, 'move fast,' 'run this side,' and so on. Furthermore, Afrikaans was often used to put others down, as illustrated by the following example:

At the end of a game, one observer (Lolo) started a conversation with one of the players (Dumi) who was fresh from the game. Dumi's team had been defeated by a score of 2–0 and Lolo was teasing Dumi about this in Afrikaans:

Lolo: *Het julle nog geklop.*
They really beat you.
(Dumi ignores Lolo.)
Lolo: *Jy wass soos 'n gans agter hulle aan.*
You were like ducks following behind them.
Dumi: *Vir wie roep jy 'n?*
Who are you calling a duck?

Lolo: Jy. *Hulle het die joos uit julle geklop.*
You. They really beat the hell out of you.
Dumi (approaches Lolo angrily): *Hou nie daarvan dat jy my 'n gans roep nie.*
I don't like being called a duck.
Langa (coach in Zulu): *Kahleni phela. Yini? Kwenzenjani?*
Hold on. What's happening? What is it?
Lolo (also in Zulu): *Angithi yilo akafuni simdlalise. Uzenza ingane yomlungu.*
It's this one. He doesn't understand a joke. He's acting like a white child.

The use of Afrikaans to put others down, especially to talk about failure, was typical of these soccer groups. Upon being asked for an explanation, they stated that the person being put down *uzwa kangcono* (hears it better) if told in Afrikaans. In the above example, it is clear that Dumi is annoyed by Lolo's comments. Whether his response was instigated by the use of Afrikaans, or by the fact that he had been defeated, or both, is not clear. However, even in normal conversations, when individuals were just talking about past soccer events, Afrikaans was used to refer to groups that had been defeated. Zulu, on the other hand, was used to level conflicts, as in the example above. Interestingly, even Lolo himself switches to Zulu to describe to the coach what was happening. Furthermore, he equates Dumi's response to his comments as being *umlungu* and by implication not black.[2]

One interpretation of why Afrikaans was used to put others down was suggested by a friend and colleague, Nhlanhla Nkosi, who argued that there was a connection between Afrikaans and the Zulu-Boer wars in which the Boers took over patches of fertile Zulu land. To support his argument, he retold the popular story in which Dingane, Shaka's brother and successor, devised a plan of getting rid of the Boers who were bothersome and took vast lands for themselves. In this plan, Dingane tricked the Boers into thinking that he was preparing a feast for them. When over twenty Boers were settled in Dingane's kraal drinking traditional Zulu beer, Dingane excused himself and left the visitors with some of his advisors and counsellors. Outside the kraal, Dingane shouted the Zulu war cry *'bulala abathakathi'* (kill the witches). The Zulus took their spears from underneath the cow dung on which they were sitting and killed the visitors. Only two of the twenty some escaped, and none of the Zulus were hurt or killed because, in traditional Zulu practice, visitors were not allowed to enter this sacred place with weapons of any kind. Although the Zulus claimed victory in this conflict, the Boers produced a controversial leather script, which they claimed Dingane had signed during the gathering, giving them ownership of parts of northern Zululand. The Boers claim that this script was signed before the killing took place, and that other Boers who later came to avenge the death of their fellow men retrieved it from the kraal. From this story, it can be deduced that although the Zulus claimed initial victory, theirs was a greater land loss. What made this loss greater than that of the Boers is that the Zulus were the ones who initiated a murder plot which initially worked, but which later cost them a fortune. Although this story is commonly told in oral history, it is one that emphasizes heartfelt defeat, and provokes images of powerlessness that the Zulu found themselves in.

Such an event of defeat and powerlessness produced an equation of

Boer equals powerful, Zulu equates with powerlessness, Afrikaans equals power and Zulu equates with defeat. Nhlanhla argued that these images, if carried to the playground, could provoke violent responses from those upon whom they are used. Although this is a convincing and well-argued suggestion, because of the code of silence, it was difficult for me to find out how much knowledge of this Zulu history these players possessed and how much got provoked in such social situations. However, if we consider such trips as the one to Dingane's kraal mentioned earlier, it is possible to conclude that these players did possess a meaningful amount of this history. Moreover, it can be deduced from the history of Afrikaans presented earlier, that in soccer, Afrikaans was a language of domination used metaphorically to express relations of power.

It is important to note, however, that the way the soccer groups used language differed from the way it was used by tsatsatsa. This was so because soccer operated mainly as a sealed Zulu space in which the possible interpretation of 'selling-out-to-the-master' (as Vukani had suggested with tsatsatsa) had been already ruled out. That is, despite the refusal to talk about social practices that made soccer possible, it is clear that it was centred mainly on valued Zulu practices, which made it possible for players to use Afrikaans without it being thought of as 'want-to-be Afrikaners.' Yet sealed as this spaced was, individuals had to leave and deal with the outside world, which did not necessarily value being Zulu, as was the case in this space. One of these places was the school.

Soccer and Schooling

As with tsatsatsa, education was the one valued resource which individuals believed could give them social mobility. In soccer, focus was given to people who wanted to use this space to understand their educational experiences. When waiting to start practice, players often spoke about what went on in their schools and classrooms, and they often sought advice and ideas regarding schooling from their coaches. It is important to remember that, unlike tsatsatsa, soccer was made up of individuals from varying class backgrounds. For example, some, like Sugar, came from an upper working-class background and attended a multiracial school, not a township one. The discussion here centres on the experience of individuals who attended model C schools, which were normally viewed as white schools and therefore better than township ones. This is the focus for two reasons. First, a sample of individuals' experiences in the township schools has already been provided through a look at tsat-satsa. Second, the experiences of individuals in the model C schools provide ideas about changes that were taking place during this period, and how these changes were experienced through schooling in previously white-defined institutions. A look at these schools, therefore, provides us with a glimpse of life in a post-apartheid situation. To develop the notion of schooling in white institutions, and the value attached to this practice, I focus on Sugar's school experiences at Greensburg High. I also look at language as a way in which schooling was experienced, and how schools assigned different values to languages as a way of assigning value to people's academic knowledge.

Language, Schooling, and Success

Language practices at Greensburg High School differed significantly from those of Umganga. The reasons for this difference were social as well as political. Greensburg is a boy's boarding school, located in one of the white suburbs that surround the city of Durban. Unlike Umganga, Greensburg is located away from the townships where political violence and economic poverty are the basic characteristics. It is known as one of the best schools in the province, admitting only those students who have excellent academic credentials. Up until 1992, Greensburg was identified as a white school, admitting only students of European heritage. By the time of the study, however, Greensburg was bending to the political reforms that were characteristic of South Africa's transformation period. Places that had been previously designated for whites only were now being opened to other racial groups, and this included academic institutions. Therefore, at the time of the study, Greensburg's student population was 80 per cent white and 20 per cent black, Indian, coloured (people of mixed races), and Chinese. The teaching staff, however, was still all white and the maintenance staff was all black. The language of instruction at Greensburg was English, and as the principal put it, 'many parents say they bring their children here to learn English. I tell them that we do not teach English at Greensburg, we learn in English.'

Greensburg was looked upon as one place where social mobility could be fostered because, unlike most township schools, Greensburg had no history of boycotts and a reputation of a high matric (the last grade before postsecondary education) passing rate. Yet two crucial factors were always at play at Greensburg. First, black parents who enrolled their children in this school had to deal with what Achebe (1988) called 'the unassailable position of English.' On the other hand, by opening the school to other racial groups, particularly to blacks, Greensburg authorities had to deal with the fact that most black South Africans spoke primarily African languages such as Zulu. However, all parties involved at Greensburg – parents, teachers, and students alike – agreed that language played a large role in accounting for differences in educational success.

Language Practices in the Classroom: Sugar's Class

Sugar's class had thirty students, twenty-five white, two Chinese, two Indian, and one African. The language of the class was English, though in rare cases, some teachers would switch from English to Afrikaans in an attempt to explain difficult concepts. Sugar was in his second month at Greensburg, and had difficulty establishing friendships. Moreover, most teachers encouraged competition rather than collaboration with one's peers, and this made it even more difficult for Sugar to relate to most of his classmates who viewed him as not very smart. Most teachers went out of their way to correct Sugar's use of English, since they believed it to be below standard. So his classmates viewed Sugar as having little command of the English language.

Sugar's situation in the township, however, was quite different. He had made a name for himself as a soccer player, and spent most of his out-of-school-time in the playground. That was where he could make friends, where his everyday experiences got analysed, shared, and understood. Sugar's soccer friends were more than just playmates; they also acted as a resource for analysing Sugar's experiences of schooling. Sugar wanted to 'belong' to Greensburg, but was well aware that the school did not consider him good classroom material. One particular incident that seemed to have helped change the perspective that the school had of Sugar was an oral presentation. The English teacher had asked all students to make an oral presentation on a subject of their choice in front of the class. Sugar wanted to speak on soccer, his favourite sport. So with the help of his friends, Sugar planned his presentation. He got tips on how to introduce the subject, on how to start by explaining the rules of soccer (how many players, how long the game is, and so on), to talk about popular soccer phrases and their meanings, and to conclude by giving information on what was going on in the National Soccer competitions. Overall, Sugar's presentation was excellent. Of course there were some attempts to discredit him by asking him difficult questions that had very little to do with his presentation, but in the end, even his teacher had to admit that Sugar's presentation had been the best in the class.

Sugar's report back at the playground felt like a festival. Those who were not there got to hear the story from others, who then congratulated him. But it seemed that in the process of congratulating Sugar, these players were also congratulating themselves as though they were the ones who actually did this presentation. For example, when asking Sugar to demonstrate to the group how he did the presentation, one player stated, *'awutshengise ukuthi sibatshele kanjani'* (show how *we* told them [about soccer]). But the person who actually expressed this victory in more illuminating terms was Nyanga, the other coach, who stated, *'awuboni – ke ndoda. UZulu wenzenjaloke'* (That's it man. That's what Zulus do). Given that Sugar was, in actual fact, of Tswana heritage, perhaps 'Zulu' in this statement referred to black people in general. Sugar was the representative of black (soccer) people in a white-dominated class.

In general, it is clear that soccer was a space that allowed certain kinds of practices while suppressing others. It attempted to give individuals a life outside party politics. It was also a window through which individuals could glance at what life would look like in a post-apartheid era, where blacks would live stable respected lives not disturbed by political violence, and would also be able to participate in valued (white) institutions such as schools. Participating in these valued institutions entailed a duty or a commitment in which Zulus had to show non-Zulus what being Zulu really meant in this case – in other words, perseverance and success. This space was able to provide this window, first by emphasizing certain kinds of traditional Zulu cultural practices uncontaminated by politics; and second, by censoring any discussions on formal politics that might have resulted in conflict; and last, by emphasizing and supporting the role of education in social mobility.

chapter 9

The Example of Ngubo: The Use of Language at Church and School

Like soccer, the church was common in all segments of South African society, playing both a unifying and dividing role. Cochrane (1987) divides the first thirty active years of the church into three periods. The first period, 1903–10 was characterized by the 'civilizing mission' in which missionaries viewed Christianity as 'the abandonment of traditionalism, and education' (p. 151). During the second period, 1911–20, the church distanced itself from imperial concerns and moved towards social issues, which were, however still secondary to concerns about the 'cure of the souls.' The third period, 1921–30, was symbolic of 'Christian socialism' in which the church began a consciousness journey towards evangelization and increased concerns with health care and education. After 1930 the National Party government used the Bible to justify apartheid. This chapter is limited to discussions about how the church offered refuge to many disenfranchised township people by providing a place and an opportunity to analyse and understand current events. This discussion will be limited to the practices of one individual whose actions sprang from the teachings of one denomination, the Jehovah's Witnesses, although the practices described here do not represent those of Witness youths in KwaMashu and elsewhere. What is of importance is the way the study participant, Ngubo, used the church and the space that it provided as a way of negotiating township hardships. Moreover, Ngubo's relatives and friends provided key information about the character of KwaMashu, which is discussed in chapter 4.

Like the soccer groups, Ngubo used this church as an alternative to participating in political activity. The difference, however, is that within soccer groups, individuals were free to participate in politics, as long as that participation occured outside the playground. Individuals such as

Ngubo, on the other hand, were prevented from participating in formal politics because church law defined politics as an unchristian practice. So while some individuals in the soccer groups might still have been involved in politics, none were in the church groups; but, like everybody else in the township, they had been affected by the political turmoil of the time.

Ngubo Kunene: Ngubo lived in KwaMashu with his parents and three siblings and attended school at Umlazi. His father was a clerk in a Kwa-Zulu government office and his mother was a homemaker. While there seem to have been conscious efforts to stay out of any political activities, members of the family knew of and discussed many political issues. Ngubo, like the rest of his family, was a strong Christian, a member of the Jehovah's Witness known in Zulu as Ofakazi. He was involved in the administration and organization of church activities, especially youth activities. For example, he organized study groups for church youth who were at the secondary school level, and was the music coordinator and conductor for the youth choir. Ngubo participated in church activities during the week after school and also partly on the weekend. On Saturdays, Ngubo worked at a place that made and sold car licence plates, located in the city centre. He was always busy and all the activities that he was involved in were part of an effort by his parents to keep him busy, and therefore out of trouble.

In Ngubo's case, 'trouble' referred to activities connected with the political struggle, be they those associated with UDF or Inkatha. Ngubo did not support participation in formal politics and he was very vocal about this position. For example, I had arranged to observe some of the key informants including Ngubo over the first weekend of May 1992. At that time, the first of May had been designated a holiday for members of the Congress of South African Trade Unions (COSATU), the UDF/ANC affiliate. One of the key participants in the study reminded me of the holiday and pointed out that observation at their work places would not be possible since they would be on holiday. As a result, I got in touch with the rest of the participants to reschedule my visit. When I contacted Ngubo his response was *'ungahlupheki, angizingeni mina lezozinto'* (do not worry, I do not care for those things). Indeed, his work place, being owned by a member of the Union of Workers of South Africa (UWUSA), the Inkatha affiliate, was open and Ngubo was at work. On the UWUSA workers' holiday Ngubo did not go to work, not necessarily because he was UWUSA but because he had no option: the place was closed.

Ngubo's non-participatory stance in formal politics was partly based on his life experiences as well as the church's position to such events. The years preceding this study Ngubo had not been able to write his final examinations because of school unrest in KwaMashu, and he had had to repeat a number of classes. He had also had to move from one school to another for similar reasons. Ngubo decided that if participating in formal politics resulted in limited academic progress, then he would be no part of it. It was in 1990 that his parents looked for an alternative school with a more stable history. They found one at Umlazi, about twenty-five kilometres away. At the time of the study, Ngubo travelled over fifty kilometres each day on public transport in order to get an education. The choices that Ngubo made have been clearly directed by the activities taking place in the townships, especially since 1985.

Language and Other Social Practices in Informal Domains

At Home

Ngubo was the eldest of four children, two boys and two girls. He was twenty-one years old, and doing his standard 9. Ngubo, like Sugar in soccer, came from what was considered a stable family since he lived with his biological parents. Also, Ngubo's economic situation was similar to Sugar's in that he did not have to work in order to survive; his parents were the full supporters of the family. Furthermore, Ngubo's home was not the usual four-room township houses that matsatsatsa lived in. His parents had bought, renovated, and extended the original four-room township house into a four-bedroom house with a working telephone, a television and video set, things that were not commonly found in the poorer working-class families. During the times I visited Ngubo's home, therefore, it was usual to find a lot his friends or his siblings' friends sitting and watching television or videos in the living room.

Most of the other youths who visited Ngubo's home were also members of Ofakazi. It is probably important to mention that in all the interviews and conversations I had with Ngubo, he denied having friends, and continuously corrected me whenever I used the word *mngani* (literally, friend) to *abantu engikhulumisana nabo* (people I talk with, associates). For example, one time I asked Ngubo, *'bahlalaphi noMashu labangani bakho obubuka nabo amavideo?'* (In which section of KwaMashu do the friends you were watching videos with live?). Ngubo responded by saying *'akubona abangani bami. Abantu nje laba engisonta nabo. Nabo bahlala lakwa K'* (These are not my friends. They are just people I go to church with. They also live here in the K section). Perhaps this refusal to admit to having friends was linked to the idea that a lot of people congregated together as a way of surviving in the township, while Ngubo felt he did not need such ties to be able to live in KwaMashu.

At first it appeared that the videos these youths watched were religious. For example, one time I found them watching a video that spoke about the origins and function of Jehovah's Witnesses and the things that this church does all over the world. Another time I found them watching a video recording of the previous year's annual youth church conference. I later realized that these videos were only watched if there were adults in the room (mainly Ngubo's parents and sometimes their friends), because adults objected to videos that portrayed violence, such as *The Terminator, Predator, Rambo*, and others.

My insight into the videos that were watched in the absence of adults was accidental, when one evening the friend who had dropped me off at Ngubo's home was late picking me up. (I had been warned not to travel on my own in KwaMashu, especially at night, because of amasinyora and other related dangers.) I arrived at Ngubo's home around 5:30; we had dinner, tidied up the kitchen, watched a video, and just chatted. When by ten o'clock my friend had not showed up, Ngubo's mother suggested I spend the night. This was towards the end of watching a video. Ngubo and his other siblings mentioned that they were not ready to sleep yet, and that they still wanted to watch another video since it was a Friday night and there was no school the next day. It was also suggested that if, by the time we finished watching the second video, my friend hadn't come, they would arrange a room for me to spend the night. At the end of the first movie, Ngubo's parents excused themselves and went to sleep. Another debate started between Ngubo and his siblings as to which movie was interesting enough for us to watch and *Predator* was finally chosen. Ngubo borrowed some of the movies from his co-workers and also rented some from the video shop next to where he worked. His parents did not approve of some of the videos because they thought there was a relationship between watching violence in the media and the actual violence in the township.

It is probably Ngubo's use of this movie as a metaphor to analyse what was going on in KwaMashu at this time, and to conceptualize his parents' reaction to these events, that interested me most. In order to understand Ngubo's analyses, it is necessary to summarize both the politics of KwaMashu and *Predator*. As stated earlier, this township was witnessing a high level of violence which emanated mainly from two sources: the Inkatha/UDF conflict and from the criminal activities of amasinyora. *Predator* is a war movie set in a South American jungle, and focuses on the efforts of a group of American soldiers trying to get rid of an unknown creature, the predator, that killed thousands in this jungle. In its essence, the reason the predator could not be killed was because it could not be visualized. The battalion was trapped in a jungle with an invisible creature that attacked and killed even the strongest.

After the movie we shared ideas about the invisible nature of the predator, and speculated on reasons for the soldiers' determination to capture it even though they were aware of its invisibility and associated dangers. While sharing these ideas Ngubo made a connection between the actions of the soldiers in the movie with those of KwaMashu residents. He argued that what was going on in KwaMashu was similar to what was happening in the movie in that both the ANC and Inkatha were in search of an enemy, yet they did not know what the enemy looked like. Similarly, ordinary KwaMashu residents lived in fear of amasinyora, yet very few could actually identify them. Ngubo stated that perhaps if residents were to direct their efforts towards identifying amasinyora, like the soldiers did in the movie, they could devise a plan to get rid of them without even soliciting help from the police. Commenting on his parents' dislike of movies that depict violence, Ngubo argued that it was basically because his parents did not know what led youths to engage in violent acts; therefore they concluded that everything that depicts violence also causes it. Again, as in the movie, it was the unknown, the unidentifiable, coupled with the uncertain and unpredictable manner of these violent attacks that caused fear in people's lives. Had they been able to identify the perpetrators of violence, perhaps they would learn how to deal with them accordingly.

Hearing Ngubo analyse events in this manner left me with a number of puzzles. Here was an individual who presented himself and was even referred to by his teachers as a religious fanatic, disinterested in formal politics, yet presented a critical understanding of events. Here was a person who was repeating his standard 9 (which was, in general, interpreted to mean that he was not very smart) yet could articulate interesting ideas. And here was a person who claimed to be untouched by and uninterested in political events, yet had an outstanding description of what was going on. What exactly was the relationship between what people said they were interested in (or not), and their actual practices?

Besides watching videos, we sat and chatted about current events, particularly about the actions of political parties in the area. It was during
these informal gatherings at Ngubo's home that I learnt about the politics of KwaMashu, and about amasinyora. Regardless of the church's policy of non-participation in political events, individuals in the church
were aware of the political events around them, and the manner in
which these events affected their lives. I also got a chance to ask questions and to note the things that people said and how they were said –
that is, to note the language of communication, as well as specific expres-
sions and statements about language and other general events. For
example, the video we watched about the origins and works of Ofakazi
documented some of the work that has been done around the Johannesburg area. It included interviews with other Ofakazi who spoke Sotho. At
this stage, Ngubo's father asked Ngubo to fast forward the tape, *'ngoba
asibezwa ukuthi bathini'* (because we don't understand what they are saying). One of Ngubo's father's friends, who had stopped by on his way
home from work, commented that it was interesting that most Zulus do
not learn other languages. I grabbed this opportunity and asked why he
thought this was the case, and his response was, *'yingoba thina Zulu
siyaziqhenya. Uyabona ndodakazi ukufunda nje, ikakhulukazi uma umuntu
esemdala, kulukhuni ngoba kufuneka umuntu aqale avume ukuthi akazi. Ama-
Zulu ayaziqhenya. Awafuni ukuthobela abanye abantu'* (it's because we Zulus
are a proud people. You see, my daughter, getting educated, especially at
an old age, is a difficult undertaking because it requires that a person
admits that he/she is ignorant. Now Zulus are proud. They do not want
to bring themselves to a subordinate position. They think that by learning other languages they would be bringing themselves to a subordinate
position of admitting that they do not know.)

I also participated in other family events, some of which indicated to
me that although this was a very Christian family, some of their practices
were based on Zulu culture. For example, one of Ngubo's sisters, who
was in standard 8, became pregnant, and despite her parents' disap-
pointments they thought it important to have umsebenzi on her behalf.
As stated, umsebenzi is a Zulu word that refers to any kind of job/work,
and also to different kinds of traditional ceremonies, including religious
ceremonies, in which the families communicate and commune with
their ancestors. In Ngubo's sister's case, the ceremony related to the
Zulu practice whereby the boyfriend sends his relatives to officially
acknowledge the pregnancy, and also to apologize to Ngubo's family
about the pregnancy.

I was honoured to be invited to this ceremony by Ngubo's mother, and I participated in the events of that day. It was interesting to know that the family was aware of the complexities that could result by performing such a ceremony, and it was during the preparationss that I was to hear how members of this family saw themselves with reference to Zulu identity, especially as they usually positioned themselves as Ofakazi. For example, Ngubo's mother sent one of her daughters to borrow a calabash from family friend, since the one she had was not big enough for the amount of beer she wanted to brew. Her daughter asked how she was to respond if she was asked why they were brewing beer because it was known that they were Christian and Christians did not do such things (as brewing beer). Ngubo's mother responded by saying, *'uyazi ukuthi singamaZulu, siyakhonza'* (she knows that we are Zulus, we perform such ceremonies). Ngubo, on the other hand, was openly worried that the ceremony would attract attention to his family, which, in turn, would result in them being labelled Inkatha supporters. His mother responded by saying that it was only people who were not Zulu who would claim not to know about such ceremonies, and that these ceremonies were not a creation of Inkatha, as they have always been practised. Overall the ceremony was carried on without any interruptions, and I did not hear that the ceremony was viewed as symbolizing some form of allegiance to a political organization.

Language and Other Social Practices in Semi-Formal Domains

At Church and at Work

Christianity was Ngubo's way of dealing with the conditions in the township, and probably it was the church that provided Ngubo with the analytic strategies which he later used to examine township events. The underlying structure of this church differed from that of many other churches. For example, I noticed was that this church did not have *intshumayelo* (a church service) as many churches do, but had *izifundo* or lessons. So instead of a preacher, every member of the church participated in presenting and analysing a biblical text and other readings from the church's books. Usually the presentations were organized according to groups: some weeks were allocated to the youths, and some weeks to the elderly people. I participated in most of the weeks that were allocated to the youths.

In these izifundo youths were given a text to talk about and analyse in their groups. One of the group members would then present the analysis to the rest of the church members on a Sunday *inkulumo* or study (*izinkulumo* literally, talks, refers to studies). After the presentation, one of the church elders would then comment on the presentation, pointing out its strengths and weaknesses. Such critiques looked at both content and structure, including vocal presentation – that is, whether people at the back could hear. The time spent in the analysis and preparation for the presentation suggested to me that one of the lessons derived from such practices was for the youths not to take any text at face value, but to analyse it fully before judging it. All church izifundo and izinkulumo occurred in the Zulu language, and I did not observe any presentations that suggested the use of a different language or language variety in these two situations.

Ngubo also participated in the church as a music coordinator and choir conductor for the youth church choir. Basically, the choir practised after the izifundo, and sang for the church before the Sunday izinkulumo. Sometimes the choir got invited to sing at other Jehovah's Witness churches around Durban, and sometimes in church weddings. Most of my participation occurred during the choir practices because this space allowed chances for conversation, and often people spoke about general things that were not church-oriented. For example, in one of the wedding practices, comments were made about who was dating whom in the church, and whether or not these people were getting married. People also spoke about how they were going to contribute to the wedding, by cooking, decorating the church, and so on. During the rehearsal, I noticed that the songs were the traditional Zulu wedding songs, ones that I did not expect the church to embrace. I also noticed that the youths were not only preparing to sing these songs, but to also dance to them as would be done in traditional weddings. I asked why they would incorporate Zulu practices into what was a Christian ceremony? The response was that the weddings *awusholutho* (do not have much meaning without these practices), and got boring without Zulu music.

During these choir practices, Ngubo was one of the two youth choir conductors. The other conductor was also a student in one of Kwa-Mushu's high schools. These observations helped me to understand the less-structured interactions between church members, and in some instances I actually participated in the practice and sang with the choir. I also noticed that Mandi, the other conductor, acquired more respect from the choir than Ngubo. This may have been because she was more knowledgeable about the songs than Ngubo, which made the choir members look up to her for leadership. The choir sang mainly written classical/European music (music that uses notes). Some songs were in Zulu and some in English. All conversations, however, took place in Zulu. Even those songs that were in English did not get commented on in English. But when Ngubo conducted the choir he did it in English (he and the other conductor took turns within each practice session). Even when there was resistance from choir members towards English songs, Ngubo did not care. One afternoon, for example, the choir practised one Zulu song. Then Ngubo called for an English song, and then another. After the call for the second English song, one member commented, 'Namhla sizoba amaNgisi impela, yini?' (Today we will be true English people, why?). The others supported this objection, and Ngubo's response was a simple 'so what?' which nobody challenged. Whenever Ngubo was asked why he conducted the choir in English his answer was that it was because they often used notes, and notes were easy to say in English. It seemed that Ngubo felt subordinated by Mandi, and needed to reinstate his position through the use of English in order to demonstrate some level of learning, since English was generally viewed as the language of education and knowledge, and, therefore, of power. Those, like Mandi, who had already established positions of power for themselves did not see the need to use English.

Another space where I observed Ngubo employing different strategies in language use, was at the garage where he worked on Saturdays. Within this environment, he used Zulu, English, and tsotsitaal. He was familiar with most of the workers in the other stores and businesses in the vicinity. The garage operated in English perhaps, because the people who worked there were EL1 speakers. Ngubo spoke to his co-workers in English, and very good English at that. Most of the customers were whites and Indians. Then one day a well-dressed black man got out of his Mercedes and walked into the store:

Ngubo (in Zulu): *Ngingakusiza mfowethu?*
  Can I help you brother?
Man (in English): I was looking for a place that can make a number
  plate for my car. Someone directed me to this road.
Ngubo (in Zulu): *kukhona lapha.*
  It's here, you have found it.
Man (in Zulu): *Niyawenza lawa asangilazi acwebezelayo ajwayele ukufakwa
  komesedisi?*

Do you make the ones that look like glass that are normally found in Mercedes?

Ngubo (in Zulu): *yebo kodwa ungathi okokwakha kusaphelile*
Yes, but for now we ran out of material for making them. (To co-worker in English): Did the material for making plastic plates arrive?

This was the pattern that Ngubo adopted whenever a black person came into the shop. Basically, Ngubo only used English with those people whom he supposed, on the basis of their racial appearance, did not know Zulu. Even those Zulu customers or friends who started their conversations in English, probably because of in the presence of Ngubo's non-Zulu speaking co-workers, were persuaded to use Zulu as demonstrated by the above example.

On other occasions, Ngubo used tsotsitaal, as in the following example:

Friend: *Yitha da.*
Hello.
Ngubo: *Wozhethi mfo?*
How are things man?
Friend: jiza ...
Not bad.

I was surprised to hear Ngubo speak a kind of tsotsitaal that was not the same as the one used by most of his friends at Umlazi. I later learnt that this is a kind that does not use Zulu as its base but equally brings together most of the Bantu languages: Zulu, Xhosa, Sothu, and Venda.

Another insight into Ngubo's language use occurred on the first time I met with him in KwaMashu. I was arranging to come to his home one afternoon when he responded by telling me not to come on my own, but rather to meet him at KwaMashu shopping centre and from there proceed to his home, otherwise *'azokubona amasinyora'* (literally, amasinyora will see you). I suspected from the way he said it that it was not safe for me to be seen by these people called amasinyora, but before Ngubo could explain, his bus came and he had to go. I had been waiting in my car for about thirty minutes at KwaMashu shopping centre when a woman came to me and said, *'Mntanami, uqiniseke kanjani ukuthi ufuna ukuhlala kanje emotweni? Kade ngikubonile uhleli. Angazi noma uyazi ukuthi ukuhlala kanje kukwenza inyama yamasinyora.'* (My child, are you sure you want to wait here like this all by yourself? It's been some time since you have been waiting here and I don't think you know that waiting like this makes you prey to amasinyora.) I thanked her and was beginning to drive away when I saw Ngubo coming towards me, running. This incident occurred at about five in the evening and in the summer, this is like midday. So I was even more puzzled because, to me, it was too early for any dangerous practices to take place. Obviously I was wrong. By the time Ngubo arrived, I was ready to ask him what exactly all this talk about amasinyora was about. Listening to my questions, he laughed and reminded me of this historic story.

At the apex of the Zulu kingdom's power, there was a series of wars of conquest throughout southern Africa. Upon their victory, Shaka's army generals would seize the conquered people's wealth, usually cattle, and give them to Shaka who then would redistribute them to the army. A story goes that one army general, Gcugcwa, kept the cattle for himself and refused to submit them to Shaka's messengers who had been sent to collect them. Being a powerful and feared king, Shaka could not believe this and decided to confront Gcugcwa himself. Greeting him in the usual Zulu salute, Shaka said *'Sawubona Gcugcwa'* (literally, I see you Gcugcwa), upon which Gcugcwa responded, *'ubona mina nje bayoze baku-bone abanamehlo'* (literally, As you see me now, those with [better] eyes will also see you). In other words, 'as you are about to punish (see) me now, I can assure you that one day you will confront some who will over-power you (with better eyes).' Gcugcwa's response was a recognition of his powerlessness. At the same time he had succeeded in doing what no man had ever done: talk down to Shaka. So in this way, Gcugcwa's response symbolized resistance, an act of defiance. But Gcugcwa had also changed the everyday meaning of 'bona' (to see or view positively to 'fix' (negatively). This is where Ngubo's meaning was coming from. I was to later learn that this meaning has become very popular and was being used in everyday speech to indicate different types of dangerous practices. For example, amasinyora used this same word as a call to action. They would say something like *'siyambona'* (literally meaning, we see her) to mean, 'Let's rob (fix) her.'

This example of Ngubo's language practices indicates that he had knowledge of both Zulu history and language, and the manner these operated in the township. He also knew the value attached to languages and the spaces where such knowledge became important. For instance, in the choir, Ngubo was eager not to be viewed as subordinate to Mandi, and used English to assert a position of power. Within this use of English, however, Ngubo did not see himself as Umlungu, an English person as tsatsatsa would have put it. In fact, in those situations where Ngubo felt he had power, such as in the study groups, or at equal level with the rest of the church members such as in the izifundo, Ngubo used Zulu. In his work place, Ngubo used English because it was the language of work, but spoke Zulu with customers whom he regarded as like him in racial terms. It was never clear, however, whether Ngubo saw these people as Zulu or just as black people. But given his refusal to be associated with the category Zulu, it is most likely that Ngubo ordinarily viewed these people as black. This was further demonstrated by his refusal to stay within a Zulu-defined tsotsitaal, but to use that which did not have any ethnic associations. In general, Ngubo challenged practices by political organizations that labelled people as ANC or Inkatha, Xhosa or Zulu respectively. Unlike tsatsatsa who manoeuvred around different practices, attempting to redefine both the Zulu and ANC identities, and unlike soccer whose practices centred on being 'Zulu,' problematic and unclear as it was, Ngubo consciously opted to remain outside any fixed identity.

Language Practices in Formal Domains

The Classroom

At school, Ngubo refused to put himself into a group or to refer to any of the students in the class as his friends. In Ngubo's Standard 9 classroom, the use of Zulu and English slightly differed from that of Standard 10. Ngubo's class had over forty-five students and this made it difficult for me to carry out discussions of language use in the same manner as in Standard 10 which had only twenty-two students. More important, however, was the fact that this Standard 9 class seemed to be made up of students of different political orientations. For instance, the mpansula student who withdrew from the study because he discovered that I was also working with tsatsatsa was PAC; others, like Ngubo, claimed they had no sympathies for any of the political organizations; some were ANC and others, I suspected, were Inkatha. This made it difficult to discuss the Zulu language without in some ways offending those students who had sympathies towards Inkatha. Informal and formal discussions that I had with tsatsatsa and the Standard 10 class as a whole had indicated to me that people's views about the use of Zulu could be critical, depending on who was saying what to whom. The analysis of language practices in this class, therefore, is based solely on classroom observations, which happened once a week for a period of four months.

The official language policy in the Standard 9 classroom was similar to that of the Standard 10 class. The way it was carried out, however, differed significantly. Students in this classroom were comfortable using Zulu in their interactions with each other and with the teachers, and made little attempt to use English, irrespective of the subject being taught. The teachers themselves often used both English and Zulu in their interaction with the students and in the actual teaching of the class, as demonstrated by the following example.

The class was observed in a forty-minute lesson, which attempted to teach English language and comprehension. In such lessons, the teacher was concerned about students' ability to comprehend and understand a given passage. Part of the lesson was devoted to general comprehension, which included general discussion about what had been read, and sometimes to answering questions about previously read material. The other part of the lesson was devoted to writing. In this particular lesson, the class began by trying to get answers to questions, which were at the end of a comprehension passage read in the previous lesson. The comprehension passage had been about a rich white woman who had been attacked and robbed in her house at night. The teacher read out the questions and those students who knew the answers raised their hands.

Teacher: What could she have done?
Student 1: She must have called the police.
Teacher: Not must, *yinto ekade phela le yenzeka*
This is something that happened a long time ago.
Student 1: She could have phoned the police.
Teacher: *Amaphoyisa, nathi siyawazi nje lapha elokishini, do they come immediately?*
Policemen, we all know them here in the township, do they come immediately?
Class: No.
Teacher: She could have avoided this, *mina ngokwami ngicabanga kanjalo.* What do you think?
She could have avoided this, I personally think so. What do you think?
Student 2: She could have screamed so neighbours could hear.
Class: She screamed.

Student 3: She could have shot them.
Student 4 (Ngubo, in Zulu): *Wayezosithathaphi isibhamu?* (Looks at teacher) *Ngaphandle* –
Where was she going to get a gun from? Except – I
Teacher: Phrase your question in English please (Class laughs – this is something they do all the time; try to sneak in some Zulu and get caught).
Ngubo: All of us here, *sihlala sinazo emakhaya* ...
All of us here, in our homes do we keep ...
Teacher: Don't you remember what I said?
Student: (Ngubo) (sits down without any further attempts to answer the question.)
Teacher: Briefly describe what ... (no hands up).
Teacher: *Siyawuzwa umbuzo?*
Do we understand the question?
Class: No.
Teacher: *uma kuthiwa* briefly describe, *kuthiwa musukushaya indandanda.*
When it says, 'briefly describe' it means don't give all the details.
Ngubo: *kafushane*
Be brief.
Teacher: Good. It means select only the few important points.
Class: O (we understand).

In this classroom, the teacher used Zulu, (a) to explain difficult things that the class could not understand such as tense or difficult phrases; (b) to express her personal views; and (c) when she thought she and the class shared an experience. This teacher's practice of using Zulu to express shared experiences is similar to that used in the Standard 10 classroom, although here the teacher monitored the use of Zulu by students. In the above example the teacher only allowed the use of Zulu by a student because it elaborated on what she had already stated, but not as a direct response to the question. In his response, like the teacher and the Standard 10 students, Ngubo tried to draw on shared experience as an attempt to answer the question, but wanted to do this in Zulu. As the teacher insisted that he used English, Ngubo gave up answering the question. Could Ngubo's practice be called resistance towards the use of English, or could it be read as an indication of his inability to express himself in English? Considering that Ngubo was able to use English in other domains, such as in the church, it is safe to conclude that his classroom attitude symbolized resistance towards English, as it would have distinguished him as 'smarter' than those who had failed to answer the question.

Ngubo was clearly aware of the power associated with the knowledge and use of English. This made it possible for him to get a job, to gain access to valuable economic resources. Also, in the choir, Ngubo's use of English gave him added status. It was this very knowledge and use of English that Ngubo needed in order to pass the end-of-year examinations. If we take it, however, that Zulu was used to express solidarity, as in the Standard 10 class, or to put individuals at the same level, as in the choir, Ngubo's refusal to use English could be seen as being in solidarity with his classmates and in defiance of the teacher at the same time. That is, in the classroom, resistance and solidarity occurred concurrently. Unlike the Standard 10 class, solidarity in the use of Zulu was not overtly understood and perhaps practised by the students in the Standard 9 class. It remained very covert.

In sum, Ngubo is an example of individuals who attempted to move away from the notion of social groups as a way of negotiating the townships. He also exemplifies an individual who consciously resisted the power of political organizations to dictate to people how to speak and what cultural practices they should engage in. Ngubo's use of tsotsitaal challenged Inkatha's interpretation that those who used tsotsitaal were ANC, and did not observe hlonipha. His language use in class, problematic as it was, challenged the institutional authority of associating academic success with the use of English. Nonetheless, Ngubo's ability to challenge authority was premised on his position as a church person: church-based youths were distinguished from other ANC youths because the church taught similar ideas as those of Inkatha, especially the culture of hlonipha abaphethe, respect for authority. Because Ngubo was already known as a church member, his acts of resistance were usually overlooked; people simply did not believe that he was capable of resisting or defying authority. Protected as Ngubo was under the umbrella of the church, even he still had to face the ambiguity of Zulu cultural practices, which positioned him and his family as Inkatha, a category with which he was not comfortable.

chapter 10

The Struggle over Symbols and the Politics of Identity

I voted on April 27, the second day of the four days of voting, and I chose to vote in Natal to show the people in that divided province that there was no danger in going to the polling stations. I voted at Ohlange High School in Inanda, a green and hilly township just north of Durban, for it was there that John Dube, the first President of the ANC was buried. This African patriot had helped found that organisation in 1912, and casting my vote near his grave site brought history full circle, for the mission he had begun eighty-two years ago before was about to be achieved.

Mandela, 1994, p. 538

Youth Challenges to the Institutionalization of Zulu Ethnicity

The arguments presented in the preceding chapters are about youths' strategies for dealing with the complex relationship between formal and interpersonal politics, for negotiating and constructing Zulu identity, and for negotiating township life at a time of political reconstruction and transition to independent South Africa. All these strategies challenged the use and interpretation of Zulu history and ethnicity that had been captured and institutionalized by both the South African state and by anti-apartheid organizations. The challenges of history and ethnicity by these youths provide new lenses with which to examine and study issues of identity formation and negotiation in politically transitional societies.

Ethnicity has different competing definitions and is sometimes used synonymously with concepts such as culture and race, which are themselves controversial. The apartheid state, for example, viewed ethnicity as primordial, as something ascribed at birth deriving from kin and clan structures of society and hence, something that is more or less fixed and permanent (Stack 1986). Such a view of ethnicity led to the declaration of racial or ethnic membership by political command. KwaZulu/Natal was defined by the South African state as the geopolitical space for the group it identified historically, linguistically, and racially as Zulu. This meaning of being Zulu was encoded in the legal system of the country, such that it became important for people to declare themselves as members of an ethnic group in order to be able to access certain kinds of state-controlled resources, such as housing, schools, and jobs. Later, with the implementation of the homeland system, the onus was on the KwaZulu authority to carry out this legacy. The practices of social groups in this study call into question the state's definition of the Zulu people. Individuals in this study demonstrate the tensions that existed as a result of the state's practices of defining people into neat racial and/or ethnic categories.

In their search for members and political power in post-apartheid South Africa, anti-apartheid organizations considered ethnic membership a boundary phenomenon to be captured and used for political gains. Viewing ethnicity in this manner is similar to Barth's (1969) presentation of group boundaries and ethnic membership. Barth argues that within boundaries members of the group share background knowledge such as history and customs and conventions of behaviour, which in turn allows them to participate in group activities through established social networks. Barth further states that to understand the manner in which ethnic membership is maintained, it is not the cultural features that are important but the nature of interaction within the boundaries of membership. That is, the activities and rules of those within the boundary are important in determining who is to be a member of the group and who is not. Also, Barth points out that the rules of the boundary are mystified; therefore, it is difficult for those members across the boundary to penetrate or to cross over. In this way, boundaries serve to separate groups from each other, to define who belongs to what group and why. To be a member of a group, one has to share the same practices, values, and ways of thinking as members within a specific boundary. An added notion of group membership is the manner in which members acquire meaning about themselves. Heller (1987, p. 187) points out that ethnic group membership 'does not acquire meaning except as a function of opposition to that which lies across the other side of the gap in social ties that differentiate one ethnic group from one another.' This implies that the function of ethnic groups is dependent on interaction with other groups, for in isolation, ethnicity has neither life nor meaning. As Barth puts it, it is precisely because of the interaction along the boundary, together with the mystification of the rules of the boundary, that ethnic membership is maintained.

Political organizations had created boundaries for defining the Zulu people and limited the sense of multiple definitions through capturing and giving politically fitted interpretations of Zulu history and other symbols of legitimatization. Moreover, to anti-apartheid organizations, ethnic membership acted as a function of opposition differentiating one political party from the other, Inkatha from the ANC. The boundaries of differentiation created by Inkatha defined the Zulu people as those black people who, first, spoke Zulu in its legitimized way; second, could trace their ancestors to KwaZulu/Natal; third, engaged in Zulu cultural practices such as hlonipha; fourth, and most importantly, showed allegiance to the KwaZulu 'state' and to Inkatha politics. Although there was never an explicit ANC definition, it was clear from its practices that Zulu people were those who, first, supported Inkatha politics; second, used Zulu and not English in specific public domains like political rallies; and third, and most importantly, behaved in ways that signalled pride in Zulu ethnic nationalism through embracing Zulu language, history, and symbols. This last point was a problem for the ANC because it went against its version of a non-racial/ethnic South Africa. In addition to these institutionalized definitions, there existed conventionalized practices that were generally associated with either Inkatha or the ANC. For instance, it was generally understood that backward/traditional and illiterate people were Inkatha, while modern and educated people were ANC. Youth challenges to these definitions varied between groups and involved strategies of differentiation that were enacted in everyday practices.

Youth everyday practices have contributed to a body of literature on ethnicity that has developed since Barth's 1969 publication of ethnicity as boundary formation. Now subjective theorists view ethnicity as 'basically a social-psychological reality or a matter of perception of "us" and "them." This view is in contradistinction to seeing ethnicity as something given which exists objectively, as it were, "out there."' While working with and developing Barth's definition of ethnicity, these theorists have also been influenced by the works of postmodern theorists, such as Michel Foucault's emphasis on the construction of the metaphor and Bourdieu's (1977) notions of practice and habitus as the basic factors that shape the structure of all social occurrences. Basically, this approach argues that ethnicity is something that gets constructed and negotiated in everyday life. In developing the notion of ethnicity as bound up with everydayness, Nigel, who equates culture with ethnicity, argues that 'we construct culture by picking and choosing items from the shelves of the past and present.' In addition to drawing from past and present symbols, Isajiw sees culture as generational, always unfolding according to necessities of everyday life, and being redefined by each generation in according to social and historical needs. Similarly, Nagata (1974) refers to the situated-ness of ethnicity, to the fact that the way ethnicity is defined changes over time and under changing social situations. Consequently, if ethnicity is situational, then ethnic identity is called into play in certain activities and not others.

The practices of youth in this study presents a picture of the processes involved in the changing of ethnicity over generations and the social situations that make this change possible. These youth practices are also a mirror to how ethnicity is negotiated in everyday life and how its situated-ness comes into play (Nigel, 1994; Nagata, 1974; Isajiw, 1977). More specifically, at that time, youth practices presented an alternative view of Zulu-ness, thus offering a different definition of Zulu identity. These youth practices demonstrate why the question 'Are you Zulu?' was less fitting of that historical period than the question, 'How do you Zulu?'

One of the challenges to institutionalized definitions of Zulu is found in the social and political practices of tsatsatsa. These challenged Inkatha's definition of the Zulu people in the following ways. First, tsatsatsa practices indicated that it was not only Inkatha followers who valued and used Zulu history, language, and culture in everyday practices. That is, tsatsatsa demonstrated that there were black people who valued and engaged in Zulu symbolic practices who, however, were not Inkatha but ANC. Tsatsatsa also challenged the ANC's use of the English language in attempts to erase ethnic divisions in order to create a nonracial state. This ANC practice implied a legitimization of the Zulu language to define Zulus from non-Zulus. Yet, as demonstrated in this study, tsatsatsa used Zulu in public ANC meetings and rallies not necessarily to define themselves as Zulus but because values of power and solidarity could be enacted through this language. Such a practice of language choice also rejected the implicit assumption that only whites used English or Afrikaans and that they had very little reason to learn an African language. In order to fully participate in these rallies, whites had to learn the Zulu language. By challenging institutionalized definitions of Zulu identity, tsatsatsa were offering an alternative version of what being Zulu meant. To tsatsatsa, Zulus engaged in more than just Inkatha-associated structures of participation. The *Zulu were those people who participated in broader social structures, forged political and social relations across racial boundaries, and participated in any political party that they chose to, while still embracing Zulu-based practices such as hlonipha.*

Furthermore, the character and practices of the soccer groups challenged both the state and political definitions of Zulu identity. As pointed out, the state, Inkatha, and to some extent the ANC, considered the Zulu people as those whose first-language was Zulu, whose ancestors could be traced to the region of KwaZulu/Natal, and who were involved in Inkatha politics. Yet some individuals who made up the soccer group were not first-language speakers of the Zulu language, had non-Zulu ancestors, and did not participate in formal politics. These individuals considered themselves and were considered by their peers as Zulu, not necessarily because they fitted the state's and political organizations' criteria of identification, but because of their everyday practices. That is, by using the Zulu language (different as this use might have been from that of Zulu first-language speakers) and by engaging in defined Zulu spaces, these individuals were then viewed as Zulu. To be Zulu in this case did not take meaning from one's claims to Zulu ancestry, political affiliation, and the use of mother tongue; rather, it took meaning from the things that people did and the spaces in which they enacted these practices. An alternative Zuluness that was offered in soccer, then, was as follows: *The Zulu people were those who chose to use the Zulu language and culture to define spaces of participation and those who participated in them, and yet to not intersect culture with politics.*

A third challenge to the institutionalized definition of Zulu was provided by the example of Ngubo, who refused to embrace the practice of giving people an identity, be it an ethnic or political identity. According to Ngubo, people could be anything they wanted, and had the choice to participate or not in any kind of practices. In his case, these choices included not participating in formal politics; not participating in cultural practices such as imisebenzi since these positioned him as overtly Zulu and therefore Inkatha; and using language to express solidarity with people whom he felt to be like him in racial terms, which he demonstrated through his practice of choosing which language to speak at his work place. *The Zulu were people who practised their right to have no ethnic ascription and political membership.*

Therefore, the character of these youth groups, together with their everyday practices, challenged institutionalized meanings of Zulu identity. Despite the official political attempts to place people into neat categories, the practices of youths in this study indicate that identities were complex since they were constructed from everyday, changing, and often-contradictory practices.

Youth Challenges to Symbolic Domination and Institutionalization of Language

Umganga High School was one area where youth enacted practices of resistance to general control over the symbolic material that was used to construct the meaning of Zulu identity. Most research studies that have investigated the process of social reproduction have emphasized the role of schools in establishing and maintaining cultural hegemony (see for example, Willis, 1976; Bourdieu, 1977), but the practices of youth at Umganga High School pose questions about this role. The discussion about the opposition to the power ascribed to formal institutions as seen through the youths at Umganga uses Bourdieu's framework of symbolic domination.

Bourdieu defines symbolic domination as a process whereby groups gain power over others through the control of resources in the marketplace. He sees linguist hegemony as being based on an integrated linguistic market, one integrated under the sponsorship of the state. In fact, Bourdieu is known for his emphasis on the role of the school and family to produce a situation whereby a uniform acknowledgment of the legitimacy of a standard exists throughout the different sectors of a community while simultaneously ensuring an unequal distribution of the knowledge or command of that legitimated resource (Bourdieu and Passeron, 1977). He argues that it is the family that first instils in children linguistic and cultural capital, but it is the school that establishes the authority and legitimacy of the scarcest and most highly valued linguistic forms, thus ensuring the recognition of this legitimacy. 'In the process that leads to the elaboration, legitimation and imposition of an official language, the school system plays a determining role' (Bourdieu 1988, 32). Linguistic authority or symbolic domination occurs when those who do not control the authoritative forms consider them more credible or persuasive, more deserving of use than the forms they control. As a result, people denigrate the very forms they know and identify with. The two aspects of linguistic hegemony, then, are knowledge or control of the legitimized standard and acknowledgment or recognition of it. Nonetheless, as recognition and control of the standard are, according to Bourdieu, unequally distributed, we cannot evaluate the hegemony of a particular variety simply from its use in the population. Rather, the legitimacy of a variety can be assessed by the extent to which authority is transferred to those who do not control that variety.

The findings in my study are in tune with Bourdieu's emphasis on the role of the family as the first institution to endow children with linguistic and other symbolic material. Most Zulu children, for example, are brought up with an emphasis on Zulu language and history that help promote or discourage certain kinds of behaviour. The practices of youth at Umganga, however, suggest a more complex interplay of events that was more than just a reproduction of cultural hegemony.

Evidence indicates that Umganga High School facilitated resistance to institutional dominance by allowing students and teachers of different socio-political backgrounds to coexist. For instance, students like those in the tsatsatsa class felt comfortable talking about their political associations, despite the fact that these were not uniform. Also, the practices in the school demonstrate that differences existed in the way that Zulu cultural practices like hlonipha were valued and interpreted. This is mainly evidenced by the incident in which the teacher punished a student for improperly referring to Chief Buthelezi. This incident and the debates that followed indicate that even in places where cultural hegemony is supposed to have been established, it is never without tension.

Language use in the school also suggests that Umganga was more than just a place for cultural reproduction. In this case, my study challenges Bourdieu's notion of how linguistic hegemony is recognized. Bourdieu cites as evidence of linguistic hegemony Labov's finding that the prestigious value of the pronouncement of 'r's' is acknowledged by all classes in New York, including those who do not pronounce them (Labov 1972). Instead, the findings in this study are in tune with Woolard's (1985) findings on the value and use of Catalan in Barcelona, Spain.

Woolard found that despite the institutional dominance of Castilian in Barcelona for many decades, the prestige and authority of the Catalan language was not destroyed. This was partly because the unauthorized Catalan enacted values of solidarity among Catalan speakers, and also because of the continued economic power of Catalans in everyday life. What Woolard's findings suggest is, first, that the role of schools and other formal institutions in establishing linguistic and cultural hegemony has been overemphasized; and second, that perhaps the success of formal institutions in establishing this hegemony is dependent on the power of the state itself to exert its authority over such institutions (see also Anderson 1977). In other words, Woolard's study of language use in Barcelona allows us to understand, as Gal puts it, 'more precisely when – in what systematic and historical circumstances – institutional support fails to assure the state language higher status than that of an ethnic minority' (1988, p. 254).

Heller's studies on francophone mobilization in Canada through the use of the French language further illuminate the language practices of groups at Umganga High School. In 1992 Heller demonstrated how francophone national mobilization from 1960 onward was aimed at accessing those economic resources centred on ethnolinguistic practices that ensured the maintenance of a self-defined francophone identity. Code-switching practices which had centred around first-language speakers of French switching to English in order to gain access to economic resources were challenged and reversed. In her 1995 study, Heller takes this notion of French ethnolinguistic mobilization further and addresses questions of how the use of French language, which had previously been marginalized and which had now assumed power, re-enacted practices of subordination, particularly in institutional structures such as the school. She demonstrates how the entry of francophones into valued Canadian industries, through taking control over mainstream structures such as the school, advanced the interests of bilinguals over those of French monolinguals and immigrants whose French did not correspond to the standard as defined by French-controlled institutions.

Heller's studies are useful in analysing the manner in which marginalized ethnolinguistic groups mobilize around language use specifically to gain access to economic resources. These studies are also useful in analysing how specific cases of resistance may, in fact, result in the reproduction of hegemonic practices similar to those that had been overthrown. These studies offer useful points of entry towards understanding the general operations of the Zulu language in KwaZulu/Natal, and how the use of this language (although it gave the Zulu people certain positions of power) resulted in the reproduction of hegemonic practices similar to those of the apartheid state which the Zulu ethnolinguistic group had subverted. The use of languages in KwaZulu/Natal was complex, and indexed both interpersonal politics as well as formal politics. In these townships, language practices and choice indicated not only who had different access to linguistic and other cultural resources but also why individuals chose to exploit these resources (Heller 1987). Also, language indicated the position of groups within the broader economy of the South African state (Gal 1988).

More specifically, however, Zulu youth patterns of language use and choice are in tune with Woolard's assertion that '[a]uthority and hegemony cannot be mechanically read out from institutional dominance' (1985, p. 743). For instance, it is clear that despite state imposition of English in schools, at this historical juncture English did not necessarily hold authority over other languages; rather, it operated in competition. The use of Zulu in key situations, including in-group interactions, asking for favours, and so on, demonstrates this competition. In fact, context-based language choices (code-switching) further illustrate the situated-ness of the identities of the people who used these languages.

Evidence that points to the esteem of English as the language of education in KwaZulu/Natal was controversial, since those who used it often demonstrated some degree of resistance towards its authority to classify people as either smart or ignorant. In fact, groups' responses to the status of English in their lives varied between situations. Within tsatsatsa, for instance, there is evidence that they acknowledged the use of English in the classroom as a way of advancing in education. At the same time, tsatsatsa and their classmates were resentful of those who used English in school-related places, such as on the school bus, and viewed this practice as an unwarranted display of power. The bus incident cited in chapter 8 indicates that those students who attended multiracial schools used English in the bus to display educational authority, since English was also used to measure this knowledge. As a response to this display of power and prestige, tsatsatsa also used English to demonstrate similar possession of educational knowledge. However, that tsatsatsa used English in this situation can be read as both compliance and resistance. To resist the power of English to position people as ignorant and illiterate, tsatsatsa had to comply with using it in that situation. To this extent, tsatsatsa language behaviour supports Woolard when she attests, 'Just as non-standard practices may accompany or conceal resistance consciousness, so it is logically possible that standard linguistic practices may accompany or conceal resistant consciousness, as a form of resistance to coercion, rather than the complicity essential to the notion of cultural hegemony' (1985, p. 741).

The findings in my study also suggest that resistance towards language and cultural hegemony was not just directed towards state institutions but also towards formal organizations that used language and culture to gain political power in the region. However, in this process there were moments of confusion experienced by individuals who resisted linguistic prescription and institutionalization. Although they resisted the control of symbolic resources, either by the state or political organizations, tsatsatsa seemed lost in trying to find something that suited their agenda; they had difficulty constructing alternative resources since others, who had different interests and occupied different positions in Zulu society, had already claimed most legitimate resources at tsatsatsa's disposal. Thus, that Zulu speakers sometimes used English among themselves could also be read to illustrate the dilemmas faced by those who attempted to redefine conventionalized meanings attached to resources: at least English did not belong to any of the political organizations competing for power.

Finally, through examining youth linguistic practices, my study offers a much-needed documentation of the politics of language in KwaZulu/Natal. This was centred on the different and often contradictory positions occupied by the three main languages in the region, Zulu, English, and Afrikaans. Zulu was positioned as (a) a neutral local language; (b) representing ethnic, Inkatha politics; and (c) indicating ignorance and illiteracy. English was positioned as (a) colonial; (b) neutral; and (c) a language of politics and education. Afrikaans was positioned as (a) apartheid and (b) an instrument for accessing economic resources. The individual's multiple linguistic practices were hallmarks of the formation of his or her identity within this highly linguistically politicized region. The use of language, then, resulted in emergent rather than conventional associations with political organizations, and individuals therefore redefined their lives through language use.

Ambiguity and Contradictions with the Use of History in Emerging Zulu Identities

Ambiguity in Zulu identity resulted from a complex representation and use of Zulu history, language, and culture in interpersonal politics. Thus, the above new meanings of Zuluness as read from the practices of groups were not always clear-cut since these meanings were drawn from a complex use of symbols. For example, I have recorded two very clear methods of historical representation. The first was to evoke certain episodes in Zulu history to legitimize an individual's everyday practices. The second was to either suppress or deny this history, or association with it, in everyday practices. These two ways of using history made it possible for individuals to identify themselves as Zulu or not Zulu, depending on the circumstances or nature of their practices.

For example, the data presented in my study, ethnographic and textual, inform us of two important episodes in Zulu history, which were evoked by individuals in then practices. The first episode is that of the consolidation of the Zulu kingdom under Shaka, and the second is that of armed resistance to colonialism under Cetshwayo, the last Zulu king who fought and defeated the British in battle in 1879. Both these episodes had been highlighted in South African black liberation politics because they presented a symbolic picture of bravery and heroism, a picture that was needed by Africans to construct a culture of resistance to colonial and later apartheid domination. Indeed, the use of the latter episode, the battle of 1879, was not limited to just South Africa but was used throughout the African continent as a whole as a way to rank active resistance to colonialism as being higher than passive resistance. Moreover, these episodes did not just present the notion of active resistance; they also presented a sense of succeeding against all odds. Thus, it is partly these episodes that were evoked by individuals such as Sizwe, in chapter 8, when he vowed to pass his final examination and to do this against all odds. Furthermore, it was such incidents that also allowed Ndabezitha to identify with Zulu royalty and to pride himself as a descendent of those who fought the Shakan wars of conquest.

Similarly, episodes that invoked Zulu military strategies employed by Shaka and other Zulu kings in consolidating and maintaining the Zulu kingdom were also retold to instil in Zulu children the culture of isibindi or bravery and to discourage cowardice and passivity. However, with the struggle for control in KwaZulu/Natal, the history of consolidation under Shaka was called into question and practices involved during this consolidation were re-examined. That this history was called into question was mainly because of the practices of Inkatha, who used this history to impose control and suppress opposition. Questions about those killed during the Shakan wars of conquest and the exact manner in which these people died were brought into the memory of those who had previously celebrated these deaths as symbolic of Zulu bravery and heroism. These questions were asked along with questions about Inkatha's methods of suppressing opposition. The consolidation of the Zulu people and the military strategies used by Shaka became a historic problem that symbolized savageness, not bravery. Similarly, Inkatha's practices were viewed by those Zulus who opposed it as subverting and not promoting democracy and freedom. Strategies of active resistance that had previously taken positive meaning from the Shakan wars of conquest, in the history of bravery, became a concern for all parties involved. It was such re-examination and re-interpretation of Zulu historic practices that made many of the tsatsatsa informants shift their identities, by calling into play other criteria of identification, such as the parents' birthplace. Invoking such interpretation of episodes sometimes made informants like Ndabezitha shift from being royalty, to being an ordinary Zulu, to not being Zulu at all. Ndabezitha's example indicates the manner in which some events in Zulu history were highlighted and others suppressed, depending on the context and the speakers' position in that context.

What, if anything, does this complex use of history in interpersonal politics reveal to us about the construction of identities in KwaZulu/ Natal? First, the use of history in KwaZulu/Natal is in line with other studies that have examined the ways some episodes in history act as symbolic markers of 'historical transition' and the process through which such markers assume a mythical dimension (cf. Shils 1975; Zerubavel 1994). The complex use of history as documented in my study supports Zerubavel's 1994 argument that even when faced with a single historical myth, individuals have a tendency to select within that episode that which is important to them and which meets their ideological intent. What has beome evident is that the myth of Shaka as the great Zulu leader is invoked by individuals who depend on this ideology. For Vukani, who was still actively involved in the MK, it became important for him not to denounce the Shakan wars of conquest because it was through the wars that his military practices could be legitimized. To Ndabezitha and Lunga, the myth of Shaka and the consolidation of the Zulu kingdom were important because, as descendants of those who fought these consolidation wars, they were positioned as more Zulu than others (Zulu Zu), which implied that they were direct products of these acts of bravery. Other inner-core tsatsatsa such as Sizwe, who did not have direct claims to these wars, looked at other episodes in Zulu history with which to associate themselves. Thus, instead of invoking Shaka to legitimize his practices, Sizwe used the myth of Cetshwayo as a great Zulu leader who, by actively resisting the British, succeeded where others had failed.

It is also clear that the complex use of history and other symbolic material indexed what in poststructuralist theory has been termed subjectivity, which is defined as 'a site of disunity and conflict, central to the process of political change and to preserving the status quo' (Weedon

1987, 21). Poststructuralists argue that people occupy different subject positions – 'ways of being an individual' – and that these positions are not always compatible with each other. Thus the shifting of identities in this study is contingent upon the social and historical context in which people operated and may change according to the subject positions occupied by individuals at different times. These shifts indicate the contradictions in subject positions and the ambiguities faced by those trying to reconcile these positions.

Nationalism and Liberation

Looking at the construction of nations, Anderson suggests three paradoxes of nationalism: '[1.] The objective modernity of nations to the historian's eye vs. their subjective antiquity in the eyes of nationalists; [2.] The formal universality of nationality as a socio-cultural concept – in the modern world everyone can, should, will 'have' a nationality, as he or she 'has' a gender; [3.] The 'political power of nationalisms vs. their philosophical poverty and even incoherence' (1991, p. 5). Anderson captures the way in which the construction of nations has assumed self-evidential proportions and has lost their historicity. National identity, national allegiance and nation have become an essential and eternal part of everyday lives.

I have examined questions about the myth of the nation and how it has played a major and sometimes positive role in liberation struggles in this book. Liberation movements are very often dominated by nationalist leaders who premise their actions primarily on an unquestionable nation as the unity of liberation. Assertions of other loyalties are often considered disruptive and disloyal to the cause of liberation and unity. Indeed, liberation struggles, especially in Africa, have been framed in terms of the nation, so that struggles that threaten the construction of a nation are seen as random or contrary to the systematized nation. These struggles are seen as biased and disruptive, that is, they are viewed as not involving national loyalty and as addressing a construct other than that of the nation. It is also common to find these struggles referred to as regional (not nation-wide) and as subversive or as threatening to the fundamental national spirit.

One of the issues I have expressed in this book and that continues to be an interesting source of research is representation in liberation struggles. At the first level of representation, my study has raised an interesting discussion about some of the conflicts that result from the use of a 'nation' to frame liberation struggles. In the South African struggle, for example, it is clear that part of the conflict was a result of the failure to deal with the multiplicity of 'nations' that made up this state, and the ways in which each of these nations viewed it as legitimate to define themselves thus in order to fight apartheid. Underlying questions remain about the position each of these 'nations' occupied within the broader South African state and about the ways in which such positioning enhanced or limited a liberation struggle whose foundation was an unquestionable black nation. I have demonstrated that issues of diversity within a nation state can no longer be ignored in liberation struggles and that liberation movements cannot continue to refer to groups such as the ones presented here as random, disruptive, and subversive because these groups are, in fact, the core of liberation itself. How and when liberation movements will begin to deal positively with the issue of nationalisms and lack of uniformity in the face of 'imagined' liberated nations remains to be seen.

At the second level of representation, I have raised questions about the uniformity of cultures and practices that constitute nations, and the position each of these cultures and the individuals who participate in them occupy within broader state institutions. It is clear, for instance, that while the Zulu group was considered by the state and political organizations as a well-defined homogeneous group, the cultures of those who made up this group thought otherwise. At the same time, it is clear that it was the institutionalized cultures of the Zulu as defined by Inkatha that had legitimacy in the eyes of the state with respect to defining who the Zulu people actually were. It is also clear that youth cultures were not viewed as part of the features that made up the Zulu nation and that youths in general occupied marginal positions within the state.

In this book I have offered something of the rhythm of life in youth groups that allows them to tell their own stories and to give characterizations of themselves. This has allowed me to present an analysis of their cultures. In this sense, my approach puts emphasis on youth autonomy and calls for an end to a generalization and top-down approach to youth policies and projects. Youths have vast amounts of responsibility and survival knowledge that need to be taken into consideration by state policymakers. If involved as part of the process and in the planning of policy construction, youths can and will reshape their sense of future and the way that they are perceived by the general public. It is clear that these youths will resist programs that attempt to control their behaviour, that label them as a problem, and that ignore their cultures and context. It will be interesting to see how, for example, the new government will legitimize youth cultures in a country where, for decades, youths have been viewed as a problem to be managed rather than a resource to be developed. It is important to re-evaluate academic achievement and advancement in education as the single most valuable measures of youth success and responsibility. Things like having a job and organizing and taking responsibility for youth activities are some of the measures that are valuable to youth. It would be interesting to see how, in places where education has always been considered the key to social responsibility and mobility, the value of other practices might be elevated.

In conclusion, I have attempted to document the controversies youths face trying to create a meaningful life for themselves and how they deal with the conflicts in formal politics. I have shown how these youths understood and engaged in practices that enhanced their lives, although their actions were not always in tune with state policies or those of formal organizations. It is hoped, then, that those who work with youths will in future consider the contribution they can make to liberation struggles and that policy-makers, be they ordained by the state or other community institutions, will work with youths in the construction of policies and programs that relate to their everyday being. By so doing, youths themselves will be given a chance to put in order, in more formally supported ways, the direction of their futures.

Epilogue

Sawubona ma [greetings mom]. I am sorry that I have not replied to your last e-mail, it is just that these computers had a virus and we were trying to fix them for the last couple of weeks. And m, I have not really told anybody about this and I want to keep it that way, but ma I am going through a difficult time with everything. It is like I do not know who I am anymore; I keep having these thoughts about life and what everyone wants from me. I mean why did the reverend want to kill me? *yini uNkulunkulu afune ukuthi kube yimina engibophisa umfundisi?* [Why is it that God chose me to be the one responsible for the imprisonment of a preacher?] How come this girl does not want to go out with me? And why are my closest friends dying and leaving me on my own? Why is life being so unfair to me especially when I am about to write my exams? You know mom I sometimes wish that I had never been born at all, no matter how hard I try to stay positive and look on the bright side I just can't, because it is like everything is against me. I know that when I ask someone else about this they will simply say it will all heal with time, but time is short and I can't keep going on like this, there has to be a way out. I sometimes wish I could get away from myself and be another person, even an animal. Mom, sorry for adding more stress to your day, you were the only option because you do not live with me and it is better that way because I won't be looking you in the eye. Phatho

My sixteen-year-old nephew, e-mail correspondence, 16 November 2003

It has been ten years since South Africa was liberated and twelve years since I undertook the study that forms the basis of this book. Because of the violence that marked the period leading up to independence, the period in which this study was conducted, many writers have equated South Africa's transitional period to a miracle, or have stressed the importance of its lessons (especially those of the Truth and Reconciliation Committee) for other so-called divided societies. The liberation of South Africa in 1994 signalled a new beginning for the country as a whole and for South African youth in particular. Yet reports about the social, political, and economic position of black youth remain pessimistic as a result of what has been called 'the burden of the present' (Zegeye 2001).

Economically, South Africa remains an extremely unequal society. Moreover, this disparity in wealth and income is, as it was during apartheid, organized along racial lines with 60 per cent of the black population being poor compared with the 1 per cent of the white population. Even though post-1994 South Africa has witnessed an increase in the African elite, this has not decreased in any meaningful way the overall level of inequality between the rich and the poor. As it was during the years of the struggle against apartheid, youth unemployment remains one of the most unresolved concerns.

At the political level, reports are mixed. Some emphasize the existence of young people in key government positions as indicative of the state recognition of the need for youth to have input in nation building. Others point to a decrease of youth's political participation since 1994. Jacobs (2003) traces this decrease in political participation to the transitional period (the period immediately after the democratic elections), and argues that this has been a trend in other democratic polities:

[The] first is the decline of traditional forms of political organizations – such as mass political parties – that have served as the means for citizens to access political power. Memberships are demobilized and parties are transformed into professional organizations geared at elections. The second development goes along with the decline of political parties are the rise of indirect forms of political organizations and narrow 'interest-based' politics. This is usually the politics that is referred to in the literature as the rise of 'civil society.' Its main expression is the myriad of well-funded nongovernmental organization and pressure groups which now take the place of civic grassroots organizations in lobbying and acting on behalf of groups of citizens (Swanson and Mancini, 1996). One consequence is that highly constricted deliberation processes replace more inclusive processes (p. 60).

Accordingly, in South Africa this new deliberation process, or as Jacobs refers to it, mediated democracy, involves professionals, the already educated and empowered, which results in the decrease in participation of the already disenfranchised populations. Jacobs writes, 'The irony is that the levels of involvement in political and civic issues were higher under the repressive machinery than under the new democratic dispensation' (p. 60).

While it may be true that post-1994 deliberation processes did not involve the youths who had been at the forefront in the struggle towards independence, this does not necessarily translate in a decrease in political participation by young people. What it means is that what is being deliberated in the new South Africa is multifaceted and involves processes of nation-building and other more urgent and pressing issues of survival. For instance, observers point to the high involvement of youth in HIV/AIDS related issues. One of these issues involved President Mbeki's infamous position of refusing the import of anti-AIDS drugs into the country. It was mainly the youth who mobilized and engineered demonstrations throughout the country protesting Mbeki's position, which had led to the loss of lives that could have been, at the very least, prolonged by the availability of these drugs. Together with pressure from other countries, Mbeki, like the apartheid regime, had to succumb to the pressure exerted on his government by the youth and today the South African government is working with young people and other non-governmental organizations in the struggle against HIV-AIDS.

Similarly, reports signal high youth involvement in protesting the treatment and ostracizing of Winnie Madikizela-Mandela, first by the ANC and later by the Truth and Reconciliation Committee (TRC). Once a significant player in ANC leadership, with an enormously significant role in the liberation struggle while her husband Nelson Mandela was in prison, Madikizela-Mandela faced trial after trial following South Africa's democratic elections. It was youth who organized demonstrations in her support, not necessarily because they believed in her innocence but mainly because of recognition that Madikizela-Mandela deserved support from the ANC which she once served. What these incidences signal is not lack of participation in civil and political issues, but involvement in what others may not consider to be important enough issues.

On the social sphere, especially with regards to issues of social identity, there have been significant developments in the way people view themselves and in the symbols they use to identify who they are. In fact, there have been volumes of literature published since independence that examine issues of social and cultural identity in post independent South Africa. Notable among these is the edited series *Social Identities South Africa (SISA)*, published by Kwela Books and South Africa History Online and the volume, *Media, Identity and the Public Sphere in Post-Apartheid South Africa*, published under the auspices of the International Studies in Sociology and Social Anthropology. Essays in these two collections examine the importance of social identities that are shaped by history as well as current events, ranging from interaction in new technologies (such as the Internet) to HIV/AIDS.

At the heart of these essays are issues of representation. Authors document concerns about the misrepresentation of groups by the media and the racist discourses that accompany these reports, which result in negative and violent consequences. For instance, in the essay 'Shooting the East/Veils and Masks: Uncovering Orientalism in South African Median,' Baderoon examines images of Islam in the South African media and argues that within reports are found regressive discourses with traces of 'orientalism' which 'gives little of the suppleness needed to distinguish between Muslims and the violence enacted in the name of Islam' (Baderon 2003, p. 129). Similarly, there exist concerns about the representation of women in public discourses. In the wake of two democratic elections, there is still a tendency to portray women as sex objects, ignore the role they played in the struggle against apartheid, undermine the sexual and other forms of abuses they suffered during the apartheid era, and disregard the ongoing violence against women.

Many of these essays further reveal the importance of social identities in the new South Africa. Efforts exists, at least at the political level, to create a new African identity. This identity is constructed and negotiated differently by groups and, not surprisingly, the formation of this identity is informed by historic events of racial categorization instituted by the apartheid regime, as well as by current socio-economic realities. For example, the coloured people of South Africa were considered next to the white group in the racial pyramid during the apartheid regime. According to Zegeye (2003), while under apartheid, this group complained of not being white enough,

> they now complain that they are not black enough to be fully acceptable to the largely black government power. It appears that in today's South Africa, large sections of the colored, Indian and Afrikaner communities are attempting to particularize their identity in an effort to legitimize a con-

ception of themselves as 'minorities'.... Political pronouncements from the
ruling African National Congress (ANC) and the government with regard
to the redistribution of wealth have threatened the position and status of
the minorities who benefited from Apartheid. (pp. 7–8)

While the above assertions may suggest that black people – who historically were the minorities in terms of power in apartheid South Africa
– are now uniformly benefiting from the new dispensation and are
working together towards the creation of a new black identity, the matter appears to be more complex. First, South Africa cannot be ruled
according to reversals in which 'the bad-old-essentially-white subject is
replaced by the new and essentially-good-black subject.' Second, while
attempts are made towards universalizing South African identity in the
new polity, there are those who would prefer them to have particular-
ized their identities as the rightful owners of the country. In this case
study, for instance, these will be the people who identify themselves as
Zulu Zu.

Yet even in the case of those people whose identities are grounded in
historic origin, whose ancestors fought in the Shaka wars of conquest,
for the Zulu Zu uncertainties and ambiguities have always marked their
existence, forcing them to shift to other criteria of identification; in a
sense occupying different positions at different times in life. As indicated by the e-mail from my nephew that begins this epilogue, uncertainties continue to be part of what mark young black identity in the
new South Africa. Phatho suggests that young people's lives are shaped
by both old and new concerns. On the one hand, my nephew indicates
that in the wake of the HIV/AIDS epidemic, which claims hundreds of
lives each day in South Africa alone, young people's identities are
shaped by attempts to understand the loss of loved ones which, consequently brings to the fore questions about their spiritual existence. On
the other hand, he suggests that young people's lives are also shaped by
their attempts to negotiate the changing social climate in which public
corruption has crossed borders and is now also found in what was once
considered a sacred and safe area, the church. While the internet has
become a viable part of young people's lives, assisting them to navigate
changes in their lives, even if it is only to ask for help, old practices such
as dating and schooling are still central to the construction of young
people's identities.

However, unlike the tsatsatsa, for post-apartheid youth, the uncer-
tainty of black identity comes with an unprecedented character of hope-

lessness. While for the tsatsatsa, the history of bravery, coupled with practices like hlonipha and imisebenzi were motivating (and protective) factors in their struggle against apartheid and its consequences (e.g., poverty), for post-apartheid youth this history renders itself impotent as it can no longer address urgent issues in their lives. In a country where in every thirty seconds a child is orphaned because of HIV/AIDS, where the gap between the rich and the poor continues to increase and evidence of extreme social inequality is abundant, and where because of severe inequalities access to the internet is limited to the wealthy few, past symbols of identification like descent become hollow entities in the lives of those struggling to survive. The challenges facing present-day South Africa are enormous, ranging from creating a more inclusive sense of national identity, to HIV/AIDS and its consequences. What is amiss for post-apartheid youth, however, is not necessarily symbols of identity but strategies of dealing with changing social practices in the wake of the freedom they fought to achieve.

Appendix: Chronology of Historical Developments

1800–25   Rival chiefdoms fight for territory and political control.

1820   Emergence of the powerful Zulu kingdom under Shaka. In
          the 1820s, the first British settlers arrive.

1828   Shaka is assassinated by brother and successor Dingane. The
          first white missionaries arrive. The first trading settlement is
          established. The first trekkers in search of fertile land
          appear.

1837   Dutch Voortrekkers arrive. The Dutch and British begin to
          fight for regional control.

1840   Mpande comes to throne, rules Zulu kingdom for over
          thirty years. Is succeeded by by son Cetshwayo's eight-year
          rule.

1843   Land Commissions sort out land controversies between
          Zulus and Voortrekkers. Colony of Natal established.

1846   Theophilus Shepstone designs system of segregation and
          indirect rule in Natal. British rule begins to take shape. The
          search for expolitable products – and white domination over
          the African population – begins.

1879   Anglo-Zulu War. Destruction of the Zulu kingdom. Zulu
          King Cetshwayo is exiled, military disbanded. The Zulu

retain their land and formal political independence. The country is divided into thirteen chiefdoms. Civil war rages between new British appointed chiefs and the old order.

1887   Civil war ends. Britain divides Zululand. The Transvaal is given some territory, while the British assume sovereignty over the rest.

1884   The Zulu begin losing control and possession of their land.

1897   Zululand is incorporated into Natal.

1903   Devastating draught.

1906   The Bhambatha rebellion. three thousand die.

1912   African National Congress (ANC) established.

1913   Under the Group Areas Act, migrant workers cannot claim permanent residence in Transvaal.

Early 1920s   Inkatha formed. More and more people are pushed into the towns in search of work. White farmers burn down ICU offices.

1924   Labour-National Party victory.

1929   White mob attacks ICU headquarters.

1936   ANC fights Native Trust and Land Act.

1940   Inkatha ka Zulu has by now ceased to function.

1948   National party captures state power, imposing philosophy of apartheid.

1949   Indian riots.

1960   Formation of ANC military wing, Umkhonto weSizwe. Nelson Mandela appointed commander. Tension mounts between ANC and the National executive. Africans must carry identity books. Non-violent resistance is crushed; violent means become popular.

1960-75   State policy and legislation to suppress African activism is increased. Profit margins of white-owned companies are high.

1962   Nelson Mandela is imprisoned.

1966   107 tribal authorities have been established throughout the Natal province for the over 280 government-recognized tribes. Leading Natal political figure, Chief Mangosuthu Buthelezi, comes into prominence.

1970   Buthelezi heads Zululand Territorial Authority (ZTA). Emergency of the Transvaal-based Black Consciousness Movement (BCM) under Steve Biko and Robert Sobukwe

1972   KwaZulu Legislative Assembly (KLA) replaces ZTA. Kwazulu constitution drafted.

1975   Inkatha ka Zulu is revived as Inkatha Yenkululko Yeizwe.

1976   20,000 students demonstrate against Afrikaans as a medium of instruction at Orlando Stadium. A thousand people are estimated to have been shot dead by the police.

1977   KLA moves into Stage 2 of self-government. Steven Biko, leader of the South African Students Organization, dies in detention.

1983   ANC begins to break links to Inkatha.

1984   Rise of the United Democratic Front. Sugar cane workers strike at Inkandla.

1985   COSTAU is launched. Buthelezi is attacked.

Glossary

amabutho: a regiment system, in which all males of the Zulu kingdom had to serve the king when they were between the ages marking puberty and marriage.

amaKholwa: converts from the African religion, mostly found on mission reserves.

amasinyora: an invented Zulu word used to refer to people who do bad deeds, and includes a group of youths involved in criminal acts within KwaMashu.

ANC: African National Congress.

apartheid: the official government policy of racial segregation, separating Europeans and non-Europeans in South Africa.

AZASO: Azanian Students' Organization.

Bantustans / Homelands: geopolitical spaces, created under apartheid, each tied to a separate black 'nation' with its own language and bureaucratic structure.

BCM: Black Consciousness Movement.

COSAS: Congress of South African Students.

COSATU: Congress of South African Trade Union.

Emandleni Camp: an Inkatha-operated youth camp in Kwazulu / Natal founded in 1981.

FOSATU: Federation of South African Trade Unions.

hlonipha: to respect.

hut tax: A homestead tax, introduced by Sir Theophilus Shepstone in colonial Natal-Zululand.

ICU: Industrial and Commercial Workers' Union.

Imisebenzi: Traditional ceremonies.

Impi: An army made out of groups of amabutho.

indaba: Literally, a story; however, the word is used here to refer to a process of negotiating meetings designed to investigate possibilities of economic and political power sharing between KwaZulu and Natal.

inhlawulo: Something material, usually cattle, given by the offender to the offended as compensation.

Inkatha: The Inkatha Freedom Party, originally Inkatha Cultural Movement.

isibindi: To be brave.

isibongo: Clan name.

isidikla: A ceremony in which a boyfriend sends his relatives to officially acknowledge a pregnancy, and also apologize to the girl's family about the pregnancy.

isiNtu: A clan name for the language and the culture of the autonomous regional people before Shaka's consolidation of the Zulu Kingdom.

izinduna: Traditional district heads.

Kangaroo courts: Peoples' courts in which individuals who had committed crimes against apartheid were tried and fined.

KDEC: KwaZulu Department of Education and Culture.

KLA: Kwazulu Legislative Assembly.

Kwazulu / Natal: A legal and independent geopolitical structure within the apartheid state, created as a home for those people defined by the Nationalist Party as linguistically, racial, and ethnically Zulu.

Land Acts: Legislative forms for land allocations, created under British colonial rule.

lobolo: A bride's wealth, the transfer of cattle from a prospective husband to the father of the bride.

matsatsatsa / tsatsatsa: An invented name referring to youth who considered themselves linguistically, culturally, and politically progressive during the period of struggle against apartheid.

MDM: Mass Democratic Movement.

NATU: Natal African Teachers' Union.

NC: National Council.

ndabezitha: A Zulu word of praise and respect used to acknowledge loyalty to Zulu royalty.

NECC: National Education Crisis Committee.

PAC: Pan African Congress.

SADF: South African Defence Force.

SASO: South African Students Organization.

SATU: South African Teachers' Union.

Separate development: The creation of separate geographic homelands for black South Africans, which was the basis of apartheid.

shantytowns: Spontaneous urban settlements that grew up mostly on the newly proclaimed KwaZulu lands in the 1970s and 1980s.

SPCC: Soweto Parents' Crises Committee.

squatting: Haphazard settlements of illegal shantytowns that developed during the early years of migration up to the 1960s.

townships: Territories that were created as a result of the events that culminated at the end of the nineteen and beginning of the twentieth centuries: the emancipation of slaves in 1833; the discovery of gold, diamonds, and other minerals; and the Native Land Acts of 1913 and 1936.

Tricameral Parliament: The 1986 race-based three-chamber parliament with one chamber for Whites, one for Coloureds (people of mixed race), and one for Indians.

Tsatsatsa: *See* Matsatsatsa.

tsotsis: Gangsters, hooligans, thieves, burglars.

tsotsitaal: A slang dialect, also called Johannesburg Zulu.

TUACC: Trade Union Advisory Coordinating Council.

ubuntu botho: A philosophy that strives for the promotion of African patterns of thought and the achievement of African humanism.

UDF: United Democratic Front.

Ukukhonza: To worship.

Umsebenzi wokuxolisa: A ceremonial dinner of apology.

UWUSA: United Workers' Union of South Africa.

ZTA: Zululand Territorial Authority.

Notes

Chapter 1

1 Recently, some research and ideas have led to a revision of the role of Shaka in the *Mfecane* story and thus of the rise of the Zulu kingdom (see, for example, Cobbing 1993).

2 There is evidence that in the early stages Inkatha was supported by and was considered the inner wing of the exiled ANC. It was only from 1980 onwards that the relationship between Inkatha and the ANC changed. Reasons for this change are beyond the scope of this study.

3 The ANC leader Nelson Mandela belonged to the state-defined Xhosa ethnic group, which was allocated the homelands of Ciskei and Transkei. The Inkatha leader Chief Mangosuthu Buthelezi belonged to the state-defined Zulu group, which was allocated the KwaZulu homeland.

4 The 1976 student uprisings were a protest against the introduction of Afrikaans as a medium of instruction along with English. During these demonstrations over twenty-thousand students marched in Soweto protesting the policy, which ended violently as the state moved in to suppress opposition. While this started as a protest against school language policy, it extended to other grievances such as housing shortages, poor public transportation, and other issues of discrimination. The 1976 uprisings put youths at the forefront of the struggle for political independence, which was recognized locally and internationally.

Chapter 2

1 By Zulu tradition and culture I mean the everyday practices that Zulu people believed in and practised which had been passed down over generations, and

had not yet become a problem in identity politics. Some of these practices are discussed in chapter six.

2   Here I am making a distinction between African legendary fairy tales and oral history, which my mother, although a product of missionary education, had knowledge of. As I explain in chapter six, most Zulu children are brought up with Zulu stories of war and conquest to instil in them some kinds of behaviour and discourage others. My mother had been brought up with this oral history, not necessarily by her parents, but by her grandmother who had not been converted into the Christian religion.

3   I use the phrase 'my mother's sister' instead of 'my aunt' because of the absence of the notion of aunts in one's mother's family. In Zulu, my mother's sisters are referred to as my other mothers, and have more power in the extended family structure than my father's sisters. They, for example, are the ones that would have acted as guardians in the absence of my parents. In some other Zulu tribes, these other mothers are even given the power to take the children away from the father, in case of the death of the biological mother. The notion of aunts is therefore expressed on one's paternal relatives.

4   Nkonzo died in a car accident in November 1999. It is in his memory and with him in mind that I have been able to revisit this study and put it in book form.

5   When the ANC was unbanned in 1990, it took over the structures and membership of the UDF since the UDF had been created as its inner wing.

6   Descent was an important criterion used to distinguish Zulus from non-Zulus. Basically, descent referred to the ability of an individual to trace his or her ancestry in the region to the years of pre-colonialism.

7   An overriding notion during this period was that immigrants were responsible for the divisions in Zulu society. It became a logistic way on the part of Inkatha and Ulundi officials to view me as a Zulu person who, however, was 'misguided' by immigrant friends – therefore shifting blame from me to the 'outsiders.' My best friend's father in the academic clique had migrated from Malawi around 1960 in search of work in the sugar plantations of Zululand. It is to her that I owe most of the information about Pietermaritzburg that I use in this study.

8   Chris Hani was the commander-in-chief of the military wing of the ANC, which was supposed to have been disbanded. However, like Winnie Mandela and other militant ANC leaders, Hani did not agree with this strategy and continued to mobilize the youth to carry out different military acts of defiance against the state and Inkatha.

9   It is worth noting that tsatsatsa avoided calling Chief Buthelezi by name, and therefore created a pseudonym for him as a way of showing respect. It is

ironic, however, that they condoned the actions of this student, who had done
something that they themselves avoided doing.

Chapter 3

1 On the issue of acculturation and colonization, there were two distinct
   approaches: the integrationist approach usually associated with Sir George
   Grey, whose aim was to gradually win Africans to civilization and Christianity,
   and thus to 'change by degrees our at present unconquered and apparently
   irreclaimable friends'; and the segregationist approach of Theophilus Shepstone, who insisted that separate reserves be set aside, and the authority of the
   chief and customary law be upheld, so that contact with whites could be mini-
   mized and Zulu culture be left relatively uncontaminated. It is the latter that
   concerns us in this chapter, although the former will be discussed in chapters
   to come since it played a significant role in development of a 'Christian African Intelligentsia' that was to help cultivate ethnic ideologies in Natal (Marks
   and Trapido, 1989).
2 Chief Mangoswthu Buthelezi is the heir to this chieftainship and his prominence in Zulu affairs was evidenced by his position as chief minister of the
   then KwaZulu homeland.
3 According to my mother, the choice of Ulundi as KwaZulu's headquarters was
   to affirm the notion that the Zulu people were not defeated in this 1879 battle, and that this was a place of negotiation and political progress.
4 The term Nguni is normally used to refer to those groups of people who occupied the area between the Drakensburg Mountains and the Indian Ocean. By
   the late nineteenth century or even earlier, they appear to have evolved a relatively homogeneous culture and way of life and to have spoken dialects of the
   Nguni sub-groups of southern Bantu languages. The political system of the
   Zulu kingdom was similar to that of the Nguni: the homestead heads or *abe-
   numzane,* the group heads or *izinduna,* the chiefs. The Zulu, however, added
   another level above the chief, the king (for details, see Marks and Atmore
   1969).
5 Citing Bishop Colenso, Marks (1970, 86) asserts:
   'the term Usuthu originated when Mpande, Cetshwayo's father, sent an *impi*
   (army) against the BaSotho and the Zulu 'brought back much cattle which
   were greatly admired, being very much larger than the Zulu cattle. So Cetshwayo's personal followers of the ukubaza homestead would boastingly say: 'We
   are the Sothu cattle...' then they took the word 'Usuthu' as their distinguishing cry and used it in their games.' When the ukubaza homestead later
   became powerful the 'Usuthu' cry was retained, becoming the war-cry of his

212 Notes to pages 43–65

party in the civil war against Mbulazi in 1856. Thereafter it became the national cry 'as the whole Zulu people are Usuthu belonging to Cetshwayo.'

6 Each of the ten 'black nations' was given its own tribal homeland. The objective of apartheid was to give each homeland independence. This would have ultimately produced a situation in which there were no black South Africans because all blacks would have been citizens of another (black) state. Four homelands were, in fact, given 'independence': Transkei (Xhosa), Ciskei (Xhosa), Bophutatswana (Tswana); and Venda (Venda). Through granting this so-called 'independence,' government in effect took away South African citizenship from over six million black South Africans. The six self-governing homelands were: KwaZulu (Zulu), Lebowa (Pedi); Gazankulu (Tsonga), KaNgwane (Swazi), Qwaqwa (Sotho), and KwaNdebele (Ndebele).

7 In September 1984 the National Party created the Tricameral Parliament. The three chambers of Parliament were race-based: one chamber for whites, one for coloureds (people of mixed race), and one for Indians. Each chamber of Parliament administered an 'Own Affairs' bureaucracy (for example, defence and foreign affairs). The proposal to launch the Tricameral Parliament gave rise to the formation of the United Democratic Front (UDF) and the growth of anti-apartheid resistance in the 1980s.

8 It is important to note that there were tensions between the Zulu king and Chief Buthelezi over issues of representation and leadership. Inkatha's representation of Zulu history and tradition differed from the Zulu history and tradition embodied in King Goodwill Zwelithini. Such differences are, however, beyond the scope of this study.

9 The KwaZulu/Natal Indaba was a process of meetings designed to investigate possibilities of economic and political power-sharing between KwaZulu and Natal. The use of the Zulu term to refer to these negotiations was indicative of Inkatha's strategy to take ownership of and give meaning to Zulu culture and symbols.

10 Popo Molefe, 'Document on the United Democratic Front.' This document was drafted for the defence lawyers in the Delmas treason trial. I owe this information to my friend Lakela Kaunda who was a journalist for and later editor of Pietermaritzburg's leading black newspaper, *The Natal Witness*. She was also witness for the defence in this trial.

Chapter 4

1 Squatting describes the kind of haphazard settlements of illegal shantytowns that developed during the early years of migration up to the 1960s. It can also refer to the spontaneous urban settlements that grew up, mostly on the

newly proclaimed KwaZulu land in the 1970s and 1980s. These settlements were also informal since the land occupied did not fall within any formally proclaimed townships.

2 This slogan is translated into English from Zulu and therefore can only be understood in its Zulu context. In Zulu, dogs are viewed as capable of doing the unthinkable and doing it without shame. Anybody therefore, who does what is different from the norm, is referred to as *uyinja* (You are a dog). The norm in Durban at this time, especially in the KwaZulu townships, was that Inkatha controlled and directed popular opposition against the state. Often Inkatha, through the KwaZulu government, embarked in long discussions with the state, which angered the youths whose interest was on military defiance rather than on negotiations. With the death of Mxenge, the UDF was seen as dividing people, by the mere fact of directing popular action against the state. Moreover, the UDF appeared to be nurturing the youths' interest by organizing protest marches, demolishing government property, and so on.

3 AZASO were affiliated with the Black Conscious Movement, while COSAS were UDF affiliates. Perhaps one of the most acknowledged achievements of the UDF was that it was able to bring together people of different political orientation. However, people who were under Inkatha Youth brigades could not join the UDF and still be considered Inkatha members.

4 As the *Sunday Express* (24 February 1984) reported: 'A young black man prodded the newspaper he was reading at the spot where a report appeared about the United Democratic Front. "The UDF," he said dismissively, "mostly Indians."'

5 Necklacing is a process by which all people suspected to be sell-outs or agents of the state were killed. During this process, the victim would have a car tire put around his or her neck, petrol added on the tire, and the tire set on fire. Participating in this brutal method of eliminating the enemy has been cited by, among other organizations, the World Health Organization, as having left the country with the highest number of mentally disturbed youths in the world. Furthermore, one of the criticisms levelled against Winnie Mandela revolved around necklacing; not only did she fail to advise the youths against it, but she condoned and perpetuated it.

Kangaroo courts, on the other hand, were a form of 'people's courts' in which individuals who had committed 'smaller' crimes against the struggle, however defined, were tried and fined. These crimes usually involved things such as refusal to house or feed victims of political unrest (usually comrades), refusal to 'lend' comrades your car in a time of 'need,' and so on.

6 Theoretically, the ANC is believed to have abandoned the armed struggle

soon after it was unbanned in 1990. But I learnt from this participant that this belief was not necessarily true, and that there is a big controversy within the ANC pertaining to the role of Umkhonto in the organization. At the time of the study, Umkhonto had not disbanded, and those members of the ANC opposed to giving up the armed struggle capitalized on the existence of Umkhonto and used it to carry out different military activities similar to those of Inkatha. The late Chris Hani and Winnie Mandela were just two ANC members who still believed in armed struggle

Chapter 5

1 In this context, outsiders referred to non-Zulu people defined not necessarily by language because we all spoke Zulu, but by descent.

2 Heath and McLaughlin (1993) point out that in North American communities, passing, the process in which small groups choose to escape ethnic labels given to them by other groups by simply moving to other regions and adopting different customs of eating, dressing, worshipping and speaking, is often viewed in a pejorative manner. In some African communities, however, such a process received no negative assessment but was considered a worthy and strategic move to improve people's station in life. For instance, during the first decades of the nineteenth century, the sub Sahara region witnessed a lot of such moves when individuals chose to shift their identities as members of a particular group because of altered regional economics or politics. For a full discussion of this process in the southern African region, see Guy (1979).

3 *Hlonipha* is not just a Zulu practice but is also found in other ethnic groups. The cited example is not from the Zulu context but from Xhosa, which explains why the names of female in-laws are included as part of the practice. Usually, in Zulu, it is only the names of elderly male in-laws that women hlonipha.

4 It is important to mention that, unlike Shaka, in whose case the place is known as *Amanzimtoti*, in Chief Buthelezi's case, those people who changed their use of *mnyama* to *mpintsholo* were subject to scrutiny as they became viewed as promoting Chief Buthelezi's politics. Such interpretations demonstrate the intersections between language, culture, and politics.

5 Some of the youths in this study mentioned that they had left the UDF because of the way UDF youths treated adults. One of these youths stated, '*angikhuliswanga kanjalo, kwakuwukungahloniphi nje lokho*' (I wasn't brought up to behave that way [towards adults], that was mere disrespect).

6 It is difficult to assess the reliability of this information given the fact that the practice was to give information that supported one's political orientation.

However, when considering that in any such project, one had to work with only one political organization, it is practical to acknowledge that the majority of those that the centre worked with were in fact ANC in orientation.

Chapter 6

1 Throughout this book, I use the terms social and cultural space interchangeable to refer to the youth groups that are the subject of this study; social because of the nature of space they occupied and cultural because of the different practices characteristic of each group.

2 It is worth noting here that despite its political stability, Umlazi schools were not always immune to the boycotts that were typical of this period. Nevertheless, compared to other townships, Umlazi schools were reasonably stable.

3 A direct translation would read like 'so what's burning in politics.' The Zulu phrase is in itself slang, or tsotsitaal, which can only be understood in its specificity. It was an indirect and informal way used by some social groups to communicate of sensitive issues. The use of this language variety was often interpreted as indicating inclusion. In this case, its use indicated to Lunga that members of this group were accepting him. Nonetheless, Lunga did not form close contact with this group. Instead, he used the strategies of communication he learned from it to establish relations with another group, tsatsatsa, which was still in the process of formation.

4 As with tsatsatsa and matsatsatsa, I use mpansula to refer to the group culture, and mampansula to refer to the members who constituted the group. It is important to note that none of the participants in this study were mpansula. One mpansula participant that I worked with at the beginning of data collection withdrew from the study when he discovered that I was also working with tsatsatsa. Three months after his withdrawal, I learnt that he was a well-known member of the Pan African Congress. This seems to contradict the common perception that mampansula did not participate in politics. Also, it can be argued that while mampansula and matsatsatsa were clearly different, these groups did not see themselves as enemies like, for example, the ANC and Inkatha. However, once a political element emerged, some hostility surfaced.

5 Smoking dagga is one practice that was disliked by tsatsatsa and was usually cited as an example of not staying clean. Mampansula, on the other hand, argued that their ancestors smoked dagga, and, in any case, they smoked it differently (distillation process).

6 It is important to remember that the late 1980s were also a period in which the state attempted some constitutional reforms. Among these reforms was

the opening of white designated areas to other races.

7 *Nkombose kababa* (literally my father's Nkombose) is a name of a bird in a Zulu legendary story about a kind family who used to share even the last of their dinner with strangers. One day, the family had to go without dinner when a bird flew in and demonstrated its magical powers and produced the most delicious dish of *amasi* and *uphuthu* (a dish made out of sour milk and corn flour). The family named the bird Nkombose, and believed that the god of harvest had sent this bird. The story goes on to relate how, because of greed and evil deeds, the family lost this bird, and how it was later retrieved because those who had committed the evil acts repented and were forgiven by the gods. Overall, the phrase *Nkombose kababa* came to symbolize life and survival. So in general this phrase is used to indicate good intent, or the power of the gods.

8 This is a Zulu saying which expresses the power of individuals over non-linguistic objects; or more precisely, over non-living things.

Chapter 7

1 The inability to find out more about the position of Inkatha students in this school also emerged from my own position as a researcher more interested in the activities of ANC-oriented students. Had I shown interest in Inkatha students, I would have been defined as an Inkatha spy and therefore a sell-out. This also would have affected my ability to pursue the study.

2 It is important to note that despite the many dangers associated with hitch-hiking, especially during this period, the city centre was a relatively safe space compared to the townships and therefore hitch-hiking was not an uncommon practice.

3 This example has to be understood in the context of South Africa's separate development where Indian people had separate residential areas from blacks, which resulted in minimum contact between racial groups. It was interesting, therefore, to hear a person whose first language was not Zulu, talk of Zulu as a choice for South Africa's national language. One would have expected that English would be this person's choice. I think, however, that this choice was reflective of the political changes of the time, which included integration of groups and the legitimization of the languages of the majority of the people in the region, the Zulu.

4 The term *nkosazane* literally translates to Miss; however, someone older than the one being addressed can also use it as a term of endearment.

5 This discussion was recorded, however, the names of those who uttered the quoted statements were not documented. What is important is that the discus-

sion occurred between people who defined themselves as Zulu and ANC, some of whom were tsatsatsa.

6 This phrase, which was translated directly from Zulu to English, means that a person is trying to do the impossible, like phoning oneself. The students translated it back into Zulu because they realized I had no clue what it means in English.

7 The teacher had applauded Vukani's essay as one that exemplified good scholarship. The fact that it was discussed in the bus was merely to demonstrate to the students from multiracial schools that township students could write critical essays. One of the typical complaints from students in multiracial schools was that their schools ruled against the use of political events in any of their writings. So the fact that students from township schools could do this was a continuous source of envy by the other students. Matsatsatsa capitalized on this envy and continued to bring in political topics as a way of legitimizing the kind of education they were receiving.

8 This is a Zulu proverb translated into English. It is used to refer to proud people, that 'they walk with their shoulders up – but should be careful because someday someone might bring them down.' (A similar saying in English would be 'to walk with your nose in the air'.) The students were surprised that I did not know the meaning of the phrase, because according to them, it was a very popular English phrase. This is a typical example of what Ndebele (1987) calls 'The Africanization of English.'

9 It is important to note that tsatsatsa footnoted most negative statements about Vukani by a request to me to not 'sell them out' (to him) and by insisting that I liked Vukani the most.

Chapter 8

1 This attitude towards my questions was not just unique to Lolo, but was found even within people like tsatsatsa with whom I had closer relations. It is safe to say that one of the limitations of being an insider is that those who knew of my cultural background were, for a variety of reasons, not comfortable responding to questions about Zulu culture. Because of the intimacy of my friendship with matsatsatsa, I was able to establish an understanding with them that my questions were not intended to test their knowledge of Zulu culture, but rather, were attempts to put those involved in a conversation at the same level of understanding.

2 A common belief in black communities is that white people's children do not like to be touched by or play with black people because they are afraid of them. Many believed that this was because of their skin colour, which white

children associate with gorillas. Moreover, black domestic workers often told stories of how white parents teach their children that black people are in fact monkeys and gorillas. Another reason why white children might be afraid of black people in general might be the result of the Group Areas Act, which made it possible for children to grow up with little or no contact with people from other groups.

References

Achebe, C. (1988) *Hopes and Impediments: Selected Essays, 1965–1987*. Ibadan: Heinemann Educational Books.

Ahluwalia, P. (2003) The Struggle for African Identity: Thabo Mbeki's African Renaissance. In A. Zegeye and R. Harris (eds.), *Media, Identity and the Public Sphere in Post-Apartheid South Africa*. Boston: Koninklijke Brill.

Alexander, P. (1989) Language Policy and National Unity. *Language Projects' Review* 4(3): 29–33.

Anderson, B. (1991) *Imagined Communities: Reflections on the Origin and Spread of Nationalism*. London: Verso.

Anderson, P. (1977) The Antinomies of Antonio Gramsci. *New Left Review* (100): 5–80.

Angogo, R. (1978) Language and Politics in South Africa. *Studies in African Linguistics* 9(2): 211–21.

Appiah, K. (1992) *In My Father's House: Africa in the Philosophy of Culture*. New York: Oxford University Press.

Baderoon, G. (2003) Shooting the East / Veils and Masks: Uncovering Orientalism in South African Media. In A. Zegeye and R. Harris (eds.), *Media, Identity and the Public Sphere in Post-Apartheid South Africa*. Boston: Koninklijke Brill.

Barth, F., ed. (1969) *Ethnic Groups and Boundaries*. Boston: Little, Brown.

Bot, M. (1985) *School Boycotts 1984: The Crises in African Education*. Durban: Indicator Project.

Bourdieu, P. (1988) *Language and Symbolic Power*. Cambridge: Polity Press.

– (1977) The Economics of Linguistic Exchanges. *Social Science Information* 16(6): 645–68

Bourdieu, P., and J. Passeron. (1977) *Reproduction in Education, Society and Culture*. Berverly Hills: Sage Publications.

Bradford, H. (1987) *A Taste of Freedom: The ICU in Rural South Africa, 1924–1930*. New Haven: Yale University Press.

Brewer, J. (1985) The Membership of Inkatha in KwaMashu, *African Affairs*: 184.

Briggs, C. (1986) *Learning How to Ask: A Sociolinguistic Reappraisal of the Role of the Interview in Social Science Research*. Cambridge: Cambridge University Press.

Burke, P. (1987) Introduction. In P. Burke and R. Porter (eds.), *The Social History of Language*. Cambridge: Cambridge University Press, pp. 1–20.

Butler, J., I. Robert, and J. Adams. (1977) *The Black Homelands of South Africa: The Political and Economic Development of Bophuthatswana and KwaZulu*. Berkeley: University of California Press.

Chakrabarty, D. (1992). The Death of History? Historical Consciousness and the Culture of Late Capitalism. *Public Culture* 4(2): 47–66.

Christianse, Y. (2003) Passing Away: The Unspeakable (Losses) of Postapartheid South Africa. In D.L. Eng and D. Kazanjian (eds.), *Loss: The Politics of Mourning*. Berkeley and Los Angeles: University of California Press.

Cluver, A. (1992) Language Planning Models for a Post-Apartheid South Africa. *Language Problems and Language Planning* 16(2): 105–36.

Cochrane, J. (1987) *Servants of Power: The Role of English-Speaking Churches in South Africa, 1903–1930*. Johannesburg: Ravan Press.

Cole, J. (1987) Crossroads: *The Politics of Freedom and Repression, 1976–1986*. Johannesburg: Ravan Press.

Collins, J. (1988) Language and Class in Minority Education. *Anthropology in Education Quarterly* 19(4): 299–326.

Crowley, T. (1989) Bakhtin and the History of the Language. In K. Hirshkop and D. Steward (eds.), *Bakhtin and Cultural Theory*. Manchester: Manchester University Press.

Dhlomo, O. (1983) The Strategy of Inkatha and Its Critics: A Comparative Assessment. *Journal of Asian and African Studies* 17: 1–2.

Doyle, A. (1955) The Future of the Bantu Languages. *Liberation* 15: 26–43.

– (1953) Language: Another View. *Liberation* 6: 1–13.

Eastman, C. (1990) What Is the Role of Language in Post-Apartheid South Africa? *Tesol Quarterly* 21 (1): 9–21.

Edwards, J. (1986) *Language, Society and Identity*. Oxford: Basil Blackwell.

Erickson, F. (1988) Ethnographic Description. In U. Ammon, N. Dittmar and K. Mattheier (eds.), *Sociolinguistics: An International Handbook of the Science of Language and Society*. Berlin: Walter de Gruyter.

– (1979) Talking Down: Some Cultural Sources of Miscommunication in Interracial Interviews. In A. Wolfgang (ed.), *Nonverbal Behavior*. New York: Academic Press.

Fairclough, N. (1989) *Language and Power*. London: Longman.

Finlay, R. (1995) Woman's Language of Respect: Isihlonipho Sabafazi. In R. Mesthrie (ed.), *Language and Social History: Studies in South African Sociolinguistics*. Cape Town: David Philip.

Foucault, M. (1979) *Discipline and Punish*. New York: Vintage.

Gal, S. (1989a) Between Speech and Silence: The Problematics of Research on Language and Gender. *Pragmatics* 3(1): 1–38.

– (1989b) Language and Political Economy. *Annual Review of Anthropology* 18: 345–67.

– (1988) The Political Economy of Code Choice: In M. Heller (ed.), *Codeswitching: Anthropological and Sociolinguistic Perspectives*. Berlin: Mouton Gruyter.

– (1979) *Language Shift*. New York: Academic Press.

Giddens, A. (1989) A Reply to My Critics. In D. Held and J. Thompson (eds.), *Social Theory of Modern Societies: Anthony Giddens and His Critics*. New York: Cambridge University Press.

– (1984) *The Constitution of Society*. Berkeley and Los Angeles: University of California Press.

Grillo, R. (1989) *Dominant Languages*. Cambridge: Cambridge University Press.

Guguske, R. (1978) The Teaching of Bantu Languages in Black Schools. In L. Lanham and K. Prinsloo (eds.), *Language and Communication Studies in South Africa*. Cape Town: Oxford University Press.

Gumperz, J. (1982) *Discourse Strategies*. Cambridge: Cambridge University Press.

Guthrie, M. (1967) *The Classification of Bantu Languages*. Norwood, NJ: ??

Guy, J. (1982) The Destruction and Reconstruction of Zulu Society. In S. Marks and R. Rathbone (eds.), *Industrialisation and Social Change in South Africa*. London: Longman.

– (1980) Ecological Factors in the Rise of Shaka and the Zulu Kingdom. In S. Marks and A. Atmore (eds.), *Economy and Society in Preindustrial South Africa*. London: Longman.

– (1979a) The British Invasion of Zululand: Some Thoughts for Centenary Year. *Reality* 1(1):13–38.

– (1979b) *The Destruction of the Zulu Kingdom: The Civil War in Zululand: 1879–1884*. London: Longman.

Gwala, Z. (1985) *Rebellion in the Last Post: The Natal Riots*. Indicator 3(2): 6–9.

Heath, S. and M. McLaughlin (eds.). (1993) *Identity and Inner-City Youth: Beyond Ethnicity and Gender*. New York: Teachers College, Columbia University.

Heller, M. (1995) Language Choice, Social Institutions, and Symbolic Domination. *Language and Society*.

– (1994) *Crosswords: Language, Education and Ethnicity in French Ontario*. Berlin: Mouton de Gruyter.

- (1992) The Politics of Codeswitching and Language Choice. *Journal of Multilingual and Multicultural Development* 13(1 and 2): 123–42.
- (1989) Speech Economy, and Social Selection in Educational Contexts: A Franco-Ontarian Case Study. *Discourse Processes* 12: 377–90.
- (1988) Introduction. In M. Heller (ed.), *Codeswitching: Anthropological and Sociolinguistic Perspectives.* Berlin: Mouton de Gruyter.
- (1987) The Role of Language in the Formation of Ethnic Identity. In J. Phinney and M. Rotheram (eds.), *Children's Ethnic Socialisation: Identity, Attitude and Interactions.* London: Sage.

Janks, H. (1990) Contested Terrain: English Education in South Africa. In I. Goodson and P. Medway (eds.), *Bringing English to Order.* London: Falmer Press.

Jessop, B. (1989) Capitalism, Nation-State and Surveillance. In D. Held and J. Thompson (eds.), *Social Theory of Modern Societies: Anthony Giddens and His Critics.* New York: Cambridge University Press.

Kotze, D. (1975) *African Politics in South Africa, 1964–1974: Parties and Issues.* New York: St Martin's Press.

Kriger, R. and A. Zegeye, eds. (2001) *Culture in the New South Africa: After Apartheid.* Volume 2. Cape Town: Kwela Books.

Labov, W. (1972) *Language in the Inner City: Studies in the Black English Vernecular.* Philadephia: University of Pennsylvania Press.

Ladlau, L. (1975) The Cator Manor Riots, 1959–1960. MA dissertation, University of Natal.

Langner, E. (1983) The Founding and Development of Inkatha Yenkululeko Yesizwe. M.A. dissertation, University of South Africa.

Lanham, L. and K. Prinsloo (eds.) (1978) *Language and Communication Studies in South Africa.* Cape Town: Oxford University Press.

Lears, J. (1985) The Concept of Cultural Hegemony: Problems and Possibilities. *American Historical Review* 90: 567–93.

Leatt, J., J. Kneifel, and K. Nürnburger (eds.). *Contending Ideologies in South Africa.* Cape Town: David Philip.

Le Roux, E. (2003) Unsung Heroines: Media Reflections of the Social Conflict in South Africa. In A. Zegeye and R. Harris (eds.), *Media, Identity and the Public Sphere in Post-Apartheid South Africa.* Boston: Koninklijke Brill.

Lodge, M. (1983) *Black Politics in South Africa since 1945.* Johannesburg: Ravan Press.

Lowe, C. (1991) Buthelezi, Inkatha and the Problem of Ethnic Nationalism on South Africa. In J. Brown (ed.), *History from South Africa: Alternative Visions and Practices.* Philadelphia: Temple University Press.

Maasdorp, G. and B. Humphreys (eds.) (1975) *From Shantytown to Township: An*

Economic Study of African Poverty and Rehousing in a South African City. Cape Town: Juta.

Magubane, B. (1988) The Political Economy of the South African Revolution. In B. Magubane and I. Mandaza (eds.), *Whither South Africa?* New Jersey: Africa World Press.

Mandela, N. (1994) *Long Walk to Freedom.* Boston: Little, Brown.

Manson, A. (1986) From Cato Manor to KwaMashu. *Reality* 13(2): 10–15.

Mare, G. (1993) *Ethnicity and Politics in South Africa.* Johannesburg: Ravan Press.

Mare, G., and G. Hamilton (1987) *An Appetite for Power: Buthelezi's Inkatha and South Africa.* Johannesburg: Ravan Press.

Marks, S. (1970) *Reluctant Rebellion: The 1906–8 Disturbances in Natal.* Oxford: Clarendon Press.

– (1986) *The Ambiguities of Dependence in South Africa: Class, Nationalism and the State in Twentieth-Century Natal.* Baltimore: Johns Hopkins University Press.

Marks, S., and A. Atmore. (1980) Introduction. In S. Marks and A. Atmore (eds.), *Economy and Society in Preindustrial South Africa.* London: Longman.

– (1970) The Problem of the Nguni: An Examination of the Ethnic and Linguistic Situation in South Africa before the Mfecane. In D. Dalby (ed.), *Language and History in Africa.* New York: Africana.

Marks, S. and R. Rathbone. (1982) Introduction. In S. Marks and R. Rathbone (eds.), *Industrialisation and Social Change in South Africa.* London: Longman.

Mbembe, A. (1992) The Banality of Power and the Aesthetics of Vulgarity in the Postcolony. *Public Culture* 4(2): 1–30.

Meer, F., ed. (1989) *Resistance in the Townships.* Durban: Madiba Publications.

– (1988) Conflict in the Community and in the Factories. *South African Labour Bulletin* 13(4/5): 89.

– (1985) *Unrest in Natal, August 1985.* Durban: Institute for Black Research.

Meillassoux, C. (1981). *Maidens, Meals, and Money: Capitalism and the Domestic Community.* New York: Cambridge University Press.

– (1972) From Production to Reproduction. *Economy and Society* 1(1): 98–100.

Milroy, J. and L. Milroy. (1985) *Authority in Language: Investigating Language Prescription and Standardization.* New York: Routledge.

Minnaar, A de V. (1992) *Squatters, Violence and the Future of the Informal Settlements in the Greater Durban Region.* Pretoria: Human Science Research Council.

– (1990) *Conflict and Violence in Natal/KwaZulu: Historical Perspectives.* Pretoria: Human Science Research Council.

Moodie, T. (1980) *The Rise of Afrikanerdom: Power, Apartheid and Afrikaner Civil Religion.* Berkeley and Los Angeles: University of California Press.

Nagata, J. (1974) What Is a Malay? Situational Selection of Ethnic Identity in a Plural Society. *American Anthropologist* 1(2): 331–50.

Ndebele, N. (1987) The English Language and Social Change in South Africa. *English Academy Review* 4: 1–16.

Nhlapo, J. (1945) *Nguni and Sotho*. Cape Town: Bookman.

Paulston, C. (1987) Linguistic Consequences of Ethnicity and Nationalism in Multilingual Settings. In D. Young (ed.), *Language: Planning and Medium in Education*. Cape Town: The Language Education Unit and SAALA.

Peires, J. (1981) Introduction. In J. Peires (ed.), *Before and after Shaka*. Grahamstown: Institute for Social and Economic Research, Rhodes University.

Pieterse, N. (1992) *White and Black: Images of Africa and Blacks in Western Popular Culture*. New Haven, CT: Yale University Press.

Potekhin, J. (1958) The Formation of Nations in Africa. *Liberation*. 34 and 35.

Said, E.W. (1978) *Orientalism*. New York: Pantheon Books.

Sanders, M. (2003) Ambiguities of Mourning: Law, Custom, and Testimony of Women before South Africa's Truth and Reconciliation Commission. In D.L. Eng and D. Kazanjian (eds.), *Loss: The Politics of Mourning*. Berkeley and Los Angeles: University of California Press.

Saunders, P. (1989) Space, Urbanism and the Created Environment. In D. Held and J. Thompson (eds.), *Social Theory of Modern Societies: Anthony Giddens and His Critics*. New York: Cambridge University Press.

Schlemmer, L. (1985) *The Politics and Social Environment of the Future in Natal/ KwaZulu* Durban: Indicator.

Schmahmann, B. (1979) KwaZulu in Contemporary South Africa: A Case Study in the Implementation of the Policy of Separate Development. PhD dissertation, University of Natal.

Seekings, J. (1993) *Heroes of Villians? Youth Politics in the 1980s*. Johannesburg: Ravan Press.

Sharp, J. (1988) Ethnic Group and Nation: The Apartheid Vision on South Africa. In E. Boonzarer and J. Sharp (eds.), *South African Keywords: The Uses and Abuses of Political Concepts*. Cape Town: David Philip.

Shils, E. (1975) *Centre and Periphery: Essays in Macrosociology*. Chicago: Universtiy of Chicago Press.

Sitas, A. (1988) Vigilantes in Durban – Social Origins and Social Implications. Paper delivered at Seminar on Violence in the Pietermaritzburg area. Pietermaritzburg, Centre for Adult Education, University of Natal.

– (1986) Inanda, August 1985: Where Wealth and Power and Blood Reign Worshipped Gods. *South African Labour Bulletin* 11(4): 85–121.

Slater, H. (1980) The Changing Patterns of Economic Relationships in Rural Natal, 1838–1884. In S. Marks and A. Atmore (eds.), *Economy and Society in Preindustrial South Africa*. London: Longman.

Stack, J. (1986) *The Primordial Challenge: Ethnicity in the Contemporary World.* Westport, CT: Greenwood Press.

Teague, P. (1983) A Study of Inkatha Yesizwe's Approach to the Youth, with Specific Reference to the Movement's Youth Brigade. MA dissertation, University of Cape Town.

Temkin, B. (1976) *Gatsha Buthelezi: Zulu Statesman.* Cape Town: Purnell.

Thompson, J. (1989) The Theory of Structuration. In D. Held and J. Thompson (eds.), *Social Theory of Modern Societies: Anthony Giddens and His Critics.* New York: Cambridge University Press.

Torr, A. (1985) The Social History of an Urban African Community: Lammont, 1930–1960. MA dissertation, University of Natal.

Turner, V. (1986) *The Anthropology of Performance.* New York: Performing Arts Journal.

– (1982) *From Ritual to Theater: The Human Seriousness of Play.* New York: Performing Arts.

Vail, L. (1989) Introduction: Ethnicity in Southern African History. In L. Vail, ed., *The Creation of Tribalism in Southern Africa.* London: James Currey.

Walshe, P. (1970) *The Rise of the African Nationalism in South Africa: The African National Congress.* London: C. Hurst.

Wasserman, H. (2003) Between the Local and the Global: South African Languages and the Internet. In A. Zegeye and R. Harris (eds.), *Media, Identity and the Public Sphere in Post-Apartheid South Africa.* Boston: Koninklijke Brill.

wa Thiong'o, N. (1986) *Decolonising the Mind: The Politics of Language in African Literature.* London: James Currey.

– (1983) *Barrel of a Pen: Resistance to Repression in Neo-Colonial Kenya.* Trenton, NJ: Africa World Press.

Watts, R. (1991) *Power in Family Discourse.* Berlin: Mouton de Gruyter.

Weedon, C. (1987) *Feminist Practice and Poststructuralist Theory.* Oxford: Basil Blackwell.

Weinstein, B. (1980) Language Planning in Francophone Africa. *Language Problems and Language Planning* 4(1): 55–77.

Welsh, D. (1971) *The Roots of Segregation: Native Policy in Natal.* Cape Town: Oxford University Press.

Whitten, N, and J. Szwed, (eds.) (1970) *Afro-American Anthropology: Contemporary Perspectives.* New York: Free Press.

William, R. (1976) *Keywords: A Vocabulary of Culture and Society.* London: Fontana.

Willis, P. (1976) *Learning to Labour.* Westemead: Saxon House.

Woolard, K. (1990) Language Convergence and Language Death as Social Process. In N. Dorian (ed.), *Obsolescent Languages.* Cambridge: Cambridge University Press.

- (1989) *Double Talk: Bilingualism and the Politics of Ethnicity in Catalonia.* Stanford: Stanford University Press.
- (1985) Language Variation and Cultural Hegemony: Toward an Integration of Sociolinguistic and Social Theory. *American Ethnologist* 12(4): 738–48.

Wright, H. (1977) *The Burden of the Present: Liberal-Radical Controversy over Southern African History.* Cape Town: David Philip.

Zegeye, A., ed. (2001) *Social Identities in the New South Africa: After Apartheid.* Volume 1. Cape Town: Kwela Books.

Zegeye, A., and R. Harris. (2003) Introduction: Media, Identity and the Public Sphere in Post-Apartheid South Africa. In A. Zegeye and R. Harris (eds.), *Media, Identity and the Public Sphere in Post-Apartheid South Africa.* Boston: Koninklijke Brill.

Zegeye, A., and I. Liebenberg. (2001) The Burden of the Present. In R. Kriger and A. Zegeye (eds.) *Culture in the New South Africa: After Apartheid.* Volume 2. Cape Town: Kwela Books.

Zerubavel, Y. (1994) The Death of Memory and the Memory of Death: Masada and the Holocaust as Historical Metaphors. *Representations* (45): 72–100.

Index

academic clique, 19,22, 210n7
African activism, 53. *See also* Black
    Consciousness Movement
African National Congress (ANC),
    66, 84, 124; conflicts with Inkatha,
    5, 11, 59–60, 105, 209n2; identity,
    9, 13; origins of, 8, 44–7; and
    tsatsatsa, 95–8; Umkhon-to
    weSizwe, 47, 77, 105–6, 108–9,
    214n6; weakness, 27
Afrikaans, 30, 122–4, 158–9, 189,
    209n4
amabutho, 19, 36, 58, 67–8
amasinyora, 73–5, 174–5
Anglo-Zulu War, 37–8, 42–3, 87–8
apartheid, 3, 5, 11, 42, 83; ethnic/
    racial divisions, 4, 7; implementa-
    tion of, 48–9; language, 159; laws
    48–52; struggle against, 12, 31, 43;
    view of ethnicity, 180; Zulu identity,
    83
Azanian Students' Organization, 66,
    69, 213n3

Bantu Authorities Act, 48
Bantu Homelands Constitution Act,
    52

Bantu language, 32, 81
bantustans, 4, 48, 49, 59
Barth, F., 181–2
Bhambatha rebellion, 43–4
Black Consciousness Movement,
    53–4, 93, 213 n3
black resistance groups. *See* ANC,
    Inkatha, UDF
Boers, 151–2, 160; tsatsatsa views of,
    107; Voortrekkers, 32–3
Bourdieu, P., 185–6
Buthelezi, Chief Mangosuthu, 7,
    18–19, 27–8, 90–1, 120, 186; rise
    of, 51, 58, 211n2; school boycotts,
    68
Butler, J., 52

Cato Manor, 65
Cetshwayo, 34, 39, 40, 88, 115, 190,
    211n5
Champion, A.W.G., 46–7
church, 165–73; music in, 172–3, 179
civil war, 39– 42
Civilized Labour Policy, 45
Cluver, A., 158
colonialism, 7, 31, 39–41, 43; struggle
    against, 4, 31, 43–4

kingdom, 6, 31, 32–43, 81–2;
language, 82–3, 123–6, 135–63;
monarchy, 6, 8, 37, 39, 52
Zulu Cultural Movement, 6, 78, 79,
81, 136
Zulu language, 81–3, 123–6; as

identity, 135, 163; usage, 127–30,
134, 176, 178, 179
Zulu Territorial Authority, 51; legiti-
mating symbol, 56; replaced by
KLA, 52

ANTHROPOLOGICAL HORIZONS

Editor: Michael Lambek, University of Toronto

Published to date: